Rethinking Your Teenager

Rethinking Your Teenager

Shifting from Control and Conflict to Structure and Nurture to Raise Accountable Young Adults

DARBY FOX

OXFORD
UNIVERSITY PRESS

OXFORD
UNIVERSITY PRESS

Oxford University Press is a department of the University of Oxford. It furthers the University's objective of excellence in research, scholarship, and education by publishing worldwide. Oxford is a registered trade mark of Oxford University Press in the UK and certain other countries.

Published in the United States of America by Oxford University Press
198 Madison Avenue, New York, NY 10016, United States of America.

Library of Congress Cataloging-in-Publication Data
Names: Fox, Darby, 1961– author.
Title: Rethinking your teenager : shifting from control and conflict to structure and nurture to raise accountable young adults / by Darby Fox.
Description: NewYork, NY : Oxford University Press, [2020] |
Includes bibliographical references and index. |
Description based on print version record and
CIP data provided by publisher; resource not viewed.
Identifiers: LCCN 2019009724 (print) | LCCN 2019011997 (ebook) |
ISBN 9780190054526 (updf) | ISBN 9780190054533 (epub) |
ISBN 9780190054519 (pbk. : alk. paper)
Subjects: LCSH: Parent and teenager. | Adolescence. | Parenting.
Classification: LCC HQ799.15 (ebook) | LCC HQ799.15.F679 2020 (print) |
DDC 306.874—dc23
LC record available at https://lccn.loc.gov/2019009724

This material is not intended to be, and should not be considered, a substitute for medical or other professional advice. Treatment for the conditions described in this material is highly dependent on the individual circumstances. And, while this material is designed to offer accurate information with respect to the subject matter covered and to be current as of the time it was written, research and knowledge about medical and health issues is constantly evolving and dose schedules for medications are being revised continually, with new side effects recognized and accounted for regularly. Readers must therefore always check the product information and clinical procedures with the most up-to-date published product information and data sheets provided by the manufacturers and the most recent codes of conduct and safety regulation. The publisher and the authors make no representations or warranties to readers, express or implied, as to the accuracy or completeness of this material. Without limiting the foregoing, the publisher and the authors make no representations or warranties as to the accuracy or efficacy of the drug dosages mentioned in the material. The authors and the publisher do not accept, and expressly disclaim, any responsibility for any liability, loss or risk that may be claimed or incurred as a consequence of the use and/or application of any of the contents of this material.

All of the names, circumstances, and at times genders have been changed for confidentiality.

1 3 5 7 9 8 6 4 2

Printed by LSC Communications, United States of America

Table of Contents

Foreword

I REMEMBER READING *The Prophet* by Kahlil Gibran many years ago, and, like so many others, being deeply moved by its message of how to live with greater consciousness in all areas of life. Perhaps the best and most well-known part of Gibran's work is his brief but powerful insight on parenting. In a short poem titled, "On Children," and in just 10 sentences, he gives the most profound advice on raising children I've ever come to know.

In his precise exposition, Gibran emphasizes the spiritual sovereignty of children. As he sees it, they are brand-new, shining souls entering this world with the express purpose of realizing their greatest potential through self-actualization, by becoming exactly the persons they were meant to be—not who we'd prefer them to be. In this light, while children may come through us into this world, they do not belong to us in a literal sense. They have come into this existence to move the world forward through their divinely ordained paths of personal development. Evolution of this nature is only concerned with what is new, the potential for change and growth—never with what already exists, and certainly not with what has been. Therefore, children are on a divine mission, playing a central role in helping humanity advance to greater levels of consciousness. It is thus not our duty nor is it our right to seek to make them like us, to replicate what has already been. To do so would not only impede their purpose and ability to evolve humanity in the unique way each child was destined to do, but also reinforce our own insecurity and worldview by making our children into clones of their parents.

Raising children is difficult. No one has all the answers, and we all make mistakes. What I do know for sure is that our job is not to turn our children into miniature versions of ourselves. Any children who think exactly the way their parents do about every issue lack the discernment to make up their own minds about almost anything. How can that be good for our children or the world? If we can provide safety and guidance while allowing our children to create their own human experience in a way that transforms them into productive and loving members of society, then we will have done our job.

As a parent, I've always intuitively known Gibran's timeless advice about raising children to be true. As a physician, however, I've been waiting many years for someone to confirm this reality in scientific terms. Fortunately (and finally), Darby Fox has done exactly that with her insightful work, which reconciles both the practical and spiritual aspects of what it means to be a parent in the 21st century. She provides us with a linguistic abstraction that clarifies the most difficult aspects of parenting and how to engage them in a way that is both inspiring and easy to understand. Her interventions emphasize maximizing connection with children, while minimizing the potential for unnecessary conflict.

When we're conscious of our true purpose as parents and focused on creating connection instead of winning a conflict, we can act from a position of authority instead of superiority over our children. Authority allows us to provide guidance through wisdom. Superiority hands out orders from ego. Authority is accommodating and objective. Superiority is about winning power struggles. Authority supports connection. Superiority creates competition. With this as the central tenet of parent–child interaction, Darby helps us keep our parenting approach grounded in the greater principles of Gibran's philosophy.

At the same time, Darby also keeps us ever mindful of perhaps the second most important aspect of parenting, of which most of us are either unaware or take for granted, and which even Gibran does not mention. In the process of becoming a better parent, our children are teaching us as much about ourselves as we're teaching them about the world. To grow, we have to be willing to be their students, too.

Dr. Habib Sadeghi
Los Angeles, CA
2018

Introduction

IF YOU'RE READING this book, it's likely that you have a teenager in your life, so you already understand how complex adolescence can be. Teenagers are changing in every way: their bodies, minds, relationships, and lives are rapidly transforming. Parents, then, are faced with the challenge of crafting rules, expectations, and standards for adolescents without a real understanding of what is going on for them, so they try to enact strict control over their increasingly independent teens. For this reason, the parent–teenager relationship is often characterized by conflict and reactivity, and someone is always on the losing end. But it doesn't have to be this way.

There's no denying that parenting teenagers is challenging, but I believe that many of the difficulties stem from misunderstanding. As a culture, we believe that teenagers are out of control, so we feel that it is our job as parents to control them. We attempt to tighten our grip over our child at the precise moment that they are pushing us to loosen it. As children grow older, many parents fail to adjust to adolescence and continue to use strategies that worked when their child was a little kid. Instead, we should shift our approach to meet adolescents where they are. Parenting teens is like teaching your child how to ride a bicycle: You move from tricycles to training wheels to the day when you run alongside your teenager as they wobble on two wheels, trying to stay up on their own. You have to let go enough so that they can learn, but you stay nearby to catch them when they fall, bandage their skinned knees, and put them back on the bicycle. When we move from an attempt to control our child to an attempt to connect with and support our child, we can embrace and enjoy them. When an adolescent feels supported, trusted, and seen for their strengths, they will build a strong foundation on which to develop their potential.

With a better understanding of what our teenager is thinking and feeling, we can parent in a more engaging and intentional way. In this book, I will explain why teenagers behave the way they do, which will put you in a position to anticipate bumps in the road and work through them with grace and calm. My hope is that this book will be a resource both for parents who are struggling with their teen and for those who simply want to feel empowered to encourage positive and healthy development through adolescence. I've chosen eight areas that I find are the most misunderstood between a parent and their teenager and, therefore, create the most turmoil in the parent–child relationship. Through a combination of neuroscience, biology, and psychology, I will shed light on a new way to think about these myths of adolescence that will make them more manageable and less contentious. With new information and strategies, you can begin to form a relationship with your child that becomes the foundation upon which they develop into the person they are meant to become.

Before you continue, take a moment to think back to your own adolescence. As parents, we often forget that we were once where our children are. What was adolescence like for you? What was on your mind? What were your primary challenges and concerns? I grew up in the middle of six kids. I don't know if it was the house full of kids or if it was just a different time, but my parents treated us like a herd. There was minimal focus on any one of us. As I entered adolescence, I craved individuality and independence, but I felt as though I lacked the guidance and support to get there. I toed the line between wanting to please the adults in my life and wanting to act beyond my years. My adolescence was largely characterized by uncertainty and loneliness: I was insecure, unsure of myself and my place in the world.

This is the push and pull of the teenage years: They think they can manage independently and they want to manage independently, but they aren't sure that they can do so. In the kids I work with every day, I see the same conflict at play: They want to seem cool and knowledgeable, experiment with new things, and assert their independence, but they are also terrified. In this way, parenting adolescents can be thankless. They want reassurance and support without wanting to admit that they want reassurance and support. So it becomes your job to manage what they don't know that they don't know. As a parent of a teenager, you should tap into your own memories of adolescence so you can empathize with this struggle and offer your child what you wish you'd had. Then, instead of trying to control your teenager, you can show them that you understand the complexities of their life and guide them through the ups and downs of these years. In other words, you can have a relationship with your teenager.

Every parent–child relationship looks different, but the key components of the most successful parent–child relationships are connection and accountability. When I first started counseling, I was somewhat intimidated by what I had learned in graduate school. I felt wary of what I perceived to be the power I had over someone else's life. But almost as soon as I began, I realized that the magic of therapy is not in theories and techniques but rather in the connection between two people. You realize this quickly as a parent, too: Each one of your children is different and you won't find the same approach to be successful with every child. There are many different parenting techniques and methods, but ultimately your success will arise from the strength of your relationship with each child. Relationships are based on the way you behave toward and regard another person. How do you behave toward and regard your adolescent? As I raised my own children and began my career in counseling, I wanted to bring a nurturing approach to my connection with each child. The single reason I most enjoy working with adolescents is that they, both teenage boys and girls, are incredibly vulnerable and sensitive. They look to me to be a trustworthy, nonjudgmental, guiding force in their life to support them as they navigate these years. Often, more than anything else, I'm a sounding board for them to talk through decisions and struggles they face; because of our connection, I'm in a position to influence their lives. A parent won't necessarily be the person that their teen confides in at every step of the way, but when you move from a control model to a relationship model, you have a better chance of being heard, particularly in difficult times. Every connection looks different, but every strong connection is based on respect, genuine caring, and quality time together.

Along with connection, the other component of a successful parent–child relationship is accountability. Accountability is twofold: We need to teach our children first to be accountable to themselves and then accountable to others. We often get this backwards: We teach our kids to uphold the standards of others, such as teachers, coaches, and disciplinarians in their lives so that they don't get into trouble, but we leave out the importance of personal accountability. *Who are you?* You don't lie or cheat or steal because *you're better than that.* This concept is more important than deferring to someone else's rule. We want our adolescents to develop personal standards to which they will be motivated to hold themselves accountable. When we attach smaller decisions to a broader sense of self, we can influence their choices in a longer-term way. Are they proud of themselves, their effort, and the decisions they make? Life is about more than getting by and checking the boxes. For the same reason, we have to step back and let go of the result on behalf of our kids so that we encourage authentic self-discovery and skill-building. This is particularly important during the adolescent years, when we know that they are highly focused on gratification and positive outcomes. It's important for them to learn early on that reward is the sum of incremental effort. Let them take charge of the results they are getting.

I have high expectations for my children and my clients, but I also accept that they won't always make the right choices. However, I always require that they be accountable for their behavior, even their mistakes. As long as they can learn to own their behavior, they can learn from their missteps and make better choices in the future. When I work with adolescents, I ask them: Where in this do you have choice? When they can identify their role in an issue or conflict, they gain perspective on and insight into their own actions. They begin to understand that different behavior will bring about a different outcome. In other words, they realize that their choices and behavior matter. Mattering is empowering. When we matter, we feel that others notice us, care about us, and depend upon us. When a child understands that their behavior impacts others, they feel worthwhile because they perceive that they belong to something greater than themselves, and they feel empowered because they understand that their choices and actions have consequences. A parent's task is to show their child that they matter. If you develop a connection with your adolescent and hold them accountable for their behavior, they will know that they matter.

Parenting adolescents can feel like juggling an infinite number of balls and hoping they don't all come crashing down at once. Yet if we simplify the task, our role becomes easier. Parenting really boils down to two fundamental questions that every child asks of their caretaker: *Am I loved? Can I have my own way?* If you think about a difficult situation you have faced with your teen, you can probably find one if not both of these questions at the core of the issue. In the simplest of terms, your answers to these questions should be *Yes, you are always loved* but *You can only have your way some of the time.* When you find yourself struggling with your teen, you can come back to this to remind yourself of the crucial distinction between love and permission. Your child needs to know that the love you have for them is unconditional and will never go away, but that love has little to do with granting permission (see Figure o.1).

As you are faced with the almost daily dilemmas of parenting teens, return to these two questions as a guide. Should you let your child go to a party without adult supervision? *Yes, I understand that you want to be with your friends, but no, you are not old enough to go to a party without parents present. Why don't you invite some of your friends over here instead?* Should you let your child sleep until the afternoon on a weekend? *Yes, you know that they need a lot of sleep, but no, they have responsibilities they need to take care of, so they need to*

HIGH-STRUCTURE AND HIGH-NURTURE: THE GOLD STANDARD FOR PARENTING

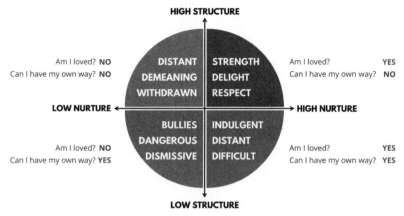

FIGURE 0.1. The Two Fundamental Questions Adolescents Ask: *Am I Loved?* and *Can I Have My Own Way?*

get up and out of bed. Try waking them up just before noon with their favorite breakfast on the table.

In the following chapters, I will address the myths of adolescence from a high-nurture, high-structure perspective so that you can understand, through real-life examples, how to put these ideas into practice. When you set up clear boundaries, clear expectations, and clear consequences (structure), you free yourself to connect with and support your teenager (nurture).

Parenting is the most challenging thing you will do. You will not be perfect—I certainly wasn't. But if you approach parenting with the mindset presented here, you will raise high-functioning, satisfied, and resilient children, with whom you will form a close bond that will be a source of immense joy for the rest of your life.

I

The First Myth

TEENAGERS ARE YOUNG ADULTS WHO CHOOSE TO ACT IMMATURELY.

WHAT WERE YOU THINKING?

If every parent of a teenager has not spoken these words aloud, every parent of a teenager has thought them. Teenagers often frustrate parents because, though they may look like adults and seem like adults, they are inconsistent in their ability to act like adults. Teenage behavior can be unpredictable and uncharacteristic. As parents, we often wish we could be inside of our child's head so we might begin to understand what causes them to behave in the ways they do. Here's the good news: We can. Over the last decade, neurological research has given us a more complete picture of the adolescent brain and how it dictates our teenagers' words, actions, and experience of the world.[1] With an understanding of where a teenager is developmentally, we can begin to understand how their brain works and embrace the role we play in shaping their mind, then adjust our expectations to fit their capabilities and break the cycle of frustration. This chapter will give you the tools to meet your child where they are and handle the challenges of the adolescent years with empathy and love.

Three Keys to Understanding the Teenage Brain

As teens grow, we often confuse their physical development with maturity. Both boys and girls are undergoing physical maturation by age 14 and have mostly finished their growth spurts by age 18. Adolescent girls tend to stop growing about 18 months after their first period, while adolescent boys can continue to grow into their early twenties. *However, the adolescent brain does not finish developing until the age of 25.* Teenagers are beginning to develop the psychological capabilities that allow them to think in flexible and abstract ways. While younger children see the world in concrete terms, we see the attainment of what Piaget calls "formal operational thought" during adolescence.[2] Teens begin to reason based on hypotheses and propositions and start solving problems creatively. They become increasingly interested in ideas, values, and social issues and start to form their own opinions. They can conceive of a broader world around them and begin to process metaphors and symbols, as well as concepts like morality and justice.

These are critical pieces of cognitive development, and parents often mistake these advancing mental functions for an adult understanding of the world.[3] Because adolescents start to articulate more mature ideas and engage in adult discussions, parents assume that their teenager is thinking at a level equal to their own. However, these processes are still developing in teens and have yet to be fine-tuned. This can't be overstated: These psychological capabilities are formed through trial and error and require practice to become skills that can be relied upon consistently. Acting mature at moments is different from executing these mental functions consistently. The teenage brain has not completely developed, so these elements remain in flux.[4]

This is the first key to getting inside of your teenager's head: The teenage brain is *not* operating at an adult level. In other words, your teenager is *not* an adult. The most simple explanation for this is that during adolescence, the teenage brain is approximately 80% developed. The brain is the only organ in the body responsible for conscious behavior, so this is a crucial piece of information. Think about it: If the adolescent brain is not fully mature, we cannot expect the adolescent to act fully maturely. Just as we would not expect a machine without all of its parts to operate at full capacity, we cannot expect our teenagers to behave as an adult might in every situation. This should come as a relief to parents who wonder what causes uncharacteristic or inconsistent behavior during the adolescent years. Simply put, until your child's brain is fully formed, they will behave in unpredictable ways and will struggle to make good decisions from moment to moment.

The second key to understanding how your child's mind works is to know *which* parts of the brain are still developing during the teenage years (see Figure 1.1). The brain develops from the back to the front. The back of the brain, well formed by adolescence, includes the **medulla**, which regulates functions such as breathing, swallowing, and digestion. The middle of the brain houses the **limbic system**, including the **amygdala**, which is in charge of memory and emotions such as stress, fear, anger, and love, as well as our

THE ADOLESCENT BRAIN UNDER CONSTRUCTION

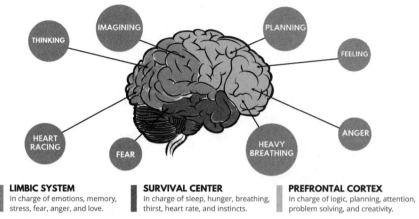

LIMBIC SYSTEM	SURVIVAL CENTER	PREFRONTAL CORTEX
In charge of emotions, memory, stress, fear, anger, and love.	In charge of sleep, hunger, breathing, thirst, heart rate, and instincts.	In charge of logic, planning, attention, problem solving, and creativity.

FIGURE 1.1. The Adolescent Brain Under Construction

"fight or flight" response. The front brain, including the **frontal lobe** and the **prefrontal cortex**, is the part of the brain responsible for more complex mental functions such as logic, planning, and problem solving. These cognitive processes are associated with judgment, insight, and instinct.

One particularly important capacity, **prospective memory**, which allows an individual to hold in their mind the intention to perform an action in the future, is also located in the front of the brain.[5] In other words, an adolescent's ability to follow through is not fully formed. It makes sense that we experience our teenagers as emotional and impulsive. *They are.* Their emotionality develops before their ability to regulate their emotions. When we feel frustration with their inability to think rationally, plan ahead, or consider the consequences of their behavior, it's important to remember that this is a result of the way their brain is developing, not of their desire to be irresponsible or unreliable.

The final key to a complete grasp of the teenage brain is to understand the impact of the very process of development. The increased neurological activity taking place in the adolescent brain makes this both a powerful and vulnerable time in the teenager's life. The adolescent brain is constantly learning, connecting, and eliminating in processes known as **pruning** and **myelination**. As neurons fire in the brain, they connect to other neurons to dictate behavior. When the same neurons connect on a consistent basis, a neural pathway is formed. Think about learning how to swing a baseball bat. The first time you take a swing, you have to remember each part of the movement: bend your knees, keep your eye on the ball, follow through. Since this is a new combination of motions, your swing is disjointed and awkward. With repetition, your brain develops a neural pathway that activates each time you're at bat, allowing you to bend your knees, swing, and follow through smoothly and without thinking. If you were able to watch a brain image of a professional baseball player, you would see strong neural pathways activate during play, formed over a lifetime of swinging.

Pruning is the process by which the brain eliminates unnecessary neurons and neural connections, reducing the **gray matter** in the brain and making room for more efficient connections. The adolescent's environment—their home, family, school, and friends—plays a major role in the pruning process, impacting which connections are used and therefore warrant further development.

Myelination, on the other hand, is the subsequent smoothing of the neural connections that remain after pruning.[6] Myelin can be thought of as insulation that protects neural connections and promotes faster impulses. Think of the difference between a dirt road and a paved road. A dirt road is rough, bumpy, and unreliable; a paved road is faster, more predictable, and easier to travel. Myelination is the "paving" of neural pathways, making the connections efficient and habitual. While pruning reduces the gray matter of the brain, myelination increases the **white matter**, which transmits information between different parts of the brain.

These processes, and the associated **neuroplasticity**, require neurons and neurotransmitters to fire at a rate twice as fast as they do in adult brains. This results in a high level of mental activity in the adolescent brain. In Frances E. Jensen's *The Teenage Brain,* she characterizes the adolescent brain as adaptable, malleable, and able to take in information at a rapid rate.[7] Adolescence is the only time these activities occur this simultaneously and at such a rapid rate and is therefore a precious window of growth and development.

Executive Functions in the Teenage Brain

Higher cognitive functions are mental processes that use the parts of the brain that involve learning skills. Cognitive functions include memory, attention, thinking, and planning, as well as what are commonly referred to as **executive functions**. I often hear parents express concern that their adolescent has "executive functioning issues." Executive functions are tasks of self-regulation, including inhibition, self-awareness, and problem solving (see Box 1.1). Each executive function requires multiple mental processes to work in conjunction.[8] Executive functions are a complex skill set that requires a

---

BOX 1.1

Common Executive Functions

Inhibition is the ability to stop what you are doing and allow your calm brain to guide you as you make decisions.

Self-Awareness is the ability to understand your role in and impact upon your relationships and environment.

Nonverbal Working Memory is the ability to hold things in your mind using visual imagery, or mental maps, to guide you toward the future and help you remember the sequence of steps necessary to achieve a goal or perform a task. It includes hindsight, foresight, and an objective sense of time.

Verbal Working Memory is self-speech or internal speech, often thought of as an "inner monologue." It is the voice that gives us instructions and asks self-directed questions about what to do in new or unfamiliar situations.

Emotional Self-Regulation is the ability to moderate strong emotions so that they don't interfere with our long-term wellbeing and goals. This means learning to use images, experience, language, and one's own self-awareness to process and manage how we feel about things. Emotional self-regulation is responsible for motivating us to act or do things a certain way.

Planning and Problem Solving, which experts sometimes call "self-play," is the way we play with information in our minds to come up with new or alternative ways of doing something. By taking things apart and recombining them in different ways, we're generating solutions to problems or obstacles we might face.

---

high level of cognitive functioning in the front of the brain, which we now know is still developing in adolescents.

I work with several high-achieving, diligent, hard-working students whose parents express confusion over what they perceive to be their child's lack of work ethic and focus. "Doesn't she know how important this is?" they ask me. Or: "I can't believe I found him watching television when he was supposed to be studying." I recently got a call from one mother who was fed up. She couldn't believe that her teenage son had asked if he could have his girlfriend over the night before a big exam. Let's remember that inhibition, emotional self-regulation, and planning are all executive functions. This is a smart and hard-working kid, but it should be entirely predictable that a teenage boy would want to spend time with his girlfriend instead of studying for his exam. His higher cognitive functions and rational brain are still developing, so he needs to *learn* the skills that would allow him to make a better choice. I told his mom to ask him to study for 15 additional minutes before his girlfriend came over. This way, she was providing structure and making her expectations clear, but she wasn't telling him what to do. She was allowing him to manage his own time so that he could hone the skill for future use.

With my own kids, I saw how challenging it was for them to manage everything in their schedules. I had a boy and a girl for whom these executive functions came more easily, and a boy and a girl who struggled with the same tasks. It had nothing to do with work ethic or intelligence; these were simply skills that they had to hone. Adolescents often struggle to plan their time in a way that's efficient and allows for everything they need to get done. Yet organization is a key executive function that needs to be developed and honed through trial and error. You can suggest a more logical plan, but if they don't take your advice, let go of it. The best way for them to learn is by wasting time or running late so that they have to figure out how to do it better the next time. Teenage girls are often stronger with organizational skills, but it's really child specific.

So I would ask each of my kids: What's your plan? Instead of taking over and telling them what to do, I would engage them so that they could practice using the functions they were still developing. Then I could offer advice if they asked for it. This isn't easy! We want to just tell our kids how to manage their time in a more efficient, sensible way, but if we do, they won't learn how to do it for themselves. When we tell them what to do, we try to control them: high structure, low nurture (see Figure 0.1). When we try to control them, we are met with resistance. On the other hand, if we aren't engaged with their lives at all, we leave them on their own to struggle without improvement: low structure, low nurture. Their executive functions don't improve because, if nobody else seems to care, they won't care either. And if we do everything for them—low structure, high nurture—we hijack their opportunity to learn how to do things for themselves. They only learn how to demand things from others.

Like all cognitive functions, executive functions must be practiced in order to become natural and habitual. Every adolescent has "executive functioning issues," because these functions involve new and unformed neural pathways.[9] Have patience with your teenager and view these skills as "in progress." Be supportive when things go wrong but let them figure out how to do it for themselves.

The Teenage Brain in Action

Let's look at the teenage brain in action. I have a client, Kate, who recently got her driver's license. On one of her first solo drives, Kate got into a fender bender in a parking lot near home. The man driving the other car sensed that she was an inexperienced driver and told Kate that if she didn't give him her credit card number, he would call the police. Kate was terrified of getting into trouble with her parents or, worse, the law. The teenage amygdala is able to sense danger and signal fear, but the frontal lobe is not developed enough to respond and guide the brain to make a decision.[10]

Kate froze. She couldn't think clearly and didn't know what to do, so she handed over her information and was slammed with a bill she couldn't pay. When her parents learned about the incident, they were frustrated. They wanted to know why Kate hadn't called them, called the police, or asked for the other driver's information, but Kate was inexperienced and incapable of thinking rationally in the moment.

Nine out of 10 teens are faced with a crisis at some point.[11] As parents, we need to anticipate that they may make the wrong decision. **If we can adjust our expectations to account for error, we will spend much less time in an exasperated state.** Alternatively, we can advance development by engaging our adolescents in discussions of judgment, decision making, and consequences, so that they recognize the importance of their actions. Drivers ages 16 and 17 are nearly nine times more likely to get into an accident than a middle-aged driver. It's important to walk through what might happen with your teen and give them specific instructions: *If you get into an accident, you can't drive away; you need to contact and wait for the police. Be sure to exchange insurance and contact information, get license plate numbers, and take pictures of both vehicles. Wait to apologize, even if you're at fault, because you never know what will happen.* The same is true for things like speeding tickets and flat tires; they are unlikely to know what to do if they haven't experienced it before. By pushing them to access these higher cognitive functions ahead of time, we can help them strengthen these crucial neural pathways. As the parent, you need to be prepared for moments when they will come up short so that you can handle these moments with clarity and patience.

Every misstep is an opportunity to teach teenagers how to do it better next time. When we tell adolescents what we expect from them, we teach them how to behave. I work with a couple in their mid-fifties; Alan has one child from his previous marriage and Julie has none. They recently bought an apartment together. Alan's son, Bobby, is with them one night per week.

Bobby, in the midst of adolescence and the child of divorce, demonstrates reactive and emotional behavior, and Julie has described feeling intimidated by him. When Bobby visits, he brings his dog and lets it run wild around the apartment. In spite of being allergic to and afraid of dogs, Julie tolerates its presence but has an agreement with Bobby that the dog is not permitted in her bedroom.

On a recent weekend, I received a text from Julie: a picture of dog feces on her pillow with the message, "HELP!" I saw Alan and Julie after the weekend and I asked Julie how she responded in the moment. Julie told me that she promptly cleaned up the mess and, somewhat jokingly, told Bobby that she was going to have a tantrum. Upon hearing this, Bobby left the room, failing to apologize for the accident or help get rid of the mess. Julie was disappointed and frustrated; she felt that Bobby acted selfish and immature. "He should have acted more grown up," Julie told me.

But Bobby *isn't* a grown-up. Adolescents are developing emotional intelligence and learning how to act in various situations. Bobby did act selfish and immature, but it's important to look at the context of his behavior. His custodial home is characterized by low structure, high nurture, so he is used to doing whatever he wants with little accountability. There are few rules and, when a mistake is made, it's swept over with reassurance and false praise. So, in this case, Bobby's behavior isn't surprising. As adults, we need to remember that teenagers are inexperienced and insecure. It's on us to teach them how to behave.

I reminded Julie that adolescents learn through experience and that Bobby hadn't previously been in a similar situation that he could refer to in the moment. I encouraged Julie, going forward, to tell Bobby how she wanted him to act. If we tell them what we would like to see happen, they have the opportunity to respond. Julie might have said, "Bobby, I know that you didn't mean for your dog to go into our room. Even when you don't mean for something like this to happen, you take responsibility, apologize for your mistake, and try to make it right. In this case, I'd appreciate an apology and I'd like you to clean it up." This would have allowed Bobby to take his cues from Julie and learn how to handle these types of situations in the future.

Of course, our teenagers won't always do exactly what we ask of them. It's still important for them to understand your expectations and to hear what the appropriate behavior would be. Reiterate that your frustration is not a reflection of how you feel about them. You can say, "I love you to death, but I need you to be responsible for your behavior." This keeps us in the high-structure, high-nurture quadrant. Over time, they will start to incorporate these instructions into their decision making and you will see their behavior begin to shift.

As parents, we should see our role as that of a disciplinarian, the goal being to shape our teens and guide them toward appropriate and productive behavior. In most cases, teens are operating from a lack of awareness and experience coupled with a brain that doesn't allow them to access a calm mind in a tense moment. They are rarely operating from an intention to do wrong or a desire to cause harm to the people in their lives. Discipline allows us to teach the power of consequences while explaining to our child where they went wrong and encouraging them to consider how they might act differently going forward.

Discipline is not the same as punishment.[12] Discipline is defined as training that corrects, molds, or perfects mental faculties and moral character. To discipline is to teach. Punishment, on the other hand, is defined as the infliction or imposition of a penalty as retribution for an offense. Try to avoid the mindset that you are the authority figure looking to catch your teenager in the wrong. Instead, view yourself as their guide through this phase in which they are experimenting with various types of behavior. In early childhood, we are able to *control* our children, simply telling them what to do and knowing that they will obey us. Adolescents, on the other hand, are developing physical and emotional independence and we can no longer control what they do.

The battle for control is one of the central challenges for parents of teenagers.[13] But as parents, we should want our teens to think independently, and we need to be aware that this comes with a tendency to question and challenge authority. Parents often fear this aspect of adolescence, but it's a welcome change. If your teenagers resist control, you are raising them to think for themselves. This is healthy behavior, but it's important that you guide them in their newfound autonomy. We want to explain the reasoning behind our expectations and the principles upon which we base our rules. We also want to set a good example. Teenagers are always watching! Contradicting the things that you say with your behavior diminishes your credibility.

When punishment is warranted and necessary, as it likely may be, ensure that the punishment fits the crime. The most successful parents of adolescents use creativity in discipline and engage their teen in problem solving. Often, you can simply allow the consequences of their actions to stand alone. I recently heard from a client whose daughter had missed her flight home from college for the holiday break, a flight that her parents had booked and paid for. She had been out late the night before and slept through her alarm. Her parents were infuriated; this was another incident in a string of irresponsible behavior. But her mom told me that she had spent the morning on the phone with the airline to try to rebook the flight because she didn't want her daughter to miss any time at home over the holidays. I urged her, as hard as it might be, to let go of losing a day or two with her daughter and ask the teen to sort the situation out for herself. Her daughter was the one to miss her flight, so she should be the one to deal with the hassle and cost of rearranging travel plans at the last minute.

To make room for the developing person that is your child, you have to be clear, and you have to let go of your agenda. You can tell them that you're disappointed or that your feelings are hurt, but then try to let go of it and move on, especially if they have solved the problem. You've already been firm with your expectations and they are dealing with the consequences. It's much easier to hold your teenager accountable for the bigger things if you have been consistent in holding them accountable all along. If they know what the consequences might be, they will be more likely to consider them at the point of decision making. It's hard to ignore information once it has been processed. If they know that missing curfew means losing the use of the car for a week, they are more likely to consider that when they are deciding whether or not to leave a party to make it home on time. Most teenagers love to suggest new and unusual ways for you to punish their siblings. Ask for their input into the consequences they face for their own behavior. You may be surprised with what they come up with!

We can see, in Alan and Julie's case, the futility of a punishment or an overly emotional response to what has occurred. Emotionality escalates the issue, and punishment without discussion often leaves your adolescent feeling judged and misunderstood. It's more effective to express what behavior is preferable and elicit the child's help in a resolution. Julie could have said, "This really grosses me out. I don't want the dog in my bedroom and I want you to clean it up. How can we make sure this doesn't happen again?" Instead of isolating and blaming Elizabeth, this response engages her in a solution and gives her the chance to make up for her mistake. Teenagers are primed to feel shame, insecurity, and self-loathing. They need reassurance and security in order to understand how to act differently according to your expectations.

There will, of course, be times when you feel that responding in a calm and rational way is beyond you. When you can, pause for poise. Take the time you need to remember that, as the adult in the situation, you are dealing with a maturing person who you have the opportunity and responsibility to teach. If emotions are involved, give them time to die down before you act. There's no harm in telling your teen that you aren't sure of the appropriate discipline. Let them wait and sit with the discomfort of uncertainty. It's this discomfort—the notion that they have let someone down and the way that makes them feel—that alters behavior over the long term.

Divorce

As parents, we want to maintain realistic expectations of our teenagers, no matter the situation. A divorce can put pressure on a child to act more mature than they are. Parents often feel that a teenager is old enough to handle divorce, when it's actually one of the most vulnerable times to experience such a change. Given what we now know about an adolescent's neurological development, we know that their brain is highly sensitive to emotional uncertainty or disruption. An emphasis on high structure and high nurture is thus especially critical during this transition. Be explicit about the fact that the divorce isn't their fault and reassure them that they are loved and cared for by both of their parents. While this may seem obvious, remember: In an emotionally charged situation, we all regress. At any age, the breaking up of a family threatens one of the most sensitive parts of ourselves and shakes our sense of stability, but adolescents are particularly sensitive and insecure. Identity is deeply tied to family and adolescents are highly focused on their self-image, self-perception, and social image. Make sure they know that while the structure of the family may change, the significant relationships between the family units can remain intact.

It's critical that parents support their children through this significant change by teaching them how to handle the new family dynamic and manage their emotions.[14] It's hard to predict how a child will react to divorce. Some might be outwardly devastated while others might internalize their emotions. Not every adolescent who experiences a divorce needs to seek professional help, but if their reaction to the divorce seems to prevent them from their normal patterns of daily living, or if you notice social withdrawal, a change in eating habits, an indication of substance use, or promiscuous or otherwise uncharacteristic behavior, it might be helpful to consult a family therapist.

As parents, we have to work to keep the tension and fighting out of the family dynamic to preserve the child's sense of security and stability at home.[15] Parents make the mistake of involving their adolescents in adult discussions or arguments because they're looking for emotional support. It's important for parents to seek support elsewhere and keep their children out of interpersonal adult issues in order to maintain the parent–child dyad. In divorce, the oldest child can often feel pressure to become a coparent to their now single mother or father. They will frequently take on responsibilities and tasks that were previously handled by the other parent. We refer to this as the **parentification** of a child.

It's completely fine to ask your kids to pitch in, whether with caring for younger siblings, helping with a meal, or getting themselves to and from their activities on their own. These are all positive developments and can actually help to refine executive functions and lead to greater independence, responsibility, empathy, and maturity. But parentification occurs when a child is asked to handle adult responsibilities. It can be difficult to reverse because it disrupts the natural parent–child relationship and forces the child to hide their own feelings in order to support their parent. It's a low-nurture, low-structure dynamic and can push a child into a relationship more mature than they have the emotional capacity to deal with. It can also add stress if and when a divorced parent develops a new intimate relationship, because the child can feel rejected and displaced by a new significant other.

I work with a family who went through a long, difficult divorce. The father was reluctant to move out. Ultimately, it fell on the oldest child to help him find a new place and then to help him settle into it, which would traditionally be spousal responsibilities. This dynamic caused a very painful rift between father and daughter when he began dating, because her role was quickly replaced by new people in his life. While it might have seemed like the father was maintaining a loving connection with his oldest child, it wasn't genuinely nurturing because it was conditional. When someone else came into his life, the dynamic shifted and his daughter was suddenly left out. Even though your teenagers rationally understand that you may begin to date other people, they can experience it as a very primal feeling of rejection.

Parents have to be highly cautious when introducing significant others to their children. It's always more successful if done on the child's timetable. I work with a father of two teenage daughters: Lisa and Jamie. Tim and his wife got divorced a couple of years ago, and Tim has been seeing someone new for several months. The divorce was not easy on the family, so Tim's daughters have had to deal with a fair amount of instability over the last few years. Tim was very clear with me that he wanted his daughters to know they were his first priority, but he also wanted to share this new relationship with them.

After we discussed what approach would be best, Tim decided to tell his daughters about his new girlfriend and give them the option to meet her whenever they felt interested and/or ready. It's important to note that Tim had been seeing this person for a substantial amount of time and that he kept the conversation with his daughters brief. There was no need for him to overshare. At any age, it's difficult for us to conceive of our parents as romantic people, whether with each other or with someone new, but it's particularly sensitive in the wake of divorce and for adolescents who are just beginning to explore intimate relationships for themselves.

All children should have the time and space to focus on themselves during a divorce; every family will mourn the end of what has been, and every child has their own process to go through. Remember: It usually takes parents a very long time to come to the decision that they are divorcing. By then, they've had at least several months to come to terms with the ramifications. Be patient and give your children the same consideration (see Box 1.2).

It's a misconception that adult children of divorce will have lifelong issues that stem from losing their sense of family during their developmental years. Adolescents can deal with divorce fairly successfully if they are exposed to a minimal amount of fighting and tension between their parents. In fact, research now indicates that individuals from healthy divorces show greater resilience and problem-solving skills as adults. By dealing with challenges and working on relationships, they engaged and developed an important skill set. For better or worse, children of divorce developed the skill of handling a new

---

BOX 1.2

Raising Children Through Divorce

Remember that the adolescent is not an adult and does not have your ability to reason and understand. Children of divorce will be happy and healthy if we provide:

- Acceptance
- Assurance of safety
- Freedom from guilt or blame for the divorce
- Structure
- A stable parent

Never burden a child with a situation they cannot control, and do not ask a child to deal with an adult situation.

Children of divorce need to avoid situations that include sabotage, being a "pawn" for adults, being used for information, absorbing adult feelings, choosing sides, or overindulgence.

relationship with each parent. They tended to see at a younger age the importance of balancing multiple personalities in relationships. Teenagers are fragile and are highly sensitive to the impact of divorce, but divorce also gives them the opportunity to grow and mature in different ways if parents focus on reassuring and protecting them throughout the breakup.

WE NOW HAVE our answer to that familiar question: *What were you thinking?* They weren't. We understand that the adolescent brain is "under construction" and that this development accounts for the teenage tendencies to be emotional, impulsive, and even irresponsible. While teenagers are able to act maturely and responsibly some of the time, this capacity is inconsistent and unreliable. Parents can be nurturing, loving, and kind but also should communicate and demonstrate expectations according to their teenager's capabilities.

Though we have our work cut out for us, we also have a unique opportunity in our children's adolescence to positively shape their growing brains. While the teenage years are a vulnerable time, they are also a chance to capture incredible strengths and hone unique skills and abilities. As we will explore in the following chapters, adolescents are wired for novelty seeking and creative exploration and are therefore primed to experiment in many areas.[16] At no other time in our lives do we have quite the same capacity. Teenagers are beginning to develop their identity and grapple with such issues as purpose, morality, and the meaning of life. It's amazing to watch the individual before you explore and interpret the world around them in increasingly complex ways. We have an opportunity in this phase to deepen and advance our teenager's development that we will not have again. As parents, we want to make sure that we encourage their creative abilities in their schoolwork, activities, and exploration of interests, while engaging their problem-solving and decision-making skills as they begin to manage their own lives.

Consider This:
Insights & Actions

- We've learned that teenagers are developing the parts of their brains that allow them to plan and think things through. As the parent, you can aid this process by talking through their choices with them. If you want to know what your child was thinking when they messed up, ask them in a genuine way. You can teach them to reflect on their choices and identify where they might have gone wrong. Provide them with options to consider, and encourage them to anticipate the potential consequences of various options as they make their decisions.

- It's always more effective to state consequences in advance: "If you come home late, you won't get the car Saturday night" or "If you don't clean up your room by Friday, you won't get to play video games over the weekend." It's easier to follow through in an unemotional way when you have been up front about the consequences for your adolescent's choices and behavior. In this way, you put the consequences back on them. When the consequence is enacted, it's because they made the choice they knew would bring about that result. It's always important to remind them: "You chose this consequence." It isn't something you're doing to them.

- When you are at the point of frustration that might make you angry or emotional, take some space from the situation so you can set an example of patience and rationality. Teenagers are hardwired for emotionality, whereas adults are better equipped to remain calm in a stressful situation. De-escalate tension by taking a deep breath and returning to the conversation in a stable and clear-headed state.

- You don't always have to have an answer for your child's behavior in the moment. It's okay to tell them that you aren't sure how you are going to handle an issue and that you need some time to think. Avoid doling out a meaningless consequence or lecturing your child about what they did wrong. It's best to address whatever might come up as calmly and clearly as you can.

- Teenagers will break the rules. Remember: They are wired for experimentation and exploration! Help your child understand the concept of consequences by tailoring consequences to each situation. If your child comes home after their curfew, ask them to get up early to do the grocery shopping or bring their sibling to their Saturday sports event. Blanket punishments, such as taking your teen's phone away, do little to give them insight into the impact of their behavior. By contrast, after spending the day tired and busy, they won't want to come home late again.

- Remember, particularly in stressful or emotional moments, that what changes behavior and decision making is *insight*. You don't unlearn insight. Random punishments don't impact long- term behavior. Ask your adolescent, "How would you do it differently now?" or "Can you think of a different solution to the issue?" These questions promote problem solving and show your teenager that you're on their team. You can offer guidance, too. The key to engaging your adolescent effectively is to eliminate the parent-versus-teen battle for control.

Notes

1. Jensen, F. E., & Nutt, A. E. (2015). *The teenage brain: A neuroscientist's survival guide to raising adolescents and young adults.* New York, NY: HarperCollins.

2. Piaget, J. (1932). *The language and thought of the child* (2nd ed.). London, UK: Kegan Paul, Trench, Trubner & Co.

3. Erikson, E. H. (1963). *Childhood and society.* New York, NY: W. W. Norton.

4. Siegel, D. J. (2013). *Brainstorm. The power and purpose of the teenage brain.* New York, NY: Penguin.

5. Siegel, D. J. (2012). *The developing mind: How relationships and the brain interact to shape who we are.* New York, NY: Guilford Press.

6. Siegel, D. J. (2013). *Brainstorm. The power and purpose of the teenage brain.* New York, NY: Penguin.

7. Jensen, F. E., & Nutt, A. E. (2015). *The teenage brain: A neuroscientist's survival guide to raising adolescents and young adults.* New York, NY: HarperCollins.

8. Barkley, R. A. (2013). *Taking charge of ADHD: The complete, authoritative guide for parents* (3rd ed.). New York, NY: Guilford Press.

9. Siegel, D. J. (2013). *Brainstorm. The power and purpose of the teenage brain.* New York, NY: Penguin.

10. Jensen, F. E., & Nutt, A. E. (2015). *The teenage brain: A neuroscientist's survival guide to raising adolescents and young adults.* New York, NY: HarperCollins.

11. Siegel, D. J. (2013). *Brainstorm. The power and purpose of the teenage brain.* New York, NY: Penguin.

12. Siegel, D. J., & Bryson, T. P. (2014). *No drama discipline: The whole-brain way to calm the chaos and nurture your child's developing mind.* New York, NY: Bantam Books.

13. Wolf, A. E. (2002). *Get out of my life, but first could you drive me and Cheryl to the mall? A parent's guide to the new teenager.* New York, NY: Farrar, Straus and Giroux.

14. Ahrons, C. (2004). *We're still family: What grown children have to say about their parents' divorce.* New York, NY: HarperCollins.

15. Ahrons, C. (2004). *We're still family: What grown children have to say about their parents' divorce.* New York, NY: HarperCollins.

16. Jensen, F. E., & Nutt, A. E. (2015). *The teenage brain: A neuroscientist's survival guide to raising adolescents and young adults.* New York, NY: HarperCollins.

2

The Second Myth

TEENAGERS BEHAVE BADLY BECAUSE OF RAGING
HORMONES AND THERE IS NOTHING
WE CAN DO ABOUT IT.

"RAGING HORMONES" MAY be the single phrase most commonly associated with the teenage years. We blame unpredictable adolescent behavior on hormones and believe that these chemicals dictate everything an adolescent does. Our culture perpetuates the image of the "sex-crazed" teenage boy and the "hysterical" and "dramatic" teenage girl. I often hear parents complaining that their adolescents are hormonal and that neither parent nor child can get a handle on it—it feels out of control and as if nothing can be done other than endure the ups and downs.

Historically, we have used the idea of hormones to encompass all of a teenager's bad behavior, yet we know little about the way hormones actually impact the adolescent. The truth is, while teens are dealing with new and changing levels of hormones in their bodies, they are capable of learning to regulate their behavior and manage the chemical shifts taking place. We can help adolescents navigate this period successfully to establish a foundation for self-regulation as they become adults. Our goal is to create standards of behavior (structure) and to support our adolescents in a loving way (nurture) as they go through this phase of development.

Hormones in the Teenage Brain

Now that we understand the structure of the adolescent brain, let's focus on the chemicals at play in their brains and bodies. Understanding your adolescent's internal environment equips you to navigate their unpredictable behavior in a firm and loving way. Teenagers do have higher concentrations of certain hormones in their bodies, including sex hormones. Their internal chemistry is in flux and their bodies are reacting to increased and varying levels of hormones. A "mood swing" is triggered by a chemical reaction. This can be difficult for both parents and teens to manage, but there are things we can do to mitigate the effect. With an understanding of the role each hormone plays, you can prepare your teen to work through these changes and learn to manage their behavior.

When we connect behavior to a chemical reaction, we approach it differently than if we think it is purely emotional. Even if your teenager's hormones are "raging," they don't get to do whatever they want. If we bring in a high-structure, high-nurture approach (see Figure 0.1), it might look like this: *I get that you aren't feeling great. I'll fix you a great meal, but you still need to go to school, go to practice, or go to work.* As parents, we don't want to give our adolescents the idea that they can't control their behavior; this is the equivalent of a free pass for teenagers to act reckless and disrespectful. Instead, we want to help our children develop the skills to anticipate and regulate their moods, desires, and emotions.

The reason hormones influence teenage behavior is twofold: one, these increased levels of hormones are new to the teenage body; and two, these chemicals are interacting with an underdeveloped teenage brain. Imagine trying a drug for the first time; it isn't always a positive experience, though you may enjoy those substances down the road. You might have an upset stomach after your first cigarette or experience the spins after your first sips of alcohol, yet become a habitual smoker or drinker. The same is true for a teenager experiencing this mix of chemicals in their body for the first time without the mental and physical capacity to adjust. It's a lot for an adolescent to handle!

As we learned in chapter 1, the adolescent brain has not yet developed to the point where it can regulate the body's response to these new and different levels of hormones. The fact that the adolescent brain is under construction helps to explain why hormones have a more intense impact on teenagers and why every teen reacts to each hormone differently. The way hormones interact with specific areas of the adolescent brain causes much of the behavior we know to be typical of a teenager. We see more emotional behavior from teens not because their hormones are "raging," but because the emotional part of their brain is developing, and this is the part of the brain that interacts with hormones most intensely.[1] The **hypothalamus**, which regulates hormones in men and women, is located in the midbrain and interacts heavily with the frontal lobe, which we know to be underdeveloped in adolescents. Eventually, the adolescent will have the ability to self-regulate and navigate changes in mood and emotion. But through most of their teenage years, they lack the skills that allow them to manage their volatility. It's our goal as parents to educate our teenagers and help them learn to manage themselves.

We talk about teenage hormones as though they are animal instincts that rage wildly in the adolescent body. The reality is that hormones are part of a complex system of regulation. A **hormone** is a chemical messenger released into the bloodstream that can affect both physiology and behavior. A **neurotransmitter** is a chemical in the brain that enables brain cells to communicate with one another and plays a vital role in the brain's ability to communicate with the body. There are glands located throughout the brain and body that release hormones. Neurotransmitters and hormones are responsible for our instinctual desires and our ability to experience emotions and pleasure. These chemicals interact with receptors in the brain and body to initiate action.[2] A chemical can have a different effect as a neurotransmitter than it does as a hormone; in other words, the same chemical can act differently in the brain than it does in the body. Neurotransmitters and hormones are present in fluctuating doses in brains and bodies that are also in flux.

Let's look at a few key hormones to better understand how they affect adolescent behavior. We see a drastic increase in the release of sex hormones in teenagers. These include **testosterone**, **estrogen**, and **progesterone**. The increased levels of sex hormones in adolescence triggers the onset of puberty and activates the testes and ovaries. Sex hormones interact with the **limbic system**, which is the emotional and instinctual center of the brain. Boys can have up to 30 times more **testosterone** in their systems as adolescents than as children. Testosterone plays a role in healthy bone development, mental clarity, and metabolism; both males and females have varying levels of testosterone in their bodies. **Estrogen** and **progesterone**, increasingly present in adolescent females, are linked to chemicals in the brain that control mood. However, I feel very strongly that we should work against the idea that "hormones" make men aggressive and violent and make women irritable or unpredictable.

Let's take a moment here to talk about periods. With the onset of puberty in adolescent girls, we begin to see mood swings in correlation to menstrual cycles because estrogen is highest right before a female gets her period each month. In a typical premenstrual cycle, we might see emotional sensitivity, unusual food cravings, physical discomfort, and even exhaustion around periods. It's important for adolescents to understand that there can be physical and emotional symptoms as the body prepares for the possibility

of pregnancy with a surge of hormones. Help your teenage boys to understand this, too; periods can have associated symptoms that they should be
sensitive to in their sisters, mothers, friends, and girlfriends. The impact
of premenstrual syndrome (PMS) is usually relatively mild and dissipates
quickly, but it isn't a free pass to be rude or impolite to family and friends.
Realistically, females will need to deal with this for the next 30 years. When
a parent acknowledges what their teen is feeling but moves on quickly, it
mitigates the drama around their discomfort and sends the message that
they can handle it. Encourage your teenage daughter to give into her food
cravings at this time, have a cookie, get more sleep than usual, and let it pass.
Hormonal changes provide an opportunity for teenagers to understand
their bodies and learn self-care. It's healthy to acknowledge that there are
times when we need to give ourselves a break, but this is different from an
excuse.

It's important to note when PMS is more severe and we are dealing with
what is known as PMDD, premenstrual dysphoric disorder, which involves
severe symptoms that interfere with daily life and may require medical attention (Box 2.1). You can't "push through" symptoms of PMDD; it is a physical
reaction in the body that needs to be addressed. I worked with a client who
began to have bouts of severe depression. She had no history of depression,
but she began to experience serious physical and emotional pain over several

---

BOX 2.1

When is it more than PMS?: Premenstrual Dysphoric Disorder

Premenstrual dysphoric disorder (PMDD) is caused by heightened sensitivity to estrogen and progesterone and presents as an almost clinically
allergic reaction. Symptoms of PMDD are severe and interfere with an
individual's ability to function in their daily life.

For example, a girl with PMDD might:

- Be almost unable to get out of bed, or struggle to concentrate on even
  simple tasks.
- Report severe physical symptoms such as vomiting, migraine, headaches, etc.
- Feel extreme, irrational rage.
- Report feelings that present as a major depressive episode, including hope-
  lessness, worthlessness, and even suicidal thoughts.

days each month. Her symptoms were so severe that she was unable to get out of bed. She began writing poetry during these episodes that included suicidal ideation.

As she and her parents described her symptoms to me, I realized they seemed to arrive cyclically, so we began to track her period and her related symptoms on a calendar. They coincided directly. Tracking symptoms on a calendar is particularly important in trying to distinguish the difference between typical PMS and PMDD. The information you can gather not only helps a teen understand her symptoms for herself, but will also help her doctor if necessary. I referred my client to a doctor and she was immediately diagnosed with PMDD. Together, they found a way to manage her condition with birth control and antidepressants, and it has been life changing for her— now she can function through her period. If the symptoms your daughter is experiencing seem unusually severe, they're worth checking out with a medical professional.

We're used to hearing about sex hormones as they relate to adolescents, but there are other hormones we need to be aware of to fully understand a teenager's chemistry (Figure 2.1). **Dopamine** is a significant hormone in your teenager's chemistry as it is the neurotransmitter that activates the reward system in the brain. During adolescence, we see an increase in the activity of the neural circuits that utilize dopamine; higher levels of dopamine prime adolescents to desire, and at times solely focus upon reward. When dopamine is released, it creates a euphoric and energetic sensation in the body.[3] This can positively translate to focus and drive, as dopamine causes us to return to something repeatedly in order to gain proficiency and skill. This is why many adolescents become obsessed with sports; physical exertion releases dopamine, which feels good, and the body in turn craves more. This feels better to an adolescent than sitting in class or doing homework.

HORMONES AND EMOTIONS

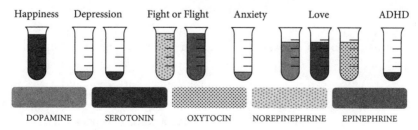

FIGURE 2.1. Hormones and Emotions

However, a craving for dopamine can lead to a ravenous desire for stimulating experiences and exhilarating sensations, which can lend itself to an obsession with an unhealthy substance or activity. Dopamine is released while playing video games and consuming alcohol, cocaine, and sugar, among other things.[4] The teenage brain is vulnerable to dependence. Be aware of anything that excessively triggers your teenager's reward system, and look out for obsessive behaviors. The dopamine pump doesn't distinguish between an Xbox, a Juul, or a Snickers bar. It just wants more. This is why it's important for parents to play a role in setting hard limits.

I often have parents ask me how they can stop their kids from partaking in these kinds of activities. You have the power to take the phone away, unplug the Xbox, throw away the vaporizer, and control their finances. If you find or catch them doing anything you have forbidden, reiterate why you're concerned about those activities and enact the established consequences. Too many parents give away their power in these difficult areas. I have numerous clients whose kids are so addicted to vaping that they're afraid taking it away will impact their performance or cause them to go into withdrawal—all the more reason to intervene immediately. If there's an addiction in place, it needs to be addressed medically. High structure means creating limits on behalf of your teenager because they aren't demonstrating the ability to do so for themselves. It is a nurturing act because you know how damaging these activities are to their growing brain and body. Permission or low structure in these areas only enables further destruction.

Oxytocin is a neurotransmitter that intensifies our feelings. Oxytocin is released in females during physical closeness and following sexual intercourse, which can often result in an increased desire for emotional connection in conjunction with sex. Physical closeness is interpreted as emotional nurturing and love sooner for girls than it is for boys. It's important to speak plainly about this to your teenage sons and daughters. This difference explains why girls have an emotional experience with physical intimacy that we haven't found to be the case for boys. Teenage boys need to understand the emotional impact of sexual intercourse on girls, and it's important for girls to know that boys aren't experiencing the same chemical reaction in connection with sex.[5] Boys will develop an emotional connection over time, but they simply don't experience the same chemical reaction.

It's a typical early experience of adolescence that a boy and a girl will want to have sex with each other for different reasons. This doesn't mean that all teenage boys are jerks! The drive for a teenage boy is often toward physical release, and the drive for a teenage girl is often toward emotional connection. This dynamic can create a disconnect in the aftermath of early sexual experiences that can be very hurtful, particularly for teenage girls. But if boys and girls have this information, they can think about it differently. We can encourage adolescent boys to be more thoughtful, and we can encourage adolescent girls to be aware that they might want to wait. These aren't hard-and-fast rules. Some boys will feel a stronger emotional attachment than some girls, and this dynamic can play out in same-sex couples in which one partner is more emotionally invested than the other. However, if you see this unfolding in a relationship your teenager is in, explaining this difference can spare them a lot of heartache.

Higher levels of **cortisol** are connected to emotions such as stress, worry, anxiety, anger, and even the sensation of loneliness. In addition, higher levels of cortisol have been found to be associated with an inability to lose weight. The level of cortisol typically fluctuates over a 24-hour period, with the highest levels occurring in the morning and decreasing throughout the day before they drop to their lowest levels around midday. Studies have found levels of cortisol to be higher in mid- to late adolescents, particularly in girls. High levels of cortisol are also associated with "brain fog," or a lack of clarity.[6] This can be helpful to know for your adolescent student. Difficulty focusing and paying attention may not be a learning disability, but in fact may be a sign of high levels of cortisol brought on by stress.

This is why it's crucial that you regulate your own anxiety around your teenager's pursuits. Parents can create more stress for their kid with their own anxiety. When we put pressure on our kids in an already charged moment, such as before an important test or a performance, all we do is create additional stress for them to manage. Would it be helpful to you if, before a big presentation or an important interview, someone reminded you of how much was riding on the moment? When a teenager is stressed, their body produces excess cortisol, which triggers the "fight or flight" response and prevents their ability to access the higher cognitive functions like reason, memory, and logic. When we add to this with our own worries or concerns, we sabotage their best shot at performing well. We interfere with their ability to perform and we negate what we are trying to accomplish. Instead, check in with them about what they have going on or ask them what their plan is—*Is there anything I can help you with?*—but then withdraw and let them do it. If anything, try to help them stay calm and remind them of their other successes and that they have your support.

Norepinephrine is another excitatory hormone. **Serotonin** and **GABA**, on the other hand, are two hormones that calm the body down. When we see a lack or an excess of these hormones, particularly serotonin, we often see a display of aggression or depression. Males are particularly sensitive to serotonin levels, demonstrating increased aggression when they are imbalanced. The recreational drug molly (aka MDMA, which is the active ingredient in ecstasy) provides us with a helpful, though extreme, example of the body's sensitivity to serotonin. Molly provides a high by using a disproportionate share of the serotonin available in the body. When someone who has taken molly is "coming down" off of the drug, they experience extreme emotional lows and depressive mood swings because the system is completely depleted of serotonin. The withdrawal is so severe in such individuals that there is an increased risk of suicide. Alternatively, an adolescent may reach for another drug in an attempt to bring themselves back "up." This might be an extreme example, but this is important information for parents to know and share with their teens to make them aware of the chemical impact of drug use and give them a sense that there is a cause and effect with their choices and the way that they feel.

Tetrahydropregnanolone, or THP, is a hormone that is released in response to stress. In the adult brain, THP acts as a tranquilizer, moderating feelings of stress and anxiety. But THP has the *reverse* effect on teens, raising levels of anxiety and exacerbating the stress response. THP is ineffective in regulating stress in teens and in fact escalates the sensation of being overwhelmed. The same hormone that signals an adult to calm down and think rationally tells a teenager to panic. This can help to explain an adolescent's inability to manage stress and intense reaction to stress-provoking situations.[7]

RAGING HORMONES

FIGURE 2.2. "Raging" Hormones

Testosterone plays a role in physical growth and mental stamina. Testosterone interacts heavily with the amygdala, which houses our fight-or-flight response. For this reason, we often see increased aggression in adolescent males. However, testosterone alone does not account for scary or violent behavior. I work with a client who struggles with anger management. He will turn his bedroom upside down, break windows, and punch car doors when he is mad. He's a big boy; he's over 6 feet tall and weighs more than 200 pounds. If you feel afraid of your child or if their behavior feels irrational or out of control, it's important to seek professional help. Another adolescent male I work with, Luis, has what are basically teenage temper tantrums. He will kick holes in the wall and kick furniture upside down over small things, like not getting the dinner he likes or being asked to clean his room. His mom will frequently say "It's his testosterone," but this doesn't have to do with hormones—this is a behavior issue. He is in a low-structure, low-nurture environment and his mom is afraid of him. He has gotten his way by having temper tantrums since he was an infant, so he continues to act this way in his teens. These demonstrations of anger will only escalate with age, particularly when alcohol and drugs are added to the mix. You might think you can handle it, but consider if you are comfortable with your child treating others that way. Someone could get hurt. Moreover, this is a real signal that your child is struggling with profound discomfort and anger that needs attention.

As parents, it's important for us to understand that our role is to help our children develop the capacity to handle their unpredictable responses to their internal chemistry. We can't expect our teens to be able to control their hormones without effort, trial, and error. Even the most resilient, precocious, and well-mannered adolescents struggle to manage their hormones and need our support. Remember, it isn't personal; hormonal development is a chemical reaction in a changing brain and body. We don't know exactly what response our adolescents will have to each hormone as they experience new and unpredictable chemical interactions. But for the most part, adolescents can work to manage their hormones and responsibly navigate their shifting moods and desires.

An effective way to encourage your adolescent to manage their moods is to distinguish between mood-dependent behaviors and goal-dependent behaviors. When an adolescent behaves according to their mood, they will avoid certain tasks and assignments with excuses such as "I don't feel like it" or "I'm tired and I don't want to." We want to encourage goal-dependent behavior, which is a willingness to do something we don't want to do in order to accomplish something that we want or complete something we simply have to do. With teenagers, we often let them make decisions based on their moods and end up frustrated when they don't take care of their responsibilities because their moods are unpredictable and unstable. Instead, we need to reorient them to decision making based on what needs to get done. We want to teach them to tolerate momentary discomfort in order to manage their daily responsibilities on an even keel. Day-to-day life largely consists of what we need to do, rather than what we would like to do or what we consider fun. The sooner we teach kids to accept this fact, the faster they can start to embrace a "make the most of it" attitude. We want adolescents to understand the importance of fulfillment and meaning, not just fun.

Teenagers will often ask: Why do I have to do this? As parents, we want to help our young adolescents connect their tasks to positive outcomes. We can encourage this perspective by making the connection for them: *Get started on your paper tonight so you don't have to worry about it while you're at your hockey tournament.* Take a minute to map out their schedule on a calendar with them. The developing brain isn't particularly attuned to sequencing and timing. When it comes to chores and menial tasks, teach them that they have a responsibility as part of a family, just like they do in any other group or community. Particularly for emotional adolescents who act as though they don't care about anyone, it's helpful to require them to stay involved in this way. Remind them that you don't necessarily enjoy the chores that are yours to do every day, but you do them because you have to.

If we can remove emotion and contention, these can be direct and simple exchanges. If they complain that "it's not fair," agree with them. My kids got tired of hearing me say "Life isn't fair, so don't look for fair." Borrow Nike's slogan: "Just Do It." Even for 18-year-olds, use tactics you employed when they were kids. Tell them that you'll time them in performing a task. It brings awareness that the task isn't usually that difficult. In the time it takes to complain about having to do one thing or another, they could have already completed the task. Or, tell them that you'll keep track of the time you spend doing things for them, and they can keep track of the time they spend doing things for you, and you can compare it. I promise you that they won't want to go down that road!

We *can't* dismiss behavioral patterns and hope that as their hormones come into balance, they will, too. We *can* anticipate and predict certain reactions and draw the line when our teens act in an unacceptable way. We want to send the message that what they are experiencing is real, but that they can learn to handle the ups and downs of this stage. If you're a woman who gave birth, remember when you were pregnant. Your hormonal mood swings didn't permit you to throw tantrums or be disrespectful (at least outside of your house!). You just had to deal with it. Talk to your children about the scientific and chemical basis of their hormonal development. Knowledge is power and they are students, eager to learn. Learning to manage ourselves is a lifelong task; teaching your children to understand themselves as physical and emotional beings during adolescence prepares them for life's highs and lows and sets the stage for self-regulation. Encourage your teenagers to take responsibility for their behavior; "raging hormones" don't let them off the hook.

Intimate Relationships and Sex in Adolescence

On top of a changing and unpredictable internal chemistry, many adolescents will experience their first intimate and sexual relationships and begin to explore their sexuality. This is a healthy, natural development. One of the central tasks of adolescence is learning to form deep, long-term relationships, including with significant others. In the absence of these connections, adolescents and young adults might experience feelings of isolation and loneliness. We want to encourage and support adolescents as they navigate and experience romance for the first time.

As parents, it is essential to have honest and open conversations with your teenagers as they begin to deal with sex in their lives.[8] Parents tend to shrink from their responsibilities in this area because it's uncomfortable; we revert to a low-structure, low-nurture approach. This avoidance makes an already confusing and uncertain element of development seem shameful and uncomfortable. In reality, this is the most important topic to discuss with your teenager because the consequences of a misstep may be life altering.

While your child's sexuality and sexual preference should be theirs to discover, you need to teach them about the nuances of emotional and physical expressions of sex. The healthy expression of sexuality, both emotionally and physically, is learned through observation and experience. When it comes to sex, the stakes are too high to take a pass on your parental responsibility. No parent looks forward to this moment with their child. I certainly didn't! But teenagers will misperceive silence or avoidance around this topic as permission. Take a deep breath and keep it short and to the point. This conversation can be broken into age-appropriate advice. For children in their early teens, talk to them about the idea of "liking" someone and avoiding pressured situations. Make sure they know that, if they don't feel ready for physical interaction with someone they are attracted to, it is perfectly fine to say so. Talk to them about showing respect for someone else's feelings and body.

Conversely, if you try to discuss sexual intercourse and intimate relationships with a young adolescent, they will likely shut you out. A better approach is a candid, unemotional conversation to ensure that they understand the adult implications and real risks of engaging in sex at a young age. There can be long-term consequences they need to be aware of before they make decisions about sex. You might not get much of a response, but you can be sure that when it comes to this topic, they are listening to what you say.

When your child is in their mid-teens, you can have a more in-depth conversation about respect, the emotional component of sex, and how to treat their significant other. Let them know where you stand on it: if you don't want your kids having sex, tell them that you think they underestimate its significance. Talk to them about the importance of forming an emotional connection before they have sex. The most effective approach with an older adolescent is to give them information and insight. They will make a stronger decision in the moment if they have knowledge of potential risks that they can understand. Cover the simple concepts of safety, such as using condoms and the risks of impregnation and sexual diseases. If you explain a **sexually transmitted disease (STD)** to your teenager in simple terms, they will understand enough to know they want to avoid anyone who might give them an STD. These are simple conversations; you don't need to get into what the sex looks like, nor should you want to. But talk to your kids about intimate relationships so that they have a resource for the healthy and appropriate way to navigate their developing sexuality.

Parents often come to me horrified by things they have heard are going on among their children and their friends, and they don't know how to talk to their teen about these things. Address the "hookup culture" with your children in straightforward terms. While you are their parent, you don't need to act oblivious to the reality of their world and the environment they are in. If you want them to develop a healthy, positive relationship to sex, you have to actively work against negative influences in their lives. Tell them what you know in very direct terms and then withdraw. *I heard that girls are giving blowjobs at the movie theater. Do you know about this?* Or: *How will you feel if this boy breaks up with you after you have sex and moves on to someone else?* Asking these questions shows you have an awareness of what their world is like and pushes them to think beyond the immediate moment to consequences they might not envision on their own. Ultimately, they will make their own choices, but if you've given them insight and a listening ear, they will be able to make a more informed and empowered decision.

Ask your kids to reflect on what they think of how other people act in their community and how they think others might perceive their behavior. Adolescents are observant, and you can encourage them to connect certain patterns of behavior with potential consequences that have broader implications than they might realize. Even though your teenage years are further behind you than you'd like to admit, the scene today is remarkably similar to what you experienced. When you point these things out to your children, they perceive that you have an understanding of their world, and you earn credibility with them. When they observe and reflect in such a way, they gain insight into the consequences of behavior, which enables them to make better decisions in the moment.

It's equally important to have this conversation with your sons as it is with your daughters. Societally, we polarize the conversation by gender when, really, the conversation is one about how we treat all people. As parents, we need to work against the cultural assumption that young men will be sexually wild and face no consequences for their behavior. In reality, nothing can change a teenage boy's life faster than impregnating a girl. We typically think of the boy having the choice to walk away or be responsible, but in terms of the decision that is made, it will be her choice to keep, give away, or terminate her pregnancy, and he may have no say in the matter.

It's also important to address the power dynamics inherent in sex, no matter the genders involved. A man usually has physical power over a woman, so they need to understand that this does not give them the right to force or pressure a woman to do anything she does not want to do. There can be different kinds of power dynamics that impact intimate relationships in various ways. As parents, we want to teach our boys and girls that they are responsible for more than their intentions. Consent is actually simple: it is a verbal, sober *yes*. Legally, it is not consent if *anyone* is impaired or compromised. Young men and women must be aware of the risks they face and the threats they pose.[9]

As parents, we want to raise our children in an environment that is inclusive of all sexual preferences. Adolescence may be the first time that your child discovers that they are attracted to members of the same sex. A healthy parental approach is to think about *all* adolescents as coming into their sexuality. They may be discovering an element of their identity that is new to them.

In the event that your child does share that their sexual orientation is different from what you believed it to be, it might take some time to adjust to this new information—which is okay—but be supportive. Say as little as possible about your fears and anxieties in the moment and reaffirm your love and support for your child. If you are having a hard time with your child's sexual orientation, I encourage you to seek guidance in the form of an individual therapist or a support group, but be careful not to put your fear and anxiety on your adolescent. Even if they are comfortable with themselves, they will likely still worry about how the news might impact their family and friends.

The discovery of one's sexuality is a process and it's important that we, as adults, treat the entire range of sexual exploration as natural. Adolescence is largely about discovering one's identity, and sexual orientation is a significant component of that. We want to leave space for this element of self-discovery to happen by demonstrating to our children that we are open to and accepting of all sexual preferences.[10]

It's important to be aware of what you say to your teen as well as what you say around them. Any time a teenager perceives that they have a thought or feeling that their parents do not approve of or accept, they will withdraw. There are enough challenges during adolescence without the added fear of losing your parents' love and support. It can be hard, particularly during adolescence, to feel different than your peers; ensure that your child feels accepted and loved unconditionally at home.

Regardless of your adolescent's sexuality, you will not be able to control who they date. When it comes to your adolescent's sexuality, your demands should be limited to safety and respect. Remember the structure/nurture quadrant: You can set limits and create boundaries so your teen doesn't get into inappropriate situations, but you need to offer unconditional support no matter what their romantic life looks like. It can be challenging to set aside the emotional investment we have in who our child chooses to be with, and we often think we know what will make them happiest. Parents often express that they are accepting of whatever their child's sexuality may be, but they fear that their child's life will be harder if they identify as a minority. This is something for a parent to work through on their own. It's not necessarily helpful to share this with your child; they likely have enough fear about "coming out" or being honest about their sexuality.

For adolescents who identify as transgender or gender nonconforming, the disconnect between their assigned gender and their affirmed gender can result in acute distress called **gender dysphoria**, which can be a source of profound suffering and discomfort (Box 2.2). Some of these individuals are treated with therapy and/or medication. For others, familial support and validation of their emotions can provide the relief they seek. I can't adequately underscore the importance of getting your teenager and yourself the support you need. The Trevor Project, which describes itself as an "organization

---

BOX 2.2

Helpful Terminology

Any time we show our teenagers that we have an awareness of their world and possible internal struggles, we defuse the tension they can feel in sharing themselves with us.

Sexual orientation refers to whom one is romantically or sexually attracted. **LGBTQ** refers to those who identify as lesbian, gay, bisexual, transgender, or queer.

Gender identity is which gender—female or male—one identifies with, regardless of biological sex. "Gender" is expressed through one's personality, appearance, and behavior, and is typically considered "masculine" or "feminine."

Trans, transgender, and **gender nonconforming** refer to people whose gender identity does not match their sex at birth. They may self-identify as more masculine or feminine, or as **nonbinary** (expressing a gender that falls outside of the two more widely recognized genders). The experience of being transgender and/or gender nonconforming means that a person's gender at birth (their assigned gender) does not match the way they feel about themselves (their affirmed gender).

Girls who transition to become boys are typically **transgender males.**

Boys who transition to girls are typically **transgender females.**

A **pansexual** individual is one who is not limited in sexual choice with regard to biological sex, gender, or gender identity.

---

providing crisis intervention and suicide prevention services" to LGBTQ teens and young adults, offers a 24/7 hotline at (866) 488–7386 and additional resources at www.thetrevorproject.org if you are looking for support. This is a highly sensitive area and can be the source of conflict and pain in a parent–child relationship. Remember, you can't figure this out for them. The best way to work through this is to try to remember a time when you felt as though your parents didn't "get" you, and all you wanted was for them to understand your point of view. If you can tap into this emotion, it's usually easier to give your child some leeway and let them make their own decisions. The specifics of your child's sexuality should be theirs to discover, and you should let them discover it on their own. In this way, you will raise children who are accepting of themselves and others. Adolescents should feel empowered in this period of self-discovery and not as though what they are doing is right or wrong; it should be fun and exciting and safe. This is a very important part of developing a healthy sense of self.

The conversation around sex is more important than ever before because adolescents today have an unprecedented level of access to pornography; they are practically inundated. Your teenagers are naturally curious, and it's very easy for them to unintentionally access highly inappropriate content. This doesn't mean that they understand it or necessarily solicited it, but pornography cannot be the only model for a teenager to develop ideas about sex and sexuality before they have their own experiences. Pornography will give your teenagers the wrong ideas about sex. If you look at what's online, you don't see examples of healthy, loving sex or a positive alternative to graphic pornography. Adolescents watch porn and believe that rough, raucous sex is the norm. Women are shown enjoying this type of sex and accepting aggressive and even violent behavior from men. In my work, I'm seeing an almost depraved indifference to significant sexual acts among my clients as young as 12 and 13 years old because they're mirroring the indifference and casual attitude they are seeing. This has to be actively countered by what they are learning at home. Address the fact that the sex in pornography is not normal or desirable.

If you can't have this conversation with your children, urge them to read this book. There are several books that can provide resources about healthy sexual exploration for both parents and teens to aid what ideally should be an open and direct dialogue (Box 2.3). Remember that, at the end of the day, the most important model of an intimate relationship is the one a teenager sees

---

BOX 2.3

Book Recommendations

- *Changing Bodies, Changing Lives: A Book for Teens on Sex and Relationships*, by Ruth Bell.
- *Our Bodies, Ourselves*, by Judy Norsigian.
- *S.E.X. The All-You-Need-To-Know Sexuality Guide to Get You Through Your Teens and Twenties*, by Heather Corinna.
- *Why Gender Matters: What Parents and Teachers Need to Know About the Emerging Science of Sex Differences*, by Leonard Sax.

every day. Model the behavior you want your adolescents to engage in and make sure to practice what you preach.[11]

Intimate relationships at such a vulnerable stage of life are complicated. As inexperienced romantic partners, teenagers are bound to hit bumps in the road. The first relationship can be a rocky one! Teens develop a capacity for intimacy through practice and experience. Adolescents begin to understand that romantic love is different from familial love or the love they might have for a friend. It's important for teens to experience heartbreak and rejection, as well as to learn how to care about somebody in a way that's special and unique.

I had a client who had dated her college boyfriend for several years when she left for college. Lucia had told me that she was ambivalent about her boyfriend, but they had been together for so long that she found it hard to imagine breaking up with him. When they were both home for winter break after their first semesters of school, he broke up with her and told her that he was already seeing someone else. When we talked, Lucia was having a hard time. For one thing, she had five long weeks at home in the place where she was used to spending time with him. She also told me that she was hurt by some of the things he had done at the end of their relationship; he had been dishonest and inconsiderate. Lucia told me she wasn't going to say anything; she was just going to try to forget about him. "Won't that give me closure?" she asked me.

Actually, this was a great opportunity for Lucia to learn about how to take care of herself within an intimate relationship. I told her I understood how hard it is to feel rejection, and we would always rather break up with someone else than have them break up with us, but she still had the right to express herself and tell her ex-boyfriend how she felt. Then, I reminded her that when she was feeling sad at school, she could remind herself that she knew she wasn't going to be with him forever, and she had a great opportunity to meet all kinds of people in college. This way, instead of trying to ignore her feelings, she could deal with disappointment and rejection in a healthy and direct way instead of trying to distract herself from her pain. If she hadn't said anything to her ex-boyfriend, her feelings would have turned into resentment and anger and she would have had a much harder time letting go.

In many ways, adolescence is the ideal time to develop a love interest, as teenagers are open to and desirous of new and exciting experiences and have the ability to rebound and come back quickly from heartbreak and rejection. It's important for adolescents to realize that, no matter what happens, they will be okay (Box 2.4).

BOX 2.4

Helping Your Child Through a Breakup

Avoid "I told you so" comments. Even if you didn't think your child's boyfriend or girlfriend was "right" for them, this type of reminder won't ease their pain.

Don't undermine or diminish what they are going through. You have the perspective to know they will move on to other people, but that can be hard for them to see, particularly if they are mourning their first love. Acknowledge what they are feeling.

Give your child the time and space to be sad. They might need a few days to be down and work through their feelings. But don't let them skip school or withdraw from their activities. It's important for them to stay busy and realize that life goes on.

Only share your own experience of a painful breakup if your child asks you whether you've been through something similar to what they're dealing with. Though it may seem sympathetic, it isn't helpful to an adolescent if they can't feel it. If they are in the mood to talk, it's more likely that they'll want to share with you about their own pain. **Listen** instead of telling them how it was for you.

Be nurturing—make their favorite meal for dinner, rent a movie, or tuck them into bed at night. These simple gestures let them know that you are there for them and remind them that they can rely on you through their ups and downs, but they will survive.

The development of intimate relationships in adolescence has taken a major hit from social media and technology. The quality of a relationship depends on our ability to move through the discomfort of vulnerability and allow others to know us in an intimate way. If teens are texting each other instead of speaking face to face and spending quality time together, the emotional connection is lost. This is a tragedy! What is a first love without butterflies in your stomach, sweat on your palms, and a pounding heart? It's important for parents to communicate expectations that prevent adolescents from conducting their relationships solely through the phone. It can be healthy for an adolescent to experience sex and intimacy in a safe way, but technology doesn't support a deep connection.[12]

Technology has also skewed the natural boundaries that used to provide time and space for solitude, reflection, and privacy. It's hard to know how we feel about someone if our mental energy is consumed with constant communication.[13] We've seen a huge decrease in what individuals are willing to share with each other because anything said over text or social media can be shared with a wider audience, and often is. It's difficult to develop or recover a sense of intimacy and trust when we don't know how many people our words will reach, and this downturn in trust can contribute to feelings of isolation and loneliness for adolescents.[14] I have had several female clients who either FaceTime a boyfriend nude or send indecent pictures over text, email, or Snapchat. This *never* ends well. These pictures can be shared, posted, or even used as blackmail, and the consequences can be devastating. Physical intimacy is private and we want to teach our children that while their sexuality is nothing to be embarrassed about, they should view sex as a private matter. Kids should consider their phones to be public domain. Nearly every teen will tell you, "It's just Snapchat, it disappears." Even on apps like Snapchat users manage to find a way to save a photo, and there is often a trace left somewhere on the internet. Most tech-savvy users can track photos down even if they have "disappeared" or been deleted. Ask your child if they would be comfortable with *anyone* seeing the things they are sending over text or through apps on their devices.[15] Most 8th- to 10th-grade relationships are short lived. Ask your adolescent if they are sending anything, whether an image or a text, they might regret if the relationship ends. The publicizing of these exchanges can be extremely shameful and humiliating for those involved.

Encouraging your children to think about the broader implications of the things they say and do when they don't think anybody else is watching is a lesson in accountability. Talk about this with your kids. Show them the volatility of these interactions through a conversation by pointing to examples in their classes or friend groups where someone's private exchange was broadcast for everyone to see. It's much more effective to give them an example from their world so that they can understand what you're talking about. If they think you "get it," you will gain respect and credibility.

The reality is, your teenager has a life online that you will always, in some way, be disconnected from. Don't get hung up on seeing everything they do. Parent as if the phone didn't exist and rely on your values and morals. By the time this book is published, there will most likely be a new app or piece of technology that has added to the challenge for parents. The same expectations for behavior, romance, and dating should hold true regardless of technological advances.

It's our responsibility as parents to combat the impact of technology on our adolescents. Talk to your teenagers about what their phones are and are not appropriate for. Encourage your children to ask someone out in person. Require that anybody picking your child up for a date come into your house to shake your hand and introduce themselves. By the same token, if your teen is having a fight with a significant other or going through a breakup, encourage them to have these difficult conversations in person. **On a neurological and emotional level, if it isn't face to face, it doesn't count.**

Hormones, which are responsible for our emotional sensations and behavior, are released based on our physical experience and environment. One of the earliest developmental milestones in life is the way a baby responds to faces. Do they laugh when they see a smile? Are they scared when they see a stranger? Humans are hardwired to connect visually and physically.[16] When we send a text, we don't consider where the other person might be or what else they are dealing with in the moment; thus we lose the ability to see their reaction to our words. Over text, meaning can be misinterpreted and we might say things we don't genuinely feel. As the iPhone has become more pervasive, we have seen people of all ages struggle with relationships, particularly intimate relationships. Teens don't have the emotional experience to treat each other with kindness and respect at every turn. Consideration for someone else's feelings and experience is learned and can only be fully understood in person.

An adolescent has a lot to handle. Their internal chemistry is changing during a highly stimulating time in their lives. Mood swings come with the flux of the brain. Help your child understand all of the factors that contribute to how they feel: their energy level, what they've eaten, and how they slept, among others. We can tweak many pieces of our daily routine if needed, but it's important to get away from the idea that we are on a hormonal roller coaster with our teen and there isn't anything anyone can do about it. If you feel that your teenager's mood swings are out of control, there may be something more serious going on. Any extreme behaviors that seem highly erratic, irrational, or out of control, or any noted withdrawal from typical behaviors, particularly social activities, indicates that there might be a more serious chemical imbalance. This is more complicated and, if you are concerned that your adolescent is struggling with these kinds of symptoms, you should consult a medical professional. For the most part, however, adolescents are well equipped for this phase of development, as the chemistry and structure of the adolescent brain create a neurological environment that is flexible and open. They can learn to manage their emotions and behavior over time through trial and error.

Parents need to help their teens learn to anticipate their unpredictable urges and volatile moods by giving them an awareness of what they are dealing with, helping them to identify their feelings, and working to use their judgment to self-regulate. We must hold our children to certain standards of behavior no matter what phase they are in, and empower them to embrace new experiences and emotions with responsibility and awareness.

Consider This:
Insights & Actions

- Encourage your adolescent to notice how various factors such as sleep, nutrition, and exercise impact their overall sense of balance. A diet high in processed foods, sugar, and/or caffeine contributes to hormonal imbalance. Encourage your family to eat plenty of fruits and vegetables, protein, and complex carbohydrates to keep their systems functioning well. This isn't about appearance or pleasure; it's important to make the connection between nutrition and health. Regular physical activity and plenty of sleep also help to regulate hormones in the body.
- Be aware of what your children are doing on their devices. Maintain oversight until you're confident that they can monitor their use on their own. As long as you're paying the bill, you are ultimately responsible. The question of privacy only comes up if they are doing something inappropriate. If you wouldn't allow your teenager to be home alone or in a room with the door locked with friends or a member of the opposite sex, you probably shouldn't allow them to have no limits in their online conversations, either.
- Teens naturally feel more comfortable saying some things over text (as do many adults!), but lewd language or images should not be tolerated. A good rule of thumb is: Would you be comfortable if your grandmother read what you were saying? I remember scrambling to turn off a Cat Stevens eight-track tape when my grandmother came into the room. Tell them that if they wouldn't say something face to face, they probably shouldn't text it. You might not prevent them from saying anything inappropriate over text or online, but you've made them aware of how you feel, and they might pause before they do something really bad.
- Up until around age 15, stay involved in your child's phone time, but only step in if they are unable to manage on their own. If their homework and chores are done, their free time is theirs. Help your teen develop their own reward system, such as getting to play a game for 30 minutes after finishing

two subjects of homework. Work with them to set up the system because if they've bought into it, they will be more likely to follow it. Remember that the goal is self-regulation. Total abstinence is unrealistic and ineffective.

- Try to establish a "no-phone time" in your family's day. Whether during family dinner or close to bedtime, ensure that there is time when everyone is off their devices and interacting with loved ones face to face. Give them a break from the constant interference. Make sure everyone in the family abides by the rule! Be present with your family during meal times so that they know they have your undivided attention, too. It's a relief to actually be off of your phone.

- Get to know your teenager's boyfriend or girlfriend. Ask them to come over for dinner or join your family on a group outing. If your child is dating someone that you have concerns about, it's useful to make concrete observations, such as "There is a big age difference between the two of you," instead of judgmental comments. It's okay to express your concerns, but keep it open ended and avoid trying to tell them what to do.

- If you see inappropriate sexual content in a movie or on the news, or hear about something in your community, point it out to your teenager. We want to encourage them to make the connection between sexual recklessness and negative consequences. A live incident can have more impact on your adolescent than your words alone. Every school deals with incidents that become public. Your kids know who is promiscuous and who is a jerk. Ask them about it directly and listen to their observations and connections. This is how things begin to make sense to them. They learn about how people are perceived when they speak about it. These are also questions that they will usually respond to, as opposed to *How are you?* or *How was your day?* It is good to show that you're aware of what's going on.

- A good cue to use with your teen is HALT. If they are feeling out of sorts, ask them if they are Hungry, Angry, Lonely, or Tired. Often times, all we need is a meal, a nap, or good company to feel better.

Notes

1. Siegel, D. J. (2013) *Brainstorm: The power and purpose of the teenage brain.* New York, NY: Penguin.

2. Brick, J., & Erickson, C. K. (1998). *Drugs, the brain, and behavior: The pharmacology of drug use disorders* (2nd ed.). New York, NY: Routledge.

3. Kestenbaum, C. J., & Williams, D. T. (Eds.). (1988). *Handbook of clinical assessment of children and adolescents* (Vols. I & II). New York, NY: New York University Press.

4. Brick, J., & Erickson, C. K. (1998). *Drugs, the brain, and behavior: The pharmacology of drug use disorders* (2nd ed.). New York, NY: Routledge.

5. Sax, L. (2017). *Why gender matters: What parents and teachers need to know about the emerging science of sex differences.* New York, NY: Harmony Books.

6. Jensen, F. E., & Nutt, A. E. (2015). *The teenage brain: A neuroscientist's survival guide to raising adolescents and young adults.* New York, NY: HarperCollins.

7. Jensen, F. E., & Nutt, A. E. (2015). *The teenage brain: A neuroscientist's survival guide to raising adolescents and young adults.* New York, NY: HarperCollins.

8. Sax, L. (2017). *Why gender matters: What parents and teachers need to know about the emerging science of sex differences.* New York, NY: Harmony Books.

9. Sax, L. (2017). *Why gender matters: What parents and teachers need to know about the emerging science of sex differences.* New York, NY: Harmony Books.

10. Brown, B. (2012). *Daring greatly: How the courage to be vulnerable transforms the way we live, love, parent, and lead.* New York, NY: Avery.

11. Siegel, J. P. (2000). *What children learn from their parents' marriage: It may be your marriage, but it's your child's blueprint for intimacy.* New York, NY: HarperCollins.

12. Turkle, S. (2012). *Alone together: Why we expect more from technology and less from each other.* New York, NY: Basic Books.

13. Gardner, H., & Davis, K. (2013). *The app generation: How today's youth navigate identity, intimacy, and imagination in a digital world.* New Haven, CT: Yale University Press.

14. Turkle, S. (2012). *Alone together: Why we expect more from technology and less from each other.* New York, NY: Basic Books.

15. Steyer, J. P. (2012). *Talking back to Facebook: The common sense guide to raising kids in the digital age.* New York, NY: Scribner.

16. Aikens, M. (2016). *Cybereffect: An expert in cyberpsychology explains how technology is shaping our children, our behavior, and our values—and what we can do about it.* New York, NY: Spiegel & Grau.

3

The Third Myth

ADOLESCENTS SHUT OUT ADULTS AND
LISTEN ONLY TO THEIR PEERS.

I CAN'T TELL you how often I hear parents complain that their teenager doesn't seem to listen to them or care about them: "He only talks to his friends" . . . "She'll never listen to me" . . . "He doesn't care about anything I say" . . . "She's always on the phone with her friends" . . . "He rips into me" . . . "She rolls her eyes at everything I say." Parents of teens often feel as though their adolescent doesn't want them in their life because they are starting to push their parents away and shut them out.[1] Based on this assumption, parents withdraw from their teenager, which in turn causes their teenager to turn away from their family and turn instead to their friends.

For parents to pull back from their child during these years is nothing short of a copout. Teenagers can only learn how to build and navigate positive relationships through the connections they have with their parents and other adults in their lives.[2] This ability is one of the most essential tools an individual can have in life, and teens learn the most from those more mature than them. The ties they have with parents, teachers, coaches, and mentors lay the foundation for the relationships they will need to build with college professors, bosses, and in-laws as they become adults.

Parenting adolescents requires a major shift in both attitude and approach. As our children enter the teenage years, we want to move from a control model to a relationship model. When we try to tighten the reins as they begin to push back, conflict becomes the singular point of contact between parent and child. The adolescent years are too formative to waste in a polarized relationship. Instead, we want to view these years as the time to build a relationship with our child. Too often, parents of teenagers hope that if they can weather the storm of adolescence, they can form a loving, nurturing relationship with their adult child, when in reality the relationship you form with your teenager establishes the type of relationship you will have with them later on. The strongest parent–child relationships grow and change with the adolescent and serve as the model for all other relationships in a teenager's life. The goal is to build self-esteem, confidence, and independence in your teen, and you can only achieve this through a relationship based on trust, listening, mutual understanding, and respect.

As we learned in chapter 2, adolescence is a wonderful and important time to form new relationships, and these ties prevent teenagers from feeling isolated, lonely, and disconnected from the world around them. According to psychological theory, the formation of a capacity for intimacy is one of the three central crises of adolescence.[3] If this crisis is confronted and resolved, we develop the ability to have meaningful connections in all areas of our lives. Adolescence is when we begin to see inferential thinking in our teen, which allows them to perceive information beyond the concrete facts in front of them and, therefore, enables them to feel empathy.[4] While we see sympathy in young children as they learn to understand when they *should* feel bad for someone else, we begin to see empathy in teens as they develop compassion for someone else's feelings and what additional stresses might impact another person's behavior. Empathy is not just the ability to imagine another person's circumstances and emotions; it's also the ability to act on that understanding. As children reach adolescence, we start to expect them to respond appropriately in various social situations as they become more aware of others. Teenagers learn to open themselves to others, set limits, and establish boundaries by testing and being tested by those around them.[5] Adolescence should be a time of trial and error during which teens can work on becoming a good son or daughter, boyfriend or girlfriend, student, leader, and friend. Remember how great it felt the first time you established a relationship independent of your family or school? There is satisfaction and even pride in building one's own relationships throughout the adolescent years.

Building a Relationship With Your Teenager
Redefining Trust

Teenagers are learning the components of a strong relationship, including trust, respect, and give-and-take. Parents and teenagers often speak about trust when they describe challenges in their relationship. Parents don't feel they can trust their teens and teens sense this lack of trust. When it comes to parenting, I define trustworthiness as a willingness to take accountability for one's actions. In other words, to trust my child does not mean I expect that they will never make a poor decision or end up in a compromised situation. However, I do trust that they will take responsibility for and be honest about their actions. This is the key difference between a mistake and a lie. Although it may seem obvious, it's important to point this out to adolescents. Simply put, a mistake is unintentional, while a lie is intentional. If they tell you they are going to be in one place and you find out that they are in another, they'll often say "I made a mistake," but what they did was lie to you. A mistake will not necessarily break your trust, but a lie will. Teenagers make mistakes when they are faced with a choice and make the wrong one; teenagers lie when they intentionally deceive you to do something they know you wouldn't condone. Often, they will make a mistake and then lie about the mistake they've made.

Suppose you suspect your teen has been doing something you have explicitly told them not to do, whether it's playing video games on a weeknight or drinking on a weekend. If you ask them about it and learn that you were right, they will have to face the consequence for breaking your rule. But they were honest with you, so you are still in a position where you can trust them. If they lie about it and you discover that they lied, it's important to let them know that when they lie, they diminish your ability to trust them. As you go through this with them, be sure to identify that it was their lie that broke your trust, not their mistake, and they made the choice to lie. This doesn't mean that their mistake doesn't have its own consequence, but a mistake shouldn't threaten your trust in them or your belief that they are capable of doing the right thing. When your teenager makes a mistake, ask yourself if the issue is really one of trust or if it's an example of your teen's inexperience and immaturity. Trust is about honesty and unconditional love, and it is at the core of your relationship with your adolescent.

Building trust with your adolescent is a process and they will earn your trust over time. You may trust them to do their homework or babysit their younger sibling before you trust them to go to a party without parental supervision. If your teenager accuses you of not trusting them, explain that trust is situational. The ability to trust in your adolescent is based on the establishment of clear expectations and boundaries. Tell them how you feel about different activities they might engage in so they know where you stand. If you tell them that you don't want them to drink, they will know that there will be consequences if they drink. Try not to be overly permissive or overly strict; set boundaries based on what is best for your child, but understand that they may not always meet them.

For the most part, your teenager will try to behave in a manner that is within your family's expectations. It's in their nature to want to please you. But you need to expect that they will make poor decisions or get themselves into trouble at some point.[6] Try not to come down hard on your child every time they do something wrong (high structure, low nurture). If they feel like you expect and anticipate that they will mess up all the time, they will. If you expect them to do the right thing, they will try to, most of the time (high structure, high nurture). Furthermore, if you react strongly to every misstep, your child won't be able to distinguish behavior that is truly unacceptable and, more importantly, they won't care because they will feel like what they do doesn't matter—it's always the same reaction.

Adolescents are very responsive to constructive criticism given in a nonpunitive demeaning way, but they respond very strongly to rejection. In fact, we can see on MRIs that rejection is experienced in the pain center in the adolescent brain.[7] **Your teenager receives reprimand as personal rejection.** If they feel judged or shamed, they will write you off and stop trying to meet your expectations because they feel that you don't understand them.[8] Judgment shuts them down and makes them feel as though it doesn't matter what they do, so they won't hesitate to engage in risky or poor behavior again. Be understanding and allow room for error, but make it clear that there is a line beyond which you will not accept certain behaviors, whatever that line may be for you.

When you're in that moment, make sure to keep your conversation short and direct. Be clear about what was wrong, where you stand, and then withdraw. Parents are prone to go on an endless tirade, bringing in irrelevant issues that compound a teen's guilt and shame. We guarantee that we will not be heard the minute we rant and rave and bring other issues into the conversation. Think of the last time you had a disagreement with a spouse or a friend. As soon as conflict becomes emotional and voices escalate, the conversation becomes unproductive. When other issues get pulled in from weeks, months, and even years prior, the only outcome is hurt feelings. When we do the same with our teenager, we put up a divider. Retain your power by keeping it specific so that your child can learn the lesson at hand. If you don't make a distinction with regard to behavior, your teen won't either.

Be aware: There is a significant difference between the message *I will help you navigate challenging situations* and the message *You can do whatever you want because I'm your friend.* Remember Amy Poehler's "cool mom" character in *Mean Girls*? You don't want to be the parent serving alcohol and gossiping with your daughter and her friends because you won't be taken seriously. **You**

aren't your child's friend. Acting as your child's friend creates a superficial sense of trust and respect in your relationship. Unconditional love and understanding do not equate to a free pass on behavior. However, you can also tell them that if something goes wrong or if they don't know what to do and they're scared, they can *always* call you. We want the message to be: I understand that you don't totally know how to handle every situation, but I **trust** that if you are in over your head, you will try to make good decisions, and you can always ask for my help. Even though there may be consequences for their behavior, you will help them get through the issue at hand.

Adolescents are often afraid to ask for help because they fear they will lose their parents' trust or get into trouble. This is a tricky area because you want to get your message across without telling your child what to do. There are several ways to get your point across without giving a directive or simply admonishing a behavior, like asking open-ended questions or making observations that aren't pointed. This is why it is so important to explain what you are looking for and explain that, just as situations will vary, your responses will, too. Parents should allow their teenager to feel that reaching out for help is a trust-building action because it demonstrates an awareness of their limitations. If your child reaches out to you for help, it's a sign of maturity and a signal that you have a strong relationship. If they trust you, they are more likely to ask for your opinion and trust you with information about their lives. In difficult situations, you want to align yourself with your teen and help them figure things out so that they know they can rely on you when they've screwed up.

Setting your kid up so that you can catch them in a mistake or a lie is not effective parenting. Again, this is a high-structure, low-nurture approach and sets up a dynamic in which their primary goal is not to be caught, instead of their primary goal being to make better choices. Avoid shaming, even when you're disappointed. Comments like "I can't believe you did this to me," "I can't trust you with anything," "You are such a liar," or "What is wrong with you?" only serve to alienate and embarrass your child. When someone is ashamed, they shut down, withdraw, and lose confidence in themselves. Instead, push them to own their behavior and help them learn from their mistakes.

As parents, remember that these can be "teaching moments." **Insight is more important than an actual, restrictive punishment.**[9] Observation and discussion are effective methods for helping your teenager learn how to make better decisions and access their judgment in the moment. When issues come up at school or they hear about classmates getting into trouble, ask them what they think about what happened and how it was handled. We often see younger siblings develop decision-making skills earlier because they've seen more. Whether it's seeing their siblings or their siblings' friends facing consequences for their mistakes, they have the opportunity to process the implications of various behavior in a rational way before they are in a position to make the same choice.

My youngest son was very focused on athletics and saw how quickly an athletic scholarship could be lost with a single slip-up. He was better able to preview the potential consequences because he had seen it happen with his siblings and older friends. He was mindful of his behavior because he could make a direct connection with a negative consequence that he wanted to avoid, so he avoided certain situations that could end badly.

Parents often avoid certain topics to try to prevent their kids from finding out about these things, but most of the time, they know more than you think. Engaging them in discussion around various incidents is a great way for them to learn. Reflecting in this way strengthens higher level functioning as these emotional, social, and behavioral capacities are utilized and stretched. You also show them that you believe in their ability to make good choices. The teenage brain grows and develops through experience; with practice, these neurological connections form and strengthen in the brain, and we start to trust our teenagers to make better decisions.[10]

Cultivating Mutual Respect

In addition to trust, another key component of your relationship with your adolescent is mutual respect. As your adolescent matures, show respect for the individual they are becoming by listening to their opinion and treating them the way you would like them to treat you. One element of this is teaching your adolescent how to acknowledge their mistakes and admit when they've done something wrong. Owning mistakes teaches us the impact of our actions.[11]

Relationships are flexible and can weather difficulties, but not without ownership and accountability. Parents are the primary people in a teen's life who show them that they will be loved and cared for even if they make a mistake. You can bolster your teenager's self-esteem by reassuring them that you love them and are proud of them in spite of mistakes or failures. The best way to get this across is with your own example. When you make a mistake, tell your teenager that you're sorry; by the same token, accept a genuine apology and demonstrate forgiveness. Kids always tell me that their parents stay stuck on their missteps. If you aren't ready to accept an apology, tell your child that you need some time. If you accept their apology, don't give them the silent treatment or continue to act irritated with them. Let go of the emotion. Give-and-take is a key element of the parent–child relationship in adolescence.

A simple, straightforward way to teach your children to show respect is by impressing the importance of manners upon them (Box 3.1). Manners are an essential piece of learning how to build relationships of all kinds. They go a long way, and people notice good manners, particularly in adolescents.

BOX 3.1

Etiquette 101

Show respect and deference to elders and those older than you. Greet the adults that you know. When you recognize someone in public, say hello and greet them by name.

Put your devices down and look someone in the eye when you speak to them. It is not only polite, it also provides a fuller emotional experience in an interaction and allows for a deeper understanding. Looking at your phone while someone is speaking to you is the equivalent of ignoring them.

A firm handshake is a key part of good communication. Make the effort to learn and remember someone's name when you meet them.

Say "please" and "thank you" when you are being served in the cafeteria, at a restaurant, or in someone's home. This should include your own home!

Hand-write a thank-you note for presents, favors, and special outings. People will be generous with you when they feel your gratitude for the things they do.

Take your shoes off in someone else's home. If you see shoes lined up at the back door, at the very least, ask if the host would like you to remove your shoes before going inside.

Demonstrate interest in the lives of those you interact with. "How was your day?" can go a long way. Asking about somebody's life shows consideration for others and their situation.

Show good manners at the table. Put your napkin in your lap, keep your elbows off of the table, and wait for everyone to be served before you begin to eat. When you're finished eating, thank whoever prepared your meal, clear your own plate, and ask if you can help clean up.

Parents often tell me that their kids don't respect them and don't seem to appreciate the small, simple things they do for them on a daily basis, such as preparing a warm meal or doing their laundry. I recently met with a group of parents who told me that they do everything for their children, yet their children appreciate nothing. I asked them why they continue to do everything for their children. They told me they continue because that's a parent's job. That's not your job. You have to be willing to stop the cycle. Your job is to teach consideration, gratitude, and respect. Another person's willingness to help us depends largely on how we treat them. If you continue to take care of your children in these ways when they are rude to you, you send the message that it's okay to treat others poorly and act spoiled. "Spoiled" is an attitude, it's not a result of material privilege.

To teach them that they are not entitled to the good favor of others in the world, you need to teach them this lesson at home. If you take the time to prepare a meal for your family and your teenager responds by criticizing your cooking or complaining about what's being served, there's no need to be emotional or defensive. Be creative; approach it differently. Remember: Teenagers are learning how to behave and how their words and actions impact others. Tell them that they're on dinner the following night. They can choose the menu and prepare the meal when they get home from school. It's important for them to understand the effort that goes into certain tasks and understand that others will not want to help them when they are ungrateful and disrespectful. By the time they are teenagers, they know what it means to show respect for another person. Parents need to hold them accountable and let them know that when they don't treat others with kindness and respect, there are ramifications.

I work with a parent whose son is constantly rude to her. She recently shared an episode with me in which Teddy was rushing to finish a term paper. She went out of her way to make herself available for help in spite of Teddy's disrespectful comments and bad attitude. He was totally ungrateful and even lashed out at her for printing his paper with the wrong margins. Parents mishandle these moments because their desire for their child to succeed overcomes their desire to teach their child the important lesson at hand. In this case, Teddy's mom continued to help him with his paper until it was done and then exploded, yelling uncontrollably at him and berating him for his bad attitude. However, Teddy faced no tangible consequence in this situation.

If your child is rude to you when you do something for them, stay calm and remove yourself from the situation. In this case, she might have said, "I can't help you if you talk to me that way. I love you, but I don't work for you.

When you treat me poorly, I don't want to be around you." Or, she may have put it back on Teddy: "It seems like you would prefer to do this on your own so I'm going to let you be." Why would the child change his or her behavior without experiencing consequences? Teddy's mom sent the message that not only is it okay for him to be rude to her, but also that the completion of his assignment is ultimately more important than the way he treats his mother.

Parents often miss these teaching opportunities because of their focus on the outcome, when these are the perfect moments to show your child the importance of the way they treat others. When you treat someone poorly, you lose their good favor, generosity, and consideration. It's important for parents to show their adolescents the consequences of acting rude and ungrateful, regardless of what's at stake. Remember, we are talking about middle and high schoolers, so the stakes shouldn't be that high in relative terms. Resist the urge to rescue your child when their behavior lands them in a situation that's difficult for them to navigate. You can support them and help them come up with a plan—high structure, high nurture—but they need to learn to find their way through.

Another one of my clients faces similar issues with her adolescent girl. Her daughter, Jane, is a motivated student and a talented dancer, but she is often overwhelmed by the demands of her schedule. On a recent weekend, she had a dance recital and a squash match with only a few hours in between. She overslept, so her mom made her breakfast. They were in the car before Jane's mom remembered to ask whether she'd brought her inhaler. Jane has asthma and often requires her inhaler during both dance and athletics. Jane insisted that they leave without it, accusing her mom of making her late on purpose. Her mom wouldn't leave without the inhaler, so Jane yelled at her that she should just leave her alone and she would take an Uber instead. Her mom called me immediately after their exchange, telling me that she was shaking and nearly in tears. She couldn't believe how Jane had spoken to her. She was in the parking lot outside of the recital, unsure of what to do next.

I asked her if there was any way she could let Jane know that she needed to find a different ride to her squash match. She said that it would be too late and Jane would have a hard time finding one. So I told her to withdraw. Jane had hurt her feelings, so it was okay for her to show that she was upset. When she picked Jane up, she was quiet in the car, said very little, and let her daughter know that they would be leaving home again at 12:30. If Jane wasn't downstairs, she wasn't going to come get her. It's important to note how Jane's mother articulated her position: She wasn't emotional and she didn't berate Jane; she simply stated what was expected and held to it. Jane was downstairs right on time and was much more pleasant to her. She had ended the cycle of emotional outburst, making it clear that she was not going to participate if Jane didn't treat her with more respect.

It worked at that time, but to achieve a shift in their daughter's attitude, her parents must continue to insist on respectful treatment. As soon as Jane is rude or demanding, they must simply say: "I can't respond when you speak and act this way." Then, they need to withdraw. If your child tells you that you are being mean or unfair, it's important to articulate that you are responding to their behavior. You're allowed to be mad, hurt, or stern when the situation calls for it. In this way, they learn that where they have the power to change the situation is through their own behavior. **As parents, if we aren't consistent with what we require from our teen, we can't expect consistent behavior from them.**

Allowing for Give-and-Take

Take a look at what you're doing for your children and ask yourself who you are doing these things for. Do you get up early to make breakfast because a "good parent" makes breakfast? While some gestures may feel important to you, they may not feel important to your child. I had a client who prepared a warm, nutritious meal for her son every morning, yet her son routinely overslept and didn't have time to eat. Every single morning, she was hurt by the lack of gratitude he showed for her effort. But it simply wasn't important to him. He cared more about a few extra minutes of sleep than getting downstairs in time to eat breakfast.

I told her to make herself a cup of coffee and hand him a granola bar on the way out the door. This came as a huge relief to her, and her son appreciated a calmer morning without his mother hassling him to get downstairs. If it doesn't matter to your child, they won't show you the gratitude you desire. Even if you feel that you know what's best for them, you can't make them want breakfast! Respect their wishes and priorities, too, when it is not detrimental to their wellbeing. It's important to pick your battles; the emphasis should be on manners and consideration for others, not your own agenda.

By the same token, it's okay to let your children fend for themselves from time to time. The morning is often hectic, when parents are trying to get all of their children out the door on time. If your teenager is routinely late, leave without them. It's not that complicated! Just go. They will have to figure out how to get themselves to school. If they are upset and accuse you of leaving them behind, make the distinction that you left because they were late. If they know what time the car leaves the driveway, they need to make sure they're in it. We confuse being a good, loving parent with doing everything for our children. Actually, doing everything for your child creates a low-structure, high-nurture environment which results in self-centered, demanding, and indulgent adolescents. **Being a good, loving parent means equipping your child to take care of themselves.**

Even if they aren't rude or disrespectful, it is still important to give teenagers small responsibilities like packing their lunch or getting their younger sibling to the bus. Siblings are a great training ground for your adolescent to learn how to care for both themselves and others. I was once panicked because I wasn't going to be home in time to make dinner for my son when he got home from lacrosse practice. I called his older brother and told him I would be out, so I needed him to make dinner for his younger brother.

When I got home, my younger son told me that his brother made him a quesadilla in the microwave with prosciutto, cheddar, and ketchup. He said it was awful, but he ate every bite because he didn't want to hurt his brother's feelings. When I asked my older son about it, he told me that the meal was really bad, but he ate it so his brother would, too. They both rose to the occasion and showed care and gratitude for each other.

Becoming an adult is, in large part, learning how to handle various situations with a degree of grace. It's important for adolescents to be in situations where they have to figure out how to do something they haven't done before. These are also opportunities for your children to realize what you do for them on a daily basis and assume a more mature role.

Sibling Relationships in Adolescence

While we're on the topic of relationships, I want to take a moment to discuss sibling relationships in adolescence. The challenges of parenting adolescents can sometimes be compounded by a family's composition, including the number of children in the family and their ages and stages of development. It's important that you don't overregulate the sibling relationship. You can have standards for how your children treat their siblings, and you can require reciprocity for family support, such as showing up at a sibling's rock concert or dance recital, but you shouldn't try to control what goes on. It's good practice for adolescents to develop their own relationships with their siblings and learn how to deal with competition, conflict, and compromise in a healthy way.

Adolescents are starting to compare themselves to those around them and they will often start with their siblings. Competition may arise between siblings in relation to external appearances (style, hair, body type, etc.) or in relation to skills (academic, athletic, artistic, musical) or social dynamics. Sibling dynamics can be strained as kids begin to develop interests and skills that set them apart from their brothers and sisters. It can also be hard for younger siblings when an older sibling begins to develop friendships or intimate relationships outside of the family. It's especially hard if siblings close in age perceive themselves to be in competition for the same friends.

Parents should refrain from comparing siblings in arguments or in attempts to motivate an adolescent. For some reason, these comparisons and criticisms are held onto far longer than any positive comments a parent makes. Adolescents have a propensity to hear rejection louder than anything else and will hold a grudge against a parent or a sibling that resurfaces frequently. Some amount of competition and jealousy is normal, but we sometimes see siblings attack or gang up on a more vulnerable sibling. Remember that adolescents are highly sensitive and self-conscious, so they are hyper-focused on their appearance, changes brought on by puberty, and how they compare to those around them. Acne, facial hair, and voice changes are all potential fodder for teasing, but a teenager's sensitivity can escalate the back and forth and the banter can become cruel very quickly. Teasing is common but should be checked by parents if it becomes constant, heated, or mean-spirited.

One of the best ways for parents to address tension between siblings is to speak separately to each adolescent and affirm their unique strengths and weaknesses as an individual. Use empathic statements, like: *You're a stronger athlete, so how do you think that feels for your older brother?* or *Math might be easier for your sister, but she struggles with writing, which you're great at!* or *Don't call your sister fat. Remember when you were a little chubby in seventh grade? How did you feel when people made fun of you?* Everyone can connect to how it feels to be inadequate in some way. Direct statements focusing on strengths and weaknesses are more effective than yelling, punishing, or separating siblings. If you feel that the sibling relationships in your family are characterized by too much conflict, it can be helpful to consult a therapist. Family dynamics can be complex and patterns of allegiance or destruction can become entrenched in day-to-day interactions. If these issues aren't addressed, they will carry into adulthood.

While research shows some definite patterns in the connection between birth order and sibling relationships, I try not to get stuck in stereotypes, like the "type-A oldest" or the "classic middle child," because I find that you get what you expect. Instead, I encourage parents try to raise all of their kids to be empathetic and accepting of the differences between them and their siblings. It's important for each child to feel that they have space to be themselves in the family. You don't need to mitigate the differences between siblings because kids will deal with this in life. Siblings are a great way for kids to learn how to manage themselves within a loving family environment. As kids get into their teens, a certain bond develops with their siblings, and they become protective of them. These bonds grow as siblings age. The sibling "subsystem" can provide a protected space where difficult aspects of a parent's behavior are lessened and shared among them. It's important for your kids to have relationships with each other that are independent of their relationship with you. A good example of this is sibling "text chains" that often leave parents off. It's actually one of the most rewarding feelings as a parent, even if you're occasionally the target of light-hearted ridicule, to realize that your kids have developed an independent bond with each other.

I recently had a mother email me that she'd had a long weekend. Two of her daughters attend the same college and her younger daughter was "rushing" the sorority where her older sister was a member. Over the weekend, the news came in that her younger daughter hadn't "gotten a bid." She was devastated. At the end of our conversation, their mother wrote: "It's so hard to see your kids in pain, but the one silver lining of all of this is how her older sister supported her. She, too, was beyond upset but was so kind and compassionate for her little sister's struggle. It's amazing to see her big sister taking care of her and being so protective of her younger sister. I couldn't ask for more as a mom." Sometimes, we don't know the extent of our kids' relationships with their siblings, and that's okay. Let it happen naturally.

Another client of mine told me that the day of her college graduation, she was so tired and so emotional that her two older sisters packed up her entire room for her. They had each been there, so they knew how they could support her and she was so grateful to them. Sometimes parents worry that their kids aren't close, but it's okay for the relationship to develop over time and, often, your kids are probably closer than you think they are.

Encouraging Independence in Your Teen

Today, parents are prone to micromanage every aspect of their child's life. Mothers and fathers are setting up appointments, calling their child's teachers, arranging for tutors, and complaining to the coach. To be clear, micromanaging is not providing structure. Structure is creating boundaries within which your child can learn about who they are and how to manage in life. Micromanaging eliminates the opportunity to learn. Parents take over in an effort to help their teenager succeed, but ultimately hijack the process by which their child can learn to handle these things for themselves.

This element of development is often hindered by constant communication between parents and their children. Children, teenagers, and even young adults ask for parental guidance in every choice they are faced with throughout the day: what to wear, what to eat, whether to go to bed or continue studying. As parents, we should use cell phones as a convenience and a mechanism to communicate simple, logistical information. It is wonderful to feel needed, particularly as our children grow older and gain independence, but what they need most is to feel capable of making their own choices. It is on us to promote self-regulation.

If you feel that your child is overly reliant on your input, put their questions back on them. Ask them what they think they should do, then withdraw. Encourage them to make healthy choices and tell them to check in with you later. This forces them to practice self-reliance and to deal with things on their own. It's okay if you don't answer your phone every time your child calls. In fact, it's healthy! I frequently advise parents to allow some time to elapse after receiving a message from their child. Parents are often uncomfortable with this out of a fear that their child will need something and they won't respond quickly enough to provide it. As a parent, you don't exist to provide for your child's every need. A child who is consistently being told what to do or having parents intervene on their behalf will not develop the ability to think independently.[12]

On the other hand, I often have adolescents complain to me that their parents are all over them. We all have tasks we want our children to accomplish, but when we smother them with reminders and requests, we send the message that we don't trust them to take care of things on their own. My children coined the term "chirping" to refer to those times when I was nagging them, like a little bird in their ear. They would say, "Mom, don't chirp me," and it was a helpful signal for me to step back and ease up.

It's more effective to establish your expectations up front. Set a deadline for the task you need them to accomplish and attach a consequence if they don't get it done. This allows you to let go of the outcome and forces them to face the consequence if they don't follow through. For example, say something like, "I need you to do this by Friday. If it's not done, you won't have use of the car over the weekend." Or, "Please return your rented tuxedo by next

Monday. If you forget, you can pay the late fee. If you can't get it done, let me know in advance."

Another effective approach is to write out short to-do lists with a deadline for each item. By short, I mean four to five tasks at most. I have had parents send me to-do lists they've given their kids and I feel exhausted by the time I'm through them. Keep it simple and limit it to those tasks that are absolutely necessary. This structure encourages independence and reinforces your teenager's ability to manage themselves. It also allows them to practice time management in a low-stakes environment, as they can work with deadlines and create a plan for what they need to get done. Most importantly, you indicate that you think your child is reliable, which will encourage them to act responsibly.

Throughout adolescence, most of the decisions your teenagers make aren't ones with the potential for catastrophic outcomes. Let them mess up so that they can learn from their mistakes and make better choices as they learn. We let our anxiety about what they need to do interfere with our responsibility to encourage their independence. A better way to motivate them to action is to ask them what they need to get done and if they need your help in any way. Then, pull back and let go of the outcome.

Teaching Your Teenager How to Build Relationships With Others

The parental role in teaching adolescents how to build relationships is twofold. On one hand, the parent–child relationship is a primary connection through which we can model healthy and nurturing bonds, and the adolescent can practice and fine-tune their own interpersonal skills in an unconditionally loving environment. On the other hand, parents can guide their teens through navigating relationships with their siblings, peers, significant others, teachers, coaches, and so on. As parents, we are teaching adolescents how to have relationships and deal with different types of people. Whether they are with a boss, colleague, subordinate, or spouse, relationships are nuanced, and navigating these connections requires perception, awareness, and thoughtfulness. The exploration of relationships and connection during adolescence should extend well beyond the home (Figure 3.1).[13]

Adolescence is a time during which teens begin to notice the world around them in a different way. They might wonder where the barista at their favorite coffee shop goes to school, or notice that the guy at the local deli gives the

NETWORK OF RELATIONSHIPS
Your Adolescent's Community

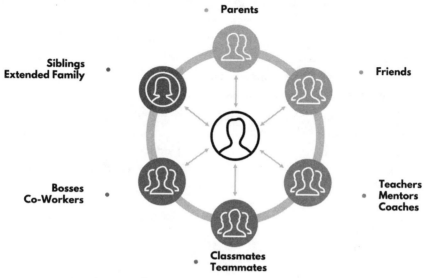

- Parents
- Siblings Extended Family
- Friends
- Bosses Co-Workers
- Teachers Mentors Coaches
- Classmates Teammates

FIGURE 3.1. Developing Self-Advocacy

more gracious customers a free bag of chips with their sandwiches. Encourage your teenager to make an effort with people in their community. Do they ask their teacher how their weekend was? Do they say "good morning" to the receptionist at school? Do they spend time with their coach's children that hang around the field after practice? Adolescents are learning how to treat other people and starting to understand the impact their behavior can have on others. The sooner they learn to treat everybody with a certain amount of respect, the better off they'll be. Social skills are not necessarily innate, so it's helpful to point out the differences in behavior we see around us so that teens can come to understand what is appropriate.[14] Encourage them to notice social cues, particularly in today's smartphone-dominated world. Even simply pointing out things like "This waiter is so friendly" or "Man, the guy at the airline counter was a jerk!" helps them understand subtle differences in interactions and how to react to different behavior from those around them. On that note, watch what you do around your children. They will take their cues from how you interact with and treat the people in your life.

Adolescents are also comprehending how relationships in their lives differ from one another. They realize they have unique connections with their parents, siblings, friends, and significant others. They are figuring out boundaries and limits; their parent may forgive behavior that their teacher will not. An adolescent's ability to build and maintain relationships with nonparental adults is essential to their ability to form meaningful connections in their community. Adolescents are beginning to observe those around them in a more reflective and self-conscious way. Remember that it's during adolescence that we start to compare ourselves to others and notice what makes us different. It's helpful to encourage your teenager to notice the behavior and attitudes of their peers and those older than them.

Talk to your child about things like leadership and work ethic (see Box 3.2). Ask them who they look up to and why. Ask them who their favorite teacher is or which of their friends' parents they admire. Encourage your kids to take stock of those around them and notice what others are good

---

BOX 3.2

Leadership Skills for Adolescents

Leadership is not a position. We want to encourage adolescents to think about leaders they admire. Here are a few leadership qualities to start with:

Integrity: A leader is someone who tries to do the right thing when no one is watching. A leader does not try to do the right thing for praise or reward.

Encouragement: A leader believes that others will succeed and encourages them to believe in themselves. A great leader pushes others beyond what they thought they could do. It's important that adolescents learn to be happy for the success of others, particularly at home in the face of sibling rivalry. Encourage your kids to support one another and show up for big events and moments.

Listening: A good leader listens to those being led, including criticism or complaints, and can tolerate hearing a different perspective than their own. A good leader always wants to improve.

Selflessness: Leadership is a service. A good leader wishes to serve others instead of be served by others. Selfless leaders are often the hardest workers and the ones you know will have your back if you run into trouble.

Influence: Leaders have the ability to obtain followers and impact those around them positively. True leaders don't need to intimidate to earn respect; they set an example that earns their peers' esteem.

at or struggle to accomplish.[15] Observing different types of people encourages teenagers to reflect on themselves and develop a sense of who they want to be.

The Importance of Mentors

A teenager's connections with nonparental adults rounds out their development because it exposes them to different mindsets, values, and approaches to life. It's easy to understand the importance of these people, as we can all remember those individuals who had an impact on us in our youth. The impression of someone who spends time with your child and takes an interest in their development and wellbeing is profound. Mentors, teachers, and coaches are wonderful figures in a child's life and can come in many forms: a music instructor, an athletic trainer, or an aunt or uncle with a shared interest.

Teens benefit from role models in their lives who hold them accountable and to high standards. It's human nature to want to perform for someone we respect and admire. It's exciting to connect with and be acknowledged by someone who is older and more experienced than you. It also expands your sense of being a member of a community. I worked in a restaurant growing up and I knew that my boss thought I was a good kid. His opinion mattered to me and I was aware of not doing anything to convince him otherwise. I act as a mentor to many of my clients and it's one of the most fulfilling elements of my job. Particularly as clients transition from high school into college, they periodically reach out when they need guidance, whether it's how to handle a difficult issue in a relationship or how to prepare for a job interview. All of my clients have my phone number, and it's amazing how frequently I get a text from an adolescent needing a little direction or even just a sounding board. I know I've had an impact if they know they can solicit advice from me in moments when they need guidance. The same can be true of a teacher, coach, instructor, counselor, or older teammate. Feeling noticed, cared for, and relied upon makes us feel as though our actions matter and can have consequences in all of our relationships.

The role of a trusted adult who believes in your child and thinks they can accomplish their goals can be the determining factor in a teen's success.[16] Adolescents will often disregard what a parent tells them because the parent has an evident bias, but the esteem of a nonparental adult can strengthen an adolescent's self-image in a far more powerful way. Think of a time you got a great grade on an assignment or received praise from a coach or instructor for a job well done. These moments are memorable because they hold significance for us. Likewise, a teacher or coach can often be

more honest with an adolescent about their strengths and weaknesses because teens assign less emotional weight to the things they say. Nonparental
adults can lay the foundation for teens' ability to see oneself clearly. When
we were growing up, we learned more from the English teacher who tore
apart our essay to make us a stronger writer, or the coach who benched us
because we showed up late to practice, than from a parent. Instead of viewing
these figures as opponents, view them as supplementing your own parenting.
Grit and perseverance are often learned at the hands of a tough teacher or
coach who expects the best from your child. Developing resilience—a positive response to adversity or failure—requires grit and determination. It's
difficult for adolescents to do this in the absence of a positive adult influence.
Angela Duckworth defines **grit** as not only the ability to be resilient in the
face of failure or adversity but also to show a deep commitment to a goal
even when it requires sacrifice.[17] As our children encounter obstacles in their
lives, nonparental adults can provide this for them. Too frequently, parents
try to protect their kids from criticism but prevent them from learning what
they're actually capable of; overcoming a challenge builds self-confidence
and self-reliance. Research shows that individuals who have overcome trau-
matic early-life events often say that a nonparental adult who was there for
them through a challenging time helped them prevail in a way they might
not have alone.[18] As our children encounter obstacles in their lives, it is essential that they have mentors, parents, and communities to shore them up and
encourage them to continue.

A relationship with a nonparental adult can also provide an adolescent
with relief from the drama of their peer group. Your teenager's friends can be
a source of stress in their lives. A more mature figure can offer perspective on
the inevitable ups and downs of adolescence. These are often the first people
a teenager might confide in about significant issues in their lives, such as
bullying or developing their first intimate relationship. Adolescents are often
willing to share information with a nonparental adult or an older friend that
they don't want their parents to know. Teenagers withhold information from
their parents for a fear that their parents will "freak out" if they know about
an issue or stop them from doing something they want to do.

It's important to make sure your child feels they have someone they can
confide in. Every child and adolescent needs to have a person with whom
they feel safe, whether that be a teacher, psychologist, coach, or friend. As a
parent, let it be okay for your child to tell another adult about their lives. Even
if you wish it were you, recognize that it's important for them to have these
relationships. Clients will often come to me when they are in a compromised

situation and are afraid that they will get in trouble if they tell their parents. I can provide more clear-headed, unemotional advice than a parent because I am less involved in the situation. This can also be true of members of your teenager's community who might have a different perspective or a better understanding of a situation than you do, as the parent.

I had a client who was at a party when one of his friends become dangerously drunk and was taken to the hospital. He faced consequences at school, though the party had occurred over a weekend, and anyone who was with him was asked to come forward. My client was nervous and was unsure of what to do, so he sought out the advice of his advisor. He wanted to do the right thing, but was terrified of the implications a punishment would have on his college prospects. His advisor told him that the school's intention was not to punish those at the party, but instead to demonstrate the importance of accountability and honesty. With her insight, he was able to make a solid decision and weigh all of the potential outcomes before proceeding. Simply put, the advisor was able to provide better guidance than a parent could have.

Similarly, a teacher or coach may have the authority to push your adolescent to beneficial action. I worked with a soccer player whose coach took a particular interest in the lives and wellbeing of those on her team. If she was concerned about the mental health of a player, she would ask them to see a school counselor. If they refused, she would tell them that they could not practice until they sought counseling. She was able to encourage positive behavior because of the way her team respected her; a parent does not always have the same position with their teen. Other adults in your child's life can help to reinforce your values. I had a client recently ask me to send a quick text to her daughter on her way up to an official visit at one of her top college choices. I didn't hesitate, as I always think it's helpful for an adolescent to get an important message from more than one source, particularly a nonparental figure. I sent a quick text saying: *Have a good trip! Remember, these visits are kind of a test so don't drink or vape, etc. Even if kids on the team encourage you. Blame it on having a paper or finals. Act nonchalant like "I wish I could." Everything gets back to the coaches.* Hearing a trusted adult echo a message reinforces its validity. This text might not necessarily have prevented her from making bad choices that night, but it's always good to have a reminder that directs behavior in the right direction.

If you know that your child respects and trusts someone, and you have a concern or issue, don't hesitate to enlist that person's guidance or support. Without betraying your child's trust or manipulating their independent relationship, you can advance your priorities and values with the help of a mentor.

As parents, we are smart to acknowledge the impact that other adults can have on our children.

It is often with nonparental adults that teens can practice self-advocacy. Starting in third and fourth grade, and definitely by seventh or eighth grade, parents should be confident that their children can mostly address their issues for themselves. Children and teenagers should want to handle matters independently and should be able to approach an adult when they have a problem. The adolescent tendency to push a parent away is an indication that they are ready to manage these situations. When we intervene on our child's behalf, we prevent adolescents from taking responsibility for their actions.[19] If they take matters into their own hands, they are faced with navigating both positive and negative outcomes; the case may be that their teacher is unfair or their coach is a jerk, in which case they will learn how to deal with difficult people early in life.

Your role is to guide adolescents by talking to them about how to manage and strengthen relationships. Help your child anticipate potential outcomes but insist that they handle the issue on their own. A signal that you have a good relationship with your child is when they ask for your guidance in handling a situation. When something comes up with a teacher, instructor, or coach, ask them what they think they should do and talk through the potential responses they might receive. Remember that they are creative: let them think about how they might approach a situation on their own. **Every resolution does not need to be perfect; even if they do it differently than you would have, it's valuable for them to practice coming to a solution independently.** If we fail to do this, our adolescents will see any setback as a crisis, and they will struggle profoundly when they get to a point in their lives, such as their college years or early adulthood, when they must trust and rely upon themselves. Let them learn how to do this when you are there to support and guide them when they really need you (Figure 3.2).

A client of mine is a talented baseball player with the ability to play at the highest level. He's the pitcher, a position that comes with a degree of leadership because it controls and commands much of the game. Jimmy is a nice boy with a great sense of humor, but he struggles with discipline and has the tendency to lash out when he underperforms. For these reasons, his peers did not elect him team captain. Understandably, Jimmy was upset. The pitcher is often a natural choice for captain, but Jimmy didn't consistently display leadership qualities. Everyone has a role to play. When we try to push our children into a role that they don't fit into, we undermine their unique strengths and capabilities. Be realistic with your child about their strengths and weaknesses.

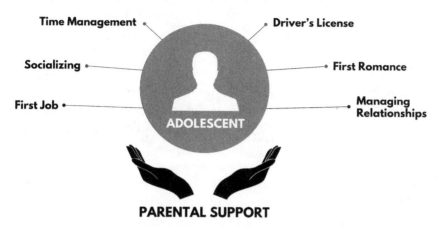

DEVELOPING SELF-ADVOCACY

FIGURE 3.2. Network of Relationships

Every player on the team is not a captain, just as every role in a play is not the lead.

When Jimmy's parents learned he would not serve as team captain, they contacted the head of school and leveraged their status in the community to contest the decision. Again, your relationship with your child is not based on your doing everything for them. Jimmy's parents could have encouraged him to ask the coach what he could do to improve as a player and how he might become a better leader. If your child is disappointed with an outcome, ask them why they think they got the result they did. Encourage self-reflection and help them come up with a plan to address their disappointment. *Okay, you didn't get what you wanted, what options do you have now?*

Even if it seems unfair, the best thing we can do as a parent is to shift our child's focus to what they *can* do. Take the opportunity to put the responsibility back on the adolescent to come up with a plan to achieve what they want. Avoid telling them to "just work harder"—this would be a low-structure, low-nurture response. In this case, Jimmy's parents showed him that they would get him what he wanted, regardless of whether he had earned or deserved such an accolade. This is a salient example of what we would consider a high-nurture, low-structure approach. Jimmy's parents surpassed the natural structure of the team and the school to manufacture the outcome they felt would please him. Children and adolescents raised in these environments are consistently unhappy and dissatisfied in their lives as they go off to college and into the working world because they haven't learned the value of self-reliance. As important as the short-term gain might seem, I strongly encourage parents to resist the urge to rescue their children and instead stay out of these issues.

It's hard to see our kids in difficult emotional situations, so it's logical that we try to steer them away from pain and getting hurt. The truth is, you can't protect your child from life's ups and downs. Let your teenager practice failure and redirect them toward improving the situation. We have to remember: Everybody gets over small obstacles in their lives and it is in doing so that we learn what we're made of. When we survive setbacks and adversity, we learn that we are capable and independent people. One of the powers of the adolescent is the ability to rebound and move past setbacks quickly. We want to raise children who believe in themselves and who are able to take advantage of this capacity during such formative years.[20]

When your child is struggling, remind them of a time they demonstrated the ability to get beyond an obstacle and overcome a challenge. It's empowering for them to see themselves reflected this way, and helps them realize they can accomplish difficult things. When outcomes are manufactured for you, you do not develop the ability to do things for yourself and you remain stuck in an adolescent mindset.[21] We all know someone who seemed to cruise through high school and even college with relative ease but faltered in adulthood. It makes sense that they got by in contained environments with supportive adults to shepherd them past obstacles, but in the absence of self-reliance or intrinsic motivation, they began to struggle in their independent lives. This can present in a myriad of ways: I've had clients struggle with eating disorders, drug and alcohol abuse, and severe depression. We often see a delayed rebellion in adolescents who have been rigidly controlled. If we think about the neurological development—pruning and myelination—occurring at this stage, we can see that if these pieces are not shaped through the teenage years, they won't be formed by adulthood. If you skip a critical developmental task, you won't be emotionally or neurologically equipped for the next stage.[22]

If adolescents don't have the opportunity to struggle through difficulties and emerge intact, they will face a complete crisis when they move beyond their parent's reach. The stakes are higher later in life, when a breakdown might mean losing a job, getting a divorce, or turning to substances to maintain emotional stability. "Helicopter parenting" produces young adults who are ill equipped to live independently, work for a challenging boss, or navigate a serious relationship.[23] The world beyond your home does not exist to make your child feel good about themselves. In their collegiate and professional lives, their professors and bosses won't give them a grade they don't deserve or sugarcoat their performance review. **As parents, we need to let go of the outcome more often so that our children learn to deal with challenging circumstances.** The best opportunity for growth is to overcome a difficult situation and reach a tolerable conclusion. A lot of life is about dealing with mundane tasks and responsibilities; we want to make sure our children are able to find happiness and success in the day-to-day and not only in the highs of life.[24] When we allow our children to navigate and learn from independent relationships, they become good citizens and contributing members of society.

It is one of the greatest feelings as a parent to recognize when the concept of relationship and community has "clicked" for your child. Perhaps your child becomes a mentor to a younger friend, or they reach out, unprompted, to help a member of the community. It's incredibly rewarding to see your child develop empathy and selflessness. It's important to notice and acknowledge these moments, particularly during what can be a challenging time for a parent and child. These connections can be built upon and strengthened.

These opportunities for reflection also help to point out both the ways your child is developing and those in which they can continue to grow. Maybe they came home after curfew on Saturday night, but they offered to pick up dinner for the family on their way home from practice on Sunday. I had a client in her senior year of high school who came home one night to find her mom waiting up for her. She had been drinking, but they said goodnight, so she thought she had gotten away with it. The next morning, her mom told her that she could tell she'd been drinking; she wanted to know what she had been drinking and where she had been.

My client was honest. She said she'd had a few beers and had been at a neighbor's house, so she had walked home. Her mom was honest in return. She told her that she wasn't thrilled she'd been drinking and cautioned her to avoid trouble with graduation around the corner, but also said she was happy that her daughter had been honest with her and hadn't gotten behind the wheel. My client was surprised by her mother's calm and reasonable demeanor. In response, my client was remorseful about her choice to drink and understood her mother's stance. If there seems to be a mutual understanding, it isn't always necessary to give a consequence.

It's a major relief for parents of adolescents to see things with a balanced perspective. We can get stuck in a mindset of discipline and punishment and see things as all bad or all good. Avoid the trap of only telling your teenager when they've done something wrong; don't overpunish or overpraise. If you're looking for mistakes, you will see them everywhere! Incorporate some humor and humanity into your parenting style and give your teenager the benefit of the doubt. Look for growth and moments where they show maturity and consideration for others. It's certainly not necessary to laud your child with praise, as this can distort the impact of their small gesture. It's better to mark these moments with a quick comment, like "That was really thoughtful of you," or a simple "Thank you" to reinforce good behavior. Attention is always a great reinforcement; whenever I receive positive feedback about my kids, no matter how small, I make sure to mention it. I'll say something like "Mr. Smith said he saw you at the grocery store and you gave him a big hug" or "Mrs. Smith said she enjoyed talking to you at the game and hearing about what you're up to." Adolescents take pride in being noticed. Sharing this feedback with them shows them that a little bit can go a long way. You want your children to see kind and thoughtful behavior as normal and, more importantly, expected.

Adolescence is a period of trial and error as teenagers learn to enrich and deepen relationships, test boundaries, and figure out what does and does not work on both sides of a relational interaction. Allowing the parent–child relationship to expand beyond a battle for control is key to a successful relationship with your child. When in doubt, come back to the high-structure, high-nurture mindset. If you provide your adolescent with a safe environment and you're able to love them through their mistakes, you're where you should be. Having the courage to empower your teenager to develop relationships with other adults is equally impactful. The ability to form strong bonds and navigate varied relationships is not something that can be learned on a test or through a phone; teens must learn by practicing at school, on teams, and in their communities. Adolescence is the time when we learn how to treat people and how we interact with those around us. You must know how to deal with people to create the relationships you want in life, and the ability to build relationships begins in adolescence. Connecting with and relating to people at a variety of levels is an essential tool for a meaningful and fulfilled adulthood.

If you feel that your adolescent has a very difficult time making friends or maintaining relationships, consider consulting a therapist for individual and/or group work. Many effective group therapy models teach social and interpersonal skills. Adolescence is an important time to learn how to relate to others. If you wait too long to address what you perceive to be an issue, you risk your teen losing confidence in social situations, fearing that they have nothing to offer, or blaming others and withdrawing. If you address these issues sooner rather than later, you can head off more significant mental illness.

Consider This:
Insights & Actions

- Your teenager wants you in their life. When they get dumped, fail a test, or get cut from the team, they will need you to reassure them that they're okay. In these moments, don't lecture them on what they should have done differently. As parents, we often want to fix whatever is bothering our children, when what they really need is warmth and support. Listen to them and let them tell you how they feel. Even if you know what they're going through, refrain from lecturing them or telling them that everything will be okay; they want to feel heard and loved, not judged. Validate their sadness, but be okay with it.

- Connection can take on many forms. One of my children always used to do her homework in the kitchen while I was making dinner. When my youngest son was in high school, all of his siblings had graduated so it was just him and me. He got plenty of time with me! Each night, I would get dinner ready and we would eat together while we watched *Chopped*. Another of my children liked to ride in the car with me while I ran errands. In all of these examples, we weren't necessarily engaged in deep one-on-one conversations, but we were spending time in each other's presences and the connection was there.

- Get out of the right–wrong game. Remember that the relationship you have with your child is one of the primary examples in their life. In the parent–child relationship, we are modeling healthy and appropriate behavior. Adolescence is much smoother if we treat our child the way we expect to be treated. Every relationship has give and take, so it's important that we don't assume we are always right and our child is always wrong. Listen to their perspective and acknowledge it before you offer yours.

- Rely on your child and give them responsibility. Ask for their help with household chores, caring for siblings, or tasks you need to complete. Once they have a driver's license, have them run errands for you. There is no quicker way to appreciate a parent than to take over the tedious errands for a day. You can teach them to be aware of others by letting them participate in your family's life and engage with you in a deeper way. When a child is treated as though they are reliable and trustworthy, they rise to the occasion and meet your expectations.

- Be careful about how you talk about other people around your kids. If they see you speaking badly about others, they won't hesitate to do the same. Here's a good lesson to teach your kids. Before they say anything, have them ask themselves: Is it true? Is it necessary? Is it kind? If the answer to any of those questions is no, then they ought to think twice before speaking.

- You don't have to be invincible as a parent. Tell them you're too tired to fix dinner and that it's a free-for-all, or ask one of them to order pizza. Or turn it into an adventure: Drive into town, give everyone the same amount of money, and tell them that they have 15 minutes to get themselves dinner. Whoever gets back to the car last is on cleanup. Show some vulnerability by letting them see that you aren't always "on." Let your adolescent help you and have fun changing it up every once in a while!

- Refrain from asking your child's teachers, coaches, or instructors about your child's status in their class or on their team. These are perfect opportunities for your adolescent to learn to advocate for themselves in a safe environment. There will always be another opportunity for them, whether another test, a new season, or the next school play, so let them figure out what they need to do in order to get what they want and experience the satisfaction of working toward and achieving a goal. Help them form a plan to talk to the coach to find out their weaknesses, suggest they look for a different team, or encourage them to pursue another extracurricular activity.

- If you struggle to engage your adolescent in discussion, try to talk to them about things that interest them, like something in the news or a sporting event. Ask open-ended questions that lead to a conversation. "How was your day?" is bound to elicit a one-word response. Teenagers are self-absorbed and will often take questions to be a personal interrogation, but they will talk about other people. Don't feel that you have to ask them a million questions—let them talk to you!

- While we want to encourage our children to form an independent connection with a role model or a mentor in their lives, we also want to be aware of who our children spend unsupervised time with. If you have a bad feeling about a person, let your child know of your concern, but pose it as a question to them. Ask them if they ever feel uncomfortable with the person in question. This spurs them to think about it and listen to their own instinct and develop an "antenna." We know that there are times where an adult in a child's life can become predatory and we want to prevent our child from such a risk. Though it's not the norm, abuse or manipulation by an adult can have a devastating impact on a life.

- Teach your children to be aware of the impression they make. The first time my son was pulled over by a police officer, he was amazed that the cop let him off with only a warning. I asked him how the conversation went, and he said he was careful to be very polite, deferential, and use "Yes, sir" and "No, sir" in addressing the policeman. I was quick to point out that people respond to the way we treat them. When you are polite or considerate of others, they will go out of their way to help you or give you a break when you need it.

- In divorce, a single parent sometimes needs to rely on someone else to stand in as a "mom" or "dad." It's a benefit of divorce that we bring nonparental adults into our family to help impart the messages we want to get across. It can benefit other adults, too, who are happy to interact with children from different families. You don't have to be divorced or widowed to tap into this resource or other adults in your kids life. Recruit trustworthy adults into your family's orbit to set an example while rounding out your parenting.

Notes

1. Siegel, D. J. (2013). *Brainstorm: The power and purpose of the teenage brain.* New York, NY: Penguin.

2. Cozolino, L. (2006). *The neuroscience of human relationships. Attachment and the developing social brain.* New York, NY: W. W. Norton.

3. Erikson, E. H. (1963). *Childhood and society.* New York, NY: W. W. Norton. (Original work published 1950)

4. Rimm, S. (1996). *How to parent so children will learn.* New York, NY: Three Rivers Press.

5. Piaget, J. (1932). *The language and thought of the child* (2nd ed.). London, UK: Kegan Paul, Trench, Trubner & Co.

6. Jensen, F. E., & Nutt, A. E. (2015). *The teenage brain: A neuroscientist's survival guide to raising adolescents and young adults.* New York, NY: HarperCollins.

7. Gold, J., Pinder-Amaker, S., Potter, M. P., Pridgen, B. C., & Palmer, C. M. (2017, November 3–4). Harvard Medical School Symposium: Middle School Through College Mental Health and Education. Cambridge, MA: Harvard Medical School.

8. Levine, M. (2008). *The price of privilege: How parental pressure and material advantage are creating a generation of disconnected and unhappy kids.* New York, NY: HarperCollins.

9. Blos, P. (1962). *On adolescence: A psychoanalytic interpretation.* New York, NY: The Free Press.

10. Levine, M. (2005). *Ready or not, here life comes.* New York, NY: Simon & Schuster.

11. Brown, B. (2012). *Daring greatly: How the courage to be vulnerable transforms the way we live, love, parent, and lead.* New York, NY: Avery.

12. Levine, M. (2005). *Ready or not, here life comes.* New York, NY: Simon & Schuster.

13. Hallowell, E. M. (1999). *Connect: 12 vital ties that open your heart, lengthen your life, and deepen your soul.* New York, NY: Pantheon.

14. Wolf, A. E. (2002). *Get out of my life, but first could you drive me and Cheryl to the mall? A parent's guide to the new teenager.* New York, NY: Farrar, Straus and Giroux.

15. Coles, R. (1997). *The moral intelligence of children: How to raise a moral child.* New York, NY: Penguin.

16. Tough, P. (2012). *How children succeed: Grit, curiosity, and the hidden power of character.* New York, NY: Houghton Mifflin Harcourt.

17. Duckworth, A. (2016). *Grit: The power of passion and perseverance.* New York, NY: Scribner.

18. Duckworth, A. (2016). *Grit: The power of passion and perseverance.* New York, NY: Scribner.

19. Hallowell, E. M. (2002). *The childhood roots of adult happiness: Five steps to help kids create and sustain lifelong joy.* New York, NY: Ballantine Books.

20. Duckworth, A. (2016). *Grit: The power of passion and perseverance.* New York, NY: Scribner.

21. Dweck, C. S. (2006). *Mindset: The new psychology of success. New York, NY: Random House.*

22. Hoffman, J. (2014, June 23). Cool at 13, adrift at 23 [Blog post]. *New York Times.* Retrieved from https://well.blogs.nytimes.com/2014/06/23/cool-at-13-adrift-at-23/

23. Tough, P. (2012). *How children succeed: Grit, curiosity, and the hidden power of character.* New York, NY: Houghton Mifflin Harcourt.

24. Hallowell, E. M. (2002). *The childhood roots of adult happiness: Five steps to help kids create and sustain lifelong joy.* New York, NY: Ballantine Books.

4

The Fourth Myth

ADOLESCENTS DON'T NEED A LOT OF SLEEP; THEY'RE JUST LAZY!

THE TRUTH IS, adolescents aren't just lazy: they need a *lot* of sleep. The current medical recommendation for teens is 9¼ hours of sleep per night.[1] However, the internal clock that signals the body for bed is significantly delayed in teenagers, so they don't feel tired as early as we do. The biological clock shifts during adolescence, starting around age 12 or 13 and lasting into the early twenties. Melatonin, known as the sleep hormone, is released a full 2 hours later in adolescents than it is in adults. Melatonin is secreted by the pineal gland in the brain, which controls and regulates sleep cycles (Figure 4.1). While adults start to feel tired around 9:00 p.m., teenagers don't experience the same sleepiness until around 11:00 p.m. Then, even if they go to bed at 11:00 p.m. sharp, they would need to sleep until 8:00 a.m. to be close to fully rested. Most schools are in full swing by 7:30 a.m. The demands of the average adolescent's daily life are such that they rarely get enough sleep. They are in a constant state of catch-up, trying to rest their growing minds and bodies. This is why your teenager might roll out of bed at noon on a Saturday. Your teenager might very well be lazy, but it's important to acknowledge that most adolescents are chronically sleep deprived. More often than not, they're just tired!

Schools have started to respond to this knowledge by opening later to allow teens to get more sleep. Research shows that even a 1-hour difference makes students more alert and refreshed in class.[2] In one study, a group of 10th graders slept on a self-selected school night schedule. During a nap opportunity at 8:30 a.m., participants fell asleep in approximately 5 minutes, nearly half the time it took them to fall asleep later in the day. Roughly half of

MELATONIN
Sleep-Inducing Hormone

RELEASE TIME
Released 2 hours later at night in a teenager's brain than it is in an adult's brain.

KNOWN AS THE "HORMONE OF DARKNESS"
Melatonin is a hormone produced in the pineal gland of the brain that is responsible for regulating sleep cycles.

THE BODY'S NATURAL PACEMAKER
It plays an instrumental role in signaling time of day and time of year, helping to regulate your body's internal clock.

HOW MUCH SLEEP DO THEY NEED?
Biological sleep patterns shift toward later times for both sleeping and waking during adolescence—meaning it is natural to not be able to fall asleep before 11:00 p.m. Average adolescent needs 9¼ hours of sleep.

FIGURE 4.1. Melatonin Facts

the participants fell directly into deep sleep in under 2 minutes. This is a clear demonstration of a teenager's delayed cycle. This delay is partly due to the fact that mature adolescents require longer periods of wakefulness in order to feel "sleep pressure," or prompting from their internal clock that it's time to rest. **Due to various changes throughout puberty, adolescents don't experience "sleep pressure" the way that children and adults do, so they are wired to stay up later into the night and wake up later in the morning.**[3] The internal changes in an adolescent's chemistry account for the behavior that is typically considered "lazy."

For many teenagers, the school day and their extracurricular responsibilities make it nearly impossible for them to get the sleep they require. Studies show that American teenagers lose a minimum of around 90 minutes of nightly sleep from sixth grade to 12th grade. The average high school senior gets under 7 hours of sleep per night.[4] We force teenagers to wake up earlier than natural and expect them to be high functioning. An adolescent consistently getting less than 7 hours of sleep per night is chronically sleep deprived. Insufficient sleep among adolescents is currently considered to be a public health concern; sleep deprivation threatens the academic success, health, and safety of teens. Parents, educators, researchers, and policy makers cannot ignore the impact that insufficient sleep has on teenagers.[5]

Many parents think they can help their teenager combat these biological shifts with over-the-counter melatonin or prescription sleep aids. The amount of melatonin in these pills is around 100 times stronger than the amount naturally produced in the body. We don't know the long-term effects of synthetic melatonin, particularly in children. We risk affecting the development of reproductive, cardiovascular, immune, and metabolic systems in the adolescent.[6] The best way to help your teenager get enough sleep is to urge them to rely on healthy nutrition, such as protein and carbohydrates, to supplement energy, and to aim to regulate sleep cycles with consistent bedtimes and good sleep hygiene.

Technology is an added obstacle to a good night's sleep. Smartphones, video games, computers, and televisions all emit what are known as **blue wavelengths** of light, which suppress melatonin and tell the body to stay awake (Figure 4.2). We experience the potency of blue light when we look at our phones in the middle of the night. The light is so strong that we squint and look away, yet we spend most of the day with our eyes fixed on these devices. A lot of the lightbulbs in homes also emit blue light, which means that your teenager might be exposed to blue light as they are doing homework or reading before bed.[7] If there is a phone nearby or a television on when your adolescent is trying to sleep, their brain will remain active in response to stimuli and works to keep them awake.

It's important to train your teens to stay off of their devices around bedtime—the earlier the better, but a good rule of thumb is to require that they power down around 10:00 p.m. When I was growing up, it was considered impolite to call someone after 9:00 p.m. If our phone rang at night, we assumed that something horrible had happened. There is nothing

LED Lights Suppress Melatonin

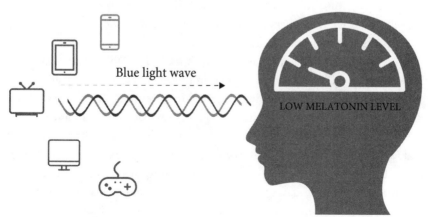

Blue light wave

LOW MELATONIN LEVEL

FIGURE 4.2. LED Lights Suppress Melatonin

wrong with reclaiming this boundary and teaching this courtesy to your teenagers today. Adolescents may want to be on their devices at night because they don't feel tired when you do, but this creates a vicious cycle. The more they use their devices around bedtime, the further melatonin is suppressed and the longer they will stay awake. Many teenagers want access to their devices at night because they like to listen to music to fall asleep. I suggest that they keep a playlist on a device that isn't a smartphone. Music can help us fall asleep, but the benefit is negated by the presence of blue light in an otherwise dark room. It's also tempting to look at your phone when you can't fall asleep, which wakes you up even more. Eye masks can also be helpful for blocking out blue light. When your eyes are covered, it allows the nervous system to relax more deeply. It is critical for everyone, not just adolescents, to power down devices before bed and shut out blue light in order to improve both the quantity and quality of sleep. If we explain that this isn't just our parental desire to "control their life" but is actually based on science, it allows them to understand the impact their devices have on their actual ability to sleep. This way, we gain credibility and can help guide them toward a different choice.

Effects of Sleep Deprivation on Teens

There is not a single part of an adolescent's life that is not adversely affected by a lack of sleep.[8] Let's begin with one of the adolescent's most important tasks: learning. A teenager's primary job is to be a student. Every day, new research consistently demonstrates how crucial sleep is to both learning and brain development. Inadequate sleep has adverse effects on attention, memory, psychomotor speed, abstract thinking, and executive functioning.[9] Sleep directly influences an adolescent's ability to absorb information. The learning process occurs through the consolidation of memories, which allows us to retain new information and reuse it in an articulate way.

This consolidation happens in two stages, *both* of which occur during sleep. **Slow-wave sleep** is believed to happen in the early stages of sleep and is the deepest part of the sleep cycle. It is during slow-wave sleep that the brain sorts through information and organizes it in a way that the mind can understand. As the deepest part of the sleep cycle, slow-wave sleep is also the most restful and rejuvenating. Because slow-wave sleep happens in the early stages of sleep, it is lost if adolescents are staying up late and falling asleep after midnight. We see this impact in the data: Slow-wave sleep is shown to decline by at least 40% during adolescence because of poor sleep habits. This critical piece of learning is cut to 60% capacity at a vital time in a child's education.[10] During the second stage, **REM (rapid eye movement) sleep**, the brain synthesizes information into a form that can be understood. Through dreams, the brain makes sense of information and creates connections between memories. Both of these processes allow adolescents to absorb what they learn and convert it into knowledge.

This is such crucial information! If you skimmed that paragraph because it seemed dense with technical terms, I urge you to reread it. Students are learning something new every day and school is a constant drain on their energy, emotions, and mental capacities. They rely on an immense number of neurodevelopmental tasks every day—attention, temporal-sequential ordering, spatial ordering, memory, language, neuromotor functions, social cognition, higher order cognition, and others—all of which are more efficient when they are well rested. It is abundantly clear how critical a good night's sleep is for adolescents to process new information and function healthily at school.[11]

As parents, it can be hard to remember that there was a time it was "cool" to have a lot of homework and to stay up all night to finish it. We want to diminish the allure of the "all-nighter," because it's totally counterproductive and diminishes the ability to work efficiently. We have the idea that the more recently you've studied or read information, the fresher it will be in your mind and therefore the easier it will be to recall. The truth is, sleep allows us to fully process information and thoroughly absorb what we've learned. For long-term retention and genuine understanding, sleep is the key. It's the difference between being able to regurgitate information on a test or quiz versus gaining a genuine understanding of a topic. A good night's sleep is more valuable to academic performance than last-minute cramming or the dreaded all-nighter. We want our adolescents to absorb new ideas and incorporate them into their worldview. The advanced processing that occurs during sleep is what allows them to assimilate new knowledge, use it flexibly, and apply it to other concepts.

Sleep is not only crucial to learning and academic performance, but also to decision making. Sleep impacts cognitive functions such as short- and long-term memory and active working memory, which is used for planning. As mentioned in chapter 1, the parts of the brain that allow for logical and sequential thinking are still developing in the teenage years. We now know that sleep not only strengthens an adolescent's ability to learn, but also organizes memories according to their emotional importance.[12] Arranging memories this way allows the brain to relate past experiences and feelings to current situations and decisions. Sleep-deprived teenagers are not triggering this essential cognitive function and are making less informed decisions. Simply put, well-rested teens make better choices. Remember the old adage "sleep on it"? It's actually based in science and is especially true for adolescents. Sleep allows the brain to sort through and make sense of daily experiences.

Pruning and myelination primarily occur during sleep when other brain functions are not actively engaged. We know from chapter 1 that these neurological processes are vital to the development of the teenage brain. Sleep is critical to overall brain development, as well as to its day-to-day functionality.[13] It is an important preventive measure against other health risks like obesity and mental health issues. Sleep loss harms energy balance and disrupts glucose metabolism, which is associated with decreased insulin sensitivity in adolescents.[14] Lack of sleep is also associated with poor nutrition choices. When you're tired, you're more likely to reach for sugar to boost your energy—important information for a generation for which obesity is a particular concern. Short sleep duration and later bedtimes (i.e., after midnight) have been linked to higher levels of depression and risky behavior, including alcohol and drug use, sexual promiscuity, and suicide.[15]

Sleep plays an active role in sculpting the adolescent brain. **We need to look at sleep as an active process.** Think about when the curtain falls in the theater during intermission. Set producers swarm the stage, rearranging the set pieces and preparing for the next act. This is like the brain asleep. Old or unnecessary neurons are pruned while new neural pathways are solidified and honed. Information and memories are consolidated and organized. The brain is essentially maturing during sleep, so ensuring sufficient, well-timed, and restorative sleep is important for optimal development (see Box 4.1).[16]

Convincing Your Teen to Sleep

Parents of adolescents are familiar with the battle over bedtime. Let's pull back and remember what we're trying to achieve. The importance of sleep is part of a bigger lesson of the value of self-care and discipline. Explain the benefits of sleep to your teens in a way they can understand. To consolidate their studies into memory, they *need* sleep—it's the essential component of processing information.[17] Tell your children that this is how their brain works and that sleep sets them up to be efficient and productive. This way, they can see sleep as part of their studying process.

Again, it's effective to prompt your adolescent to notice how they feel based on how much sleep they got the night before. By age 12, your adolescent should

---

BOX 4.1

Sleep for the Adolescent Athlete

A study performed on the Stanford basketball team tracked player performance in conjunction with sleep and found that consistent, high-quality sleep is an important predictor of peak athletic performance.[22]

- REM sleep, which typically begins 90 minutes into sleep, provides energy to both the brain and the body and allows the body to consolidate memories and release hormones.
- Studies show that sleep deprivation and low-quality sleep result in a decline in split-second decision making, whereas well-rested subjects showed increased accuracy.
- Sleep deprivation decreases the production of glycogen and carbohydrates that are stored for energy demands during physical activity.
- Sleep is crucial for muscle repair and recovery. A lack of sleep makes athletes prone to illness and injury.
- The sleep we get two nights before an event is the most crucial. If there is a big game on Saturday, Thursday night's rest makes the difference.

---

start to have a sense of when they have the most energy, whether they are a morning person or a night owl, and whether they are better served by an extra hour of sleep or an extra hour of studying. Everyone is different; in my family, two of my children are night owls like me, and two are religiously in bed early. So two of them would study late into the night to get things done because they didn't function that well in the morning, while the other two would go to bed early and wake up early to finish what they needed to get done. Help your children start to understand how they work and what their natural rhythm is. Self-awareness is a sign of maturity. By the time an adolescent is in college, they should know exactly how much sleep they need to perform well. The better we know ourselves, the more efficient and productive we will be.

When it comes to bedtime, we want to set boundaries within which a teenager can learn to manage and take care of themselves. This requires finesse on a parent's part, as the ability to regulate one's own bedtime is a privilege to be earned. We want to give them enough rope to practice making choices, but enforce an expectation appropriate to their age and academic requirements. In other words, we want to provide the right balance of structure and nurture.

As frustrating as it is, teenagers sometimes resist guidance simply because it comes from their parent. Your teenager will push back when they feel that you are trying to control them; teenagers want to make their own choices. Adolescents are interested in factors that benefit them personally and will be more receptive to facts than emotional pleas. If they understand how sleep benefits them, they will start to regulate it for themselves. The best we can do is to require that they fulfill their obligations regardless of how much sleep they've gotten. If they make a poor choice, they have to get up and go to school, despite how tired they are. They want to make their own choices, so let them deal with the consequences. Just make sure they are connecting the dots: a poor night's sleep impacts their entire day.

Over time, they should begin to regulate themselves. You only need to step in if it becomes a prolonged pattern. It's important not to step back entirely. A low structure approach around sleep is usually a recipe for disaster if they struggle to manage their own time. Teens become increasingly dysregulated and we start to see disorganization, bad behavior, and dipping grades from sleep deprivation. Hold them accountable and acknowledge moments when they make a mature decision. This way, they will make the shift and begin to take ownership for themselves.

I've tried this with my own kids and recommend it to clients all the time. Suggest to your adolescent that you're going to do an experiment: For one night, you want them in bed by 11:00 and in the morning, you want them to eat a good breakfast before they leave the house. For the rest of the week, they can do it however they want to do it, but you want them to notice how they feel. When did they feel most productive? When did they feel most exhausted? As parents, we don't need to be overly involved or inundate teens with directives. It doesn't work and we end up in a battle for control. Just prompt them to notice and then let them make choices based on what they discover about themselves. Let them figure it out for themselves because, one way or another, they will.

When an adolescent can make a solid decision that does not adversely impact his or her weekly schedule, they can determine their own bedtime. Here are two examples that demonstrate different stakes and require unique parental approaches. It's crucial that we stay involved as parents to prevent our children from developing habits that significantly harm their health or their ability to function, but we also need to let go enough so that they can learn to self-regulate.

I work with a client whose son suffers from serious health issues, including an autoimmune disorder. Spencer is an intelligent, athletic, and talented boy, yet in addition to his physical ailments, he struggles with an unmedicated learning disability. Adolescents have a lot on their plates and they often lose a handle on time management. This can be especially true for those with learning disabilities, which are exacerbated by a lack of sleep.[18] Spencer desperately needs sleep, yet he stays up until 1:00 or 2:00 in the morning every night. Although Spencer is performing at a high level in all areas of his life, it's unsustainable, and sleep deprivation exacerbates his health issues.

Spencer feels he is old enough to go to bed when he wants to, but he is not making a healthy decision about his bedtime. Spencer's parents instated a rule that Spencer could not attend early-morning hockey practice if he wasn't in bed by 11:00 p.m. the night before. When their child's self-regulation is not yet in place, parents need to intervene to ensure their adolescent is getting the sleep they need, to prevent long-term consequences. Sleep is the best medicine for emotional regulation, stress management, and cognitive functioning and protects our children against complete physical and emotional breakdown.

When a lack of sleep does not pose as serious a threat to health, parents can give teenagers more rope to try to manage independently. Another client of mine called me in a state of total frustration with her sophomore, Lily. Lily put off writing a paper until the night before it was due and stayed up until 1:30 in the morning to finish it. She had been distracted by social media and became stressed and emotional when she realized that she had to finish her assignment. When her alarm sounded at 6:30 the following morning, she was exhausted and couldn't get out of bed. Lily's mom called in to school to say Lily would be coming in late. The following night, Lily wasn't tired at the appropriate time because she had slept in. What's more, she hadn't suffered the consequences of trying to function at school without enough sleep, so she repeated the same behavior on a regular basis. Lily and her mom were in a cycle of rescue and lecture, and Lily's mom was taking responsibility for Lily's inability to make healthy choices. This cycle would fall in the low-structure, high-nurture category. It's not beneficial for either one of them.

Lily's mom should have required that Lily get up in time for school so that she would have to get through the day in an exhausted state. If she *really* couldn't get out of bed, Lily's mom should have insisted that Lily be the one to call into school. If Lily had to call the school herself, she would be much less likely to sleep in. This is an important point: Lily wants control over what time she goes to bed, so she has to take on the responsibility of her choice. Lily's mom can remove herself from the struggle by putting it back on Lily: "If you want to go into school late, you need to call the administrator and let her know." Nine out of 10 kids would rather get up and go to school than explain the situation to someone there. Whereas in Spencer's case, it was important for his parents to intervene to prevent a serious health risk, Lily's mom should let her learn the true impact of sleep by feeling the full effect of total exhaustion. Mental and physical exhaustion is the best teacher of the importance of sleep. Teaching our adolescents to prioritize sleep lays the foundation for self-discipline (see Box 4.2).

In spite of everything we now know about the importance of sleep, the reality is, teenagers don't get enough of it, particularly during the school week. A teenager has a completely full day of academics, athletics, extracurricular activities, family time, and homework. If you think about it, most adults don't

---

BOX 4.2

"I Can't Sleep": Simple Suggestions

Many adolescents struggle to fall asleep at night. If your teen has occasional difficulty falling asleep, encourage them to try these exercises when stress or an overactive mind is keeping them awake.

- Focus on breathing to bring your mind to rest. Count your breaths on each exhale.
- Count backwards, starting with a high number such as 100 or 500. When you focus on counting backwards, your mind engages in a task and allows the brain to rest.
- Read a hard copy of something that isn't related to schoolwork in bed. Reading allows the eyes to grow tired. As an adult, I can barely get through a page before I'm fast asleep!
- Keep a piece of paper by your bedside. If you're tossing and turning, write down the top five things on your mind, big or small. Writing these things down allows your brain to stop trying to remind you of them and clears them from your head.
- Listen to music or a podcast as a distraction.
- Drink a mug of warm milk or chamomile tea before bed. Warming beverages are soothing and contain chemicals that trigger melatonin production in the body.
- Walk your child through their upcoming day. The ability to know and envision what is in store allows them to feel in control and unafraid of what's to come.

have a schedule as packed as any teenager. Teenagers are tired! And it isn't (always) their fault.

So, what can we do? Adolescents will also need to catch up on sleep at some point, which may happen on the weekend or even over the summer. The most beneficial sleep is the sleep we get every night, but sleep is *never* bad. During sleep, adolescents can recharge over an extended period off of technological devices. However, adolescents can also recharge throughout the day during periods of **downregulation**. Downregulation occurs when the brain can go on "automatic" and doesn't function at full capacity. During downregulation, the brain shifts into a less-engaged state in which it can relax.[19] There is a reason we build recess and nap time into the kindergarten day. Adolescents need these breaks as badly as toddlers! When the brain isn't actively processing information, higher cognitive functions are not engaged and the brain can regain energy. This might be during a break in the school day, study hall, music rehearsal, or physical activity. Athletics are a particularly good break, as physical activity activates the limbic system and nourishes the brain with oxygenated blood. The risk of almost every disease, illness, and mental health challenge is decreased by regular physical activity. Aside from exercise, a 15- to 20-minute power nap is ideal, but any time away from devices and academics can have a positive impact. Frequently, if they have a few minutes between their academic schedule and their extracurriculars, high schoolers will grab a snack or a quick nap. This is a great choice; both options allow them to recharge. "Minis" are short, simple exercises that don't require a lot of time and can be done anywhere. Encourage your adolescent to try these when they are feeling especially stressed or tired but don't have time to take a nap or catch up on sleep (see Box 4.3).

Some children and adolescents have more difficulty with sleep than others. It's completely normal for adolescents to have trouble falling asleep or to resist going to bed on occasion. However, a prolonged inability to sleep might point to a more serious issue. If your adolescent is struggling to fall asleep or waking up through the night over a couple of weeks in a row, ask their pediatrician if the pattern needs to be looked at more closely. Similarly, if your teen is lethargic through the day and experiences severe swings in energy or extreme exhaustion, they might be dealing with something more serious like mononucleosis, Lyme's disease, Epstein-Barr virus, or depression. Adolescents in college are less experienced with monitoring their own symptoms. Some kids will have full-blown strep throat or mono before they signal that something isn't right. A good clue to how tired they are is what they are or aren't willing to miss. If they want to get out of school but they

BOX 4.3

Minis

- Take a minute to close your eyes and take a few deep breaths. Simply closing your eyes allows the nervous system to relax. If you can, take 10 to 20 minutes to lie down on the floor with legs supported, eyes closed, and palms facing up.
- Step away from the constant stimulation of school and give yourselves a few minutes of silence. Silence allows your nervous system to rest.
- Visualize relaxing. Imagine yourself taking a deep breath, rolling your shoulders back and down, and sighing.
- Pick up a magazine, book, or newspaper about a random subject to read for 5 minutes. This can draw your brain into a different space and bring your heart rate down.
- Go out into crisp, cold air. The body uses energy to generate heat, which shifts the body into an automatic function and pulls us out of stress.
- Any type of physical movement can be beneficial. Stretching, jumping jacks, a yoga pose, or even running in place can create energy in the body.[23]

still want to go to sports practice, they're probably okay, and you should insist that they go to school. But if they're missing activities they enjoy or are committed to, they might have something else going on. It's typical for teens to be worn out by their schedules, but they should be able to get through it and bounce back.

Consistent tiredness or exhaustion might also be a cue to look to other habits. Teens with particularly poor diets are often exhausted throughout the day and then struggle to fall asleep. If you have a teen who is wired throughout the day and isn't tired at night, you should check this out with a pediatrician or a psychiatrist. Extremes on either end or a marked change in sleep patterns that isn't situational (i.e., when they are anxious about an upcoming test or event) might indicate that something more serious is going on and needs to be examined.

Sleep can help an adolescent in just about every way imaginable. We can help teens care for themselves with plenty of rest and teach them tools to use when they aren't operating on a full night's sleep. Set a good example for your child by powering down your own devices and prioritizing sleep for yourself. Sleep is good for everyone.

Consider This:
Insights & Actions

- Parents should regulate bedtime until the child can. Instead of arguing with your teenager over an appropriate bedtime, let the built-in structure of school dictate their wakeup time, which will in turn determine when they need to go to bed. Enforce a set bedtime so that your teen has a plan for sleep, and encourage your teen to stick to their schedule on weekends. It's okay to catch up on sleep, but try not to stray too far from the routine.

- It's a sweet, loving gesture to wake someone up, but waking ourselves up is an important element of self-regulation. Nurture your teen with a nutritious breakfast or a cup of hot chocolate, but let them learn how to get themselves out of bed. Have an idea of your child's schedule. If they sleep through an alarm, you can help them out on occasion, but it isn't harmful to let them practice managing their time through trial and error.

- Take your adolescent's devices out of their room at night, especially from Sunday through Thursday, up to age 15 and/or if they aren't monitoring their own schedule. Make it a privilege they can strive to earn.

- If your teenager has a brutally hard time getting up or seems especially groggy throughout the day, make sure they aren't on devices when you think they're asleep. If you don't want to be in a constant battle over technology, trying turning off the house Wi-Fi at 10:00 p.m. Or, check on them at night before you go to bed. It could be that your child is in bed with the lights off by 10:00 p.m. but is using a cell phone or computer until late at night.

- Purchase an alarm clock so that adolescents aren't reaching for their phones first thing in the morning. Again, it's healthy for children to learn to wake themselves up, particularly before they get to college. If they struggle to respond to their alarm, put the alarm clock far enough away from the bed that they have to get up to silence it. The power of putting two feet on the ground is immense.

- Getting bright light in the morning has been shown to align the internal clock with sunrise and sunset. While we want teens to avoid light at night, exposure to natural sunshine in the morning hours can help with earlier wake ups and encourage healthy sleep cycles.

- Recent studies have suggested that attention-deficit/hyperactivity disorder (ADHD) may also impact sleep. Teens with ADHD may be producing melatonin up to 2 hours later than peers, causing them to feel sleepy up to 3 or 4 hours after a typical adult.[20] In addition, many of the most common

ADHD medications are stimulants and will keep teenagers awake. If your child has ADHD, ensure that dosing takes this into account and doesn't further impact sleep cycles.

- Set expectations for periods of time when your child is off from school, but encourage them to manage their own time. If they want to sleep in until the afternoon, that is acceptable, and even beneficial, as long as they handle their responsibilities. Let them know in advance what you need them to do by what deadline so that you aren't irritated by their sleeping in.
- Encourage your teenager to take short naps during busy days. Even 10 minutes of closed eyes calms the nervous system and allows the brain to recharge. However, napping after 4:00 p.m. can interfere with sleepiness at bedtime, so stick to early-afternoon naps.
- Inform adolescents that caffeine late in the day can delay sleepiness for up to 2 hours. Suggest limiting caffeine intake beyond midday or after school, particularly during the week.[21]

Notes

1. Paruthi, S., Brooks, L. J., D'Ambrosio, C., Hall, W. A., Kotagal, S., Lloyd, R. M., . . . Wise, M. S. (2016). Recommended amount of sleep for pediatric populations: A consensus statement of the American Academy of Sleep Medicine. *Journal of Clinical Sleep Medicine, 12*(6), 785–786. doi:10.5664/jcsm.5866

2. Jensen, F. E., & Nutt, A. E. (2015). *The teenage brain: A neuroscientist's survival guide to raising adolescents and young adults.* New York, NY: HarperCollins.

3. Hummer, D., & Lee, T. (2016). Daily timing of the adolescent sleep phase: Insights from a cross-species comparison. *Neuroscience & Biobehavioral Reviews, 70,* 171–181.

4. Tarokh, L., Saletin, J. M., & Carskadon, M. A. (2016). Sleep in adolescence: Physiology, cognition and mental health. *Neuroscience & Behavioral Reviews, 70,* 182–188.

5. Hummer, D., & Lee, T. (2016). Daily timing of the adolescent sleep phase: Insights from a cross-species comparison. *Neuroscience & Biobehavioral Reviews, 70,* 171–181.

6. Kennaway, D. J. (2015). Potential safety issues in the use of the hormone melatonin in paedeatrics. *Journal of Paediatrics and Child Health, 51*(6), 584–589. doi:10.1111/jpc.12840

7. Jensen, F. E., & Nutt, A. E. (2015). *The teenage brain: A neuroscientist's survival guide to raising adolescents and young adults.* New York, NY: HarperCollins.

8. Siegel, D. J. (2013). *Brainstorm: The power and purpose of the teenage brain.* New York, NY: Penguin.

9. Hummer, D., & Lee, T. (2016). Daily timing of the adolescent sleep phase: Insights from a cross-species comparison. *Neuroscience & Biobehavioral Reviews, 70,* 171–181.

10. Brand, S., & Kirov, R. (2011). Sleep and its importance in adolescence and in common adolescent somatic and psychiatric conditions. *International Journal of General Medicine, 4,* 425–442. doi:10.2147/IJGM.S11557

11. Campbell, I. G., Kraus, A. M., Burright, C. S., & Feinberg, I. (2016). Restricting time in bed in early adolescence reduces both NREM and REM sleep but does not increase slow wave EEG. *Sleep, 39*(9), 1663–1670. doi:10.5665/sleep.6088

12. Jensen, F. E., & Nutt, A. E. (2015) *The teenage brain: A neuroscientist's survival guide to raising adolescents and young adults.* New York, NY: HarperCollins.

13. Casey, B. J., Jones, R. M., & Hare, T. A. (2008). The adolescent brain. *Annals of the New York Academy of Sciences, 1124,* 111–126. doi:10.1196/annals.1440.010

14. Hummer, D., & Lee, T. (2016). Daily timing of the adolescent sleep phase: Insights from a cross-species comparison. *Neuroscience & Biobehavioral Reviews, 70,* 171–181.

15. Tarokh, L., Saletin, J. M., & Carskadon, M. A. (2016). Sleep in adolescence: Physiology, cognition and mental health. *Neuroscience & Behavioral Reviews, 70,* 182–188.

16. Tarokh, L., Saletin, J. M., & Carskadon, M. A. (2016). Sleep in adolescence: Physiology, cognition and mental health. *Neuroscience & Behavioral Reviews, 70,* 182–188.

17. Telzer, E. H., Fuligni, A. J., Lieberman, M. D., & Galvan, A. (2013). The effects of poor quality sleep on brain function and risk taking in adolescence. *Neuroimage, 71,* 275–283. doi:10.1016/j.neuroimage.2013.01.025

18. Van Veen, M. M., Kooij, J. J., Boonstra, A. M., Gordijn, M. C., & Van Someren, E. J. (2010). Delayed circadian rhythm in adults with attention-deficit/hyperactivity disorder and chronic sleep-onset insomnia. *Biological Psychiatry, 67*(11), 1091–1096. doi:10.1016/j.biopsych.2009.12.032

19. Fonagy, P., Target, M., Cottrell, D., Phillips, J., & Kurtz, Z. (2002). *What works for whom? A critical review of treatments for children and adolescents.* New York, NY: Guilford Press.

20. Van Veen, M. M., Kooij, J. J., Boonstra, A. M., Gordijn, M. C., & Van Someren, E. J. (2010). *Biological Psychiatry, 67*(11), 1091–1096. doi:10.1016/j.biopsych.2009.12.032

21. Lee, K. A., Mcenany, G., & Weekes, D. (1998). Gender differences in sleep patterns for early adolescents. *Journal of Adolescent Health, 24*(1), 16–20. doi:10.1016/S1054-139X(98)00074-3

22. Mah, C. D., Mah, K. E., Kezirian, E. J., & Dement, W. C. (2011). The effects of sleep extension on the athletic performance of collegiate basketball players. *Sleep, 34*(7), 943–950. doi:10.5665/SLEEP.1132

23. Gold, J., Kaplan, C. S., Pinder-Amaker, S., & Palmer, C. M. (2015, November 6–7). Harvard Medical School Post-Graduate Symposium, 2015. Cambridge, MA: Harvard Medical School.

5

The Fifth Myth

ADOLESCENTS ARE AMAZING MULTITASKERS, AND MULTITASKING ALLOWS THEM TO ACCOMPLISH EVERYTHING THEY NEED TO DO.

"MULTITASKING" HAS BECOME synonymous with efficiency, productivity, and the ability to accomplish more in a day than we have time for. When it comes to teenagers, parents are often amazed by their ability to juggle tasks and activities. They'll eat dinner in the back of the car on their way to practice while studying for an upcoming exam, or text their friend while playing a video game and singing along to their favorite song on the radio. Parents encourage their teenagers to do more than they seem capable of to get through their endless to-do lists, but the myth that adolescents are great at multitasking is misleading.

Adolescents aren't great at multitasking because the brain is not designed to multitask. **Multitasking** is defined as attempting to perform two complex cognitive tasks at the same time. The key word is *attempting*; the human brain is actually incapable of doing more than one thing at a time. If you've tried to write an email while talking on the phone and ended up sending the recipient a tidbit from your call, or if you've checked your phone while driving and missed a turn, this is because the brain can only focus on a single task. Any task that uses the prefrontal cortex, such as studying or driving, is considered "complex," and requires the brain's full attention. When we think we're multitasking, the brain is actually switching rapidly between two or more tasks with independent goals. By doing so, we significantly reduce the efficiency of the brain.

Multitasking is particularly problematic for teenagers, who are developing the cognitive functions that allow them to perform and complete tasks. If they don't practice sustaining focus and following through, they fail to develop these essential mental functions. Teens already struggle to focus, but they're also overscheduled and stretched too thin. The constant attempt to multitask creates fractured attention and a distracted mind. Multitasking not only reduces the efficiency with which teenagers can perform tasks, but it also prevents them from engaging deeply and meaningfully with their academics, activities, and relationships. Technology and social media add to the number of potential distractions and have troubling implications for teenage mental health because they undermine identity formation, relationship building, and internal motivation. This isn't merely a matter of productivity; multitasking robs adolescents of a healthy and productive brain and contributes to psychological problems.

To understand how counterproductive and damaging multitasking really is, we first need to understand what goes into completing a single task. Task completion is a complex and fragile function of the brain. We are constantly working to stay on task and follow through. When we set a goal to perform a task, such as completing a homework assignment or remembering to pack for an upcoming trip, we employ executive functions such as decision making, organization, and planning. Executing those goals requires attention and focus, for which we rely on our **working memory**. Working memory is a primary skill of the prefrontal cortex and serves as the critical bridge between perception and action. **Working memory is at the core of decision making**. It allows us to process various external factors and devise a plan based on what we see around us. Interestingly, the cognitive control necessary to enact goals has not evolved to the same degree as the cognitive abilities required to set those goals. In other words, the part of the brain that determines what needs to be done is more advanced than the part of the brain that can perform those tasks.

Our cognitive control is limited; we have a restricted ability to distribute, divide, and sustain attention.[1] Given this, it seems irrational that we would attempt to concurrently manage, let alone rapidly switch between, independent tasks. Multitasking is like trying to carry six things out to the car. You have your gym bag, your work papers, your dry cleaning, your keys, your wallet, and a cup of coffee. Something is bound to drop, and when you bend over to pick it up, you drop everything else. When we multitask, we divide our attention, lower our focus, and make ourselves susceptible to distractions of all kinds.

When something distracts us, it lowers our ability to accomplish what we need to do. In other words, it interferes. Let's look at how a distraction becomes an interference. **Goal interference** occurs when you decide to work toward a specific goal and something takes place to hinder its successful completion.[2] The interference can be internal or external: You might remember you need to make a dinner reservation (internal) or you might turn your attention to an incoming call (external). An interference becomes a **distraction** or an **interruption** based on how you manage it. Interruptions happen when you decide to simultaneously engage in more than one task at a time, even if you repeatedly switch between them. As the brain tries to multitask, it doesn't fully engage with either task, so efficiency drops. We also tap into a limited amount of brainpower when we multitask because so much of our mental energy is being used for simultaneously managing multiple tasks. In other words, multitasking is an interruption. Multitasking drains all aspects of cognitive control, reduces efficiency, and prolongs the amount of time it takes to accomplish a single goal. The brain is like a piece of technology: It functions best when only one application is open at a time. When too many windows are open, a computer slows down and even crashes. This is the nature of the demand we put on our brains when we attempt to multitask. If a task is difficult or requires considerable thought (like an academic assignment), carries a risk of harm (like driving), is critical or of high value (like a conversation with a loved one), or is time sensitive (like an exam), it requires our full attention to be completed **successfully**.[3]

Figure 5.1 is a helpful visual to understand how multitasking impacts a teenager's ability to absorb information. If the teen is distracted while they

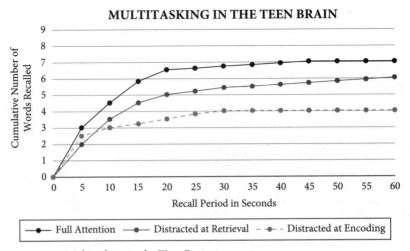

FIGURE 5.1. Multitasking in the Teen Brain

are trying to remember information (retrieval), their capacity for recall will be notably lower. Parents often feel that their teenager doesn't listen to them. You know the feeling of asking your adolescent a question when they're on their phone. They will give you information in fragments and probably get some of it wrong. If you have their full attention, they are likelier to remember the answer to your question in full. They do listen, but if they're distracted, they'll struggle to come up with the information. The dashed line in Figure 5.1 shows us that if they are distracted while they are taking the information in (encoding), their recall is **50% lower** than at full attention. This is significant. If teenagers are distracted while they are trying to learn, whether in class or at home, their capacity to take in new information is essentially cut in half. So often our kids are on their phones or computers while they're in class or studying. Then, when they take a test, they struggle to recall the needed information. This is important for them to understand, so I would encourage you to show them this graph. Their understanding is more effective than you simply putting their phone in another room.

To "solo-task," we have to limit interference so that we can successfully accomplish what we need to do. Adolescents already struggle to suppress interference because their brains are wired for novelty and stimulation. Parents of teens know that they are easily distractible and it can be hard to hold their attention. I was always amused by what my kids could come up with to distract themselves from studying, whether it was silly games or finding new music to listen to while they worked. I'm consistently impressed by how current teenagers are; they always know the latest music, the newest game, the recent releases in on television and in the movies. We don't want to dampen this instinct, because it allows for creativity, curiosity, and spontaneity, but we want to encourage them to channel it in the right way so that it doesn't interfere with what they need to get done.

Interference management is maintained by the front of the brain, so it's forming throughout adolescence and it can only fully develop through practice and exercise. The **parietal lobes** are neurological structures that process sensory information. In the context of attention, they serve to dampen extraneous activity to allow the brain to focus. The parietal lobes are located behind the prefrontal cortex, so they mature throughout adolescence. A strong connection between the parietal and temporal lobes and the prefrontal cortex allows the brain to effectively switch between tasks. This connection is called the **insula,** which is part of the executive functioning network and allows for smooth switching between tasks. The insula is like a muscle, through which we can develop mental stamina. If it is called upon to switch too often, we become mentally fatigued. Mental fatigue weakens our ability to manage interference. In other words, **multitasking hinders a teenager's ability to resist interference and makes it challenging to execute and complete a task.** When we constantly attempt to multitask, the brain is drained of energy and functionality. This is even more significant for teenagers because their schedules demand mental effort from the moment they wake up to the moment they fall asleep. We use the phrase "my brain is fried" to describe the feeling of mental depletion. It can be helpful to think about multitasking as an activity that drains your reserve of mental energy and gets you to that state sooner. Multitasking "fries" the teenage brain.

Adolescence is the time when these mental processes need to be honed and refined, but multitasking creates a frazzled and disjointed state in the brain and prevents the development of focus and attention. In fact, the brain actually *grows* when attention is focused in a sustained way without frequent distractions. When the prefrontal cortex is activated and engaged in a task, connections form between neurons and neural pathways are optimized. When you solo-task, you build mental stamina that allows you to focus and sustain attention over longer periods. During such a crucial time of neurological development, we want adolescents to solo-task as much as possible so they develop and strengthen the executive functions required to perform complex cognitive tasks (see Box 5.1). Focusing on one thing at a time develops industry and proficiency in an adolescent.[4] When the brain is deeply engaged in a task, whether mental or physical, neural pathways form that allow for the development of skill and ability.

As parents, we want to teach our teens to manage distraction and interference by encouraging them to focus on one thing at a time. It's important to let them know that multitasking is unproductive and inefficient. This is different from a parent's demand, which is often perceived as a desire to control their behavior. Multitasking has also been shown to increase cortisol levels in the body which, as we know from chapter 2, correlate directly to higher stress levels. Increased levels of cortisol engage the fight-or-flight response and thereby interfere with the brain's capacity for learning and other higher functioning.

We want to teach our teenagers the important skills of organization, scheduling, and planning to encourage goal execution and interference management. When it comes to juggling busy schedules and managing a full plate, ask your teenagers if you can help them create a schedule or write down reminders for what needs to get done. Teenagers often resist making a to-do list, but the act of writing out what we we need to do and when we need to

---

BOX 5.1

Retraining the Mind: Solo-Tasking for Teens (and Parents!)

- **Meditation** improves cognitive control and promotes sustained attention, processing speed, and **working memory** capacity.
- **Physical exercise** is associated with increased brain activity in the prefrontal cortex. Exercise allows the brain to **downregulate** and effectively frees up neural channels to allow for increased focus.
- Decreasing **access** to phones during times assigned to important work such as schoolwork, studying, or driving.
- **Time management** and **scheduling** your day into designated segments has been proven to increase productivity and enable prioritization of the most important tasks.
- Regular **breaks** facilitate brain function and improve attention. Try this: Every 20 minutes, take a 20-second break in which you stand up, stretch, or simply focus your eyes on something far away. These simple movements shift blood flow and allow for a quick return to work.
- Take a 10-minute **nap** to improve cognitive function, or even just close your eyes. You'll still feel more rested than you had.
- Have a small snack or something to drink. Staying hydrated and nourished keeps the brain energetic and reduces "brain fog" when we need to focus.
- Read a chapter in a fictional book (and preferably in print as opposed to on a screen or an e-reader!) Research shows that there's a major brain shift when we are immersed in fiction.

---

do it allows us to organize and prioritize our tasks. If you help them by jotting it down for them or printing out schedules they can fill in, they will see how painless and helpful scheduling is for both short- and long-term planning. Post-its are useful tools for color-coordinated to-do lists and reminders that allow us to cross things off and gain a sense of accomplishment each time. Time management, focus, and task execution are not innate, but they are essential lifelong skills.

THE MOST RECENT technological advances combined with overscheduled lifestyles have made focus and attention increasingly difficult. Social media, the internet, and smartphones drive both internal and external interference and aggravate an already distracted mind. These relatively new technologies are immediate, constant, and accessible at unprecedented levels.

Studies show that people of all ages are addicted to their smartphones:

- Four out of 10 young adults check their phone immediately upon receiving a notification.
- Seventy-five percent of teenagers sleep next to their phones with notifications on.
- Three out of four smartphone users admit to being within 5 feet of their phone day and night.
- Eighty-nine percent of young adults reach for their phone immediately upon waking.

A recent study showed that, over the course of an hour, young adults switched between tasks once every 2 minutes. A similar study of middle-school to college-aged students examined a 15-minute study period and found that participants could not focus for more than 3 to 5 minutes at one time. A study that measured GPA confirmed four predictors of a lower GPA, including total media time during a typical day and a preference for task switching rather than working on one task until completion. A fifth predictor of a lower GPA was also uncovered: **One visit to Facebook or Instagram while studying was enough to predict a lower academic performance.**[5] This is a staggering statistic.

Why do we behave this way if it's distracting and less productive? Simply put, it's more fun, especially for a teenager. Remember that the teenage brain is highly active and is wired for stimulation, novelty, and information. Novelty is associated with the reward center of the brain. When we switch to something new, we experience it as a reward. From an evolutionary perspective, our appetite for technology satisfies our innate drive to seek information. Greater accessibility feeds this instinctive drive and counters feelings of boredom.[6] But when we constantly jump between stimuli, our brain begins to crave this connectivity and becomes unable to focus for extended periods of time. When was the last time you went more than 10 or 15 minutes without taking a peek at your phone? It's mindless, easy entertainment. And it isn't going anywhere. It's up to us as parents to redirect our adolescents and teach them to separate technology from learning and relationships. Overuse of technology permanently alters brain development and cognitive functioning. The growing brain is easily frazzled. Exposure to screens overstimulates and agitates the brain, which in turn hinders executive functioning, causes cognitive delays, and impairs learning.

In my work, I see a problematic cycle arising, in which distractibility is immediately equated to a learning disability. Instead of looking at potential causes, we are quick to diagnose and medicate children at younger and younger ages. During the years when iPhones and iPads began to saturate American homes, we saw a spike in the number of young people being treated with medication for attention-deficit disorder (ADD)* and attention-deficit/hyperactivity disorder (ADHD).[7] Diagnoses of learning disabilities are rising. The number of teenagers diagnosed with ADHD jumped 25% in the last 10 years. Research shows that the more a baby or toddler watches television or other screens, the more likely they are to have attention issues by early childhood. Quite shockingly, even 2- and 3 year-olds are taking medication for learning disabilities.[8]

This contradicts what we know about psychological development: *All* 2-year-olds lack focus and attention and we don't expect them to have object constancy. We want them to be exploring and playing and constantly shifting their attention! At such a young age, medication can change the fundamental structure of the growing brain. **We're fixated on identifying a learning disability and treating it with medication without looking at the root cause of this increased distractibility.**

There is a connection between screen exposure and learning disabilities because developing brains have not honed the ability to focus and follow through on a task. We naturally protect our babies from sensory overload in other ways; we see young children with earplugs in loud public places, and we ensure that our kids stick to a strict sleep schedule so they can recharge. Likewise, we should look at screens as sensory overload. Excessive screen time is also connected to increased impulsivity and a decreased ability to self-regulate.[9] These are the exact capacities and functions that we are trying to teach and encourage in our adolescents. Technology and social media, when not limited, interfere with every single one.

There is a significant difference between a frazzled, distracted mind and a learning disability. Learning disabilities come in many forms, such as dyslexia, auditory processing disorder, language processing disorder, spatial processing disorder, dysgraphia, dyscalculia, visual motor deficit, and ADHD, among others. Recent studies show that the diagnosing of ADD and ADHD among U.S. schoolchildren increased by 43% between 2003 and 2011.[10] This is

---

* We will refer to both ADD and ADHD as ADHD. While there is a clinical difference between these two diagnoses, it is not significant enough for the purpose of this manual to warrant a distinction.

a drastic jump, yet the brain has not evolved in a way that can account for this difference. It is important to make a distinction between the brain, the organ and the structure, and the mind, the white and gray matter that is malleable and shaped by external inputs. While this increase may indicate overdiagnosis, environmental factors may also be contributing to these shifts.[11] As parents, we should understand what these are and how to combat them.[12]

Learning disabilities can be thought of as a part of the brain that is under-developed or not fully functioning. In other words, there is a weaker neural connection of some sort that accounts for the challenges these disabilities present. Given that the adolescent brain is not fully developed, this weaker connection is more detrimental in the teen brain than in an adult's. The most recent data show that the executive functioning in an adolescent with ADHD can be up to 2 years behind the level of their peers. We often see a drastic de-cline in the performance of students with learning disabilities starting in the sixth or seventh grade. At this age, they should be able to keep up with the pace of their classes, develop academic capabilities, and maintain a stamina and energy for learning. If you see a lag in these areas, it is a signal to take a closer look at what might be going on for your child. Undiagnosed learning disabilities can impact a child's self-esteem and diminish their willingness to try new activities as they feel left behind by their peers.

I worked with a boy named Nico who was around 12 years old when his parents brought him to me. They told me that Nico had low self-esteem, hated going to school, struggled with focus, and had difficulty sustaining en-ergy through the day. He was performing at grade level only in activities out-side of the traditional classroom, like open art time and music class. Subjects that had a visual processing component appeared to be very difficult for him. His teachers described him as having behavioral issues: He didn't pay atten-tion in class and seemed to be daydreaming instead.

Nico was referred for a neuropsychological evaluation and came to me for anxiety treatment. His parents and teachers assumed that he would be diagnosed with ADHD, prescribed medication to treat it, and given extra time on assignments and tests. After beginning to work with him, the neuro-psychologist and I began to suspect that there was something more complex going on. Further testing showed that Nico actually had a vision problem. He was classically cross-eyed. He didn't actually have attention issues at all, but he was trying to learn every day with impaired vision. How could he possibly have learned to process appropriately? Imagine trying to read with uncor-rected crossed vision. He was exhausted by trying to manage this, so of course he dreaded going to school. The classroom environment created a lot of anxiety for him, and he struggled as much with athletics because he couldn't see well enough to coordinate his movements. Nico didn't need medication or extra time; he needed special glasses.

As soon as Nico was fitted with the right prescription, he began to remediate right away. It took some time to get him back on track completely, but medication and extra time would not have addressed the root of the issue. Moreover, he would have had increasing difficulty as academic demands grew in high school, and this would have taken a severe toll on his self-esteem and emotional state. It was so important that Nico underwent a thorough evaluation so that the problem could be addressed quickly and correctly.

There are many, many learning disabilities. We used to primarily diagnose two: dyslexia and ADHD. Today, we know that there are nuanced processing differences that are often grouped in with or misunderstood to be more common learning disabilities. If we reflexively label every learning difference as ADHD, the unique challenges for that child are masked and left untreated. We have the ability to teach to individual learning styles and to help students overcome deficiencies.[13] For example, auditory processing disorders are frequently overlooked. If a child struggles to hear and comprehend verbal information, they will struggle to follow along in a classroom setting, and it will present as an inability to pay attention and a lack of focus. Children with auditory processing disorders often don't realize when they've missed something and feel that they are unable to connect because of their own inadequacy or stupidity. If you suspect that your child might learn differently, take the time to do comprehensive neuropsychological testing to identify exactly which part of their brain is not functioning properly so that they can strengthen and develop those connections over time.

Similarly, parents often complain that their teenager is disorganized or struggles to manage their academic workload. Parents believe this to be a sign of laziness or disinterest and don't realize that organization must be taught. Though some children, like adults, are more prone to neatness than others, it is not innate. Organization is a function located in the front brain, which we now know is not fully developed in the adolescent. As academic and extra-curricular requirements increase in high school, we need to help our teens develop a system to keep track of their schedules and assignments. Organization is a lifelong skill and allows for execution at every level. Challenges with organization do not necessarily point to ADHD.[14]

I worked with Lee, an engaged and curious boy who was selected for his school's gifted program. Just before Lee turned 12, his teachers noted a sudden decline in his academic performance and described him as unfocused and disengaged. Lee described feeling bored with what he was studying in school. His teachers suspected that Lee might have ADHD and recommended testing. Something didn't add up: Lee was charismatic, excellent at imitations based on a keen memory, able to recite sports statistics about any team or athlete, and could fly-fish for hours without distraction. Lee's parents didn't think that he had ADHD and believed that there must be something else going on.

They brought Lee to a neuropsychological testing facility where he had a complete evaluation. The findings were inconclusive regarding ADHD and there were no other perceived learning disabilities, so the neuropsychologist referred them to a psychiatrist, but also figured it couldn't hurt to get him a prescription for ADHD medication. His parents dutifully took him to a psychiatrist, who reviewed all of the testing and told them that he couldn't find a medical need for ADHD medication, but he would still be willing to prescribe it for him. This is a red flag! It's important to be aware that doctors may be willing to prescribe medication in spite of an uncertain diagnosis. We are fortunate that we now have medications that, in combination with behavioral therapy, are very effective. However, we want to make sure we are confident in the diagnosis before we determine the best course of action.

His parents weren't satisfied with the diagnosis, so they continued to seek medical help on their son's behalf. As it turned out, Lee had suffered a severe concussion in football that had knocked his pituitary gland out of place so that it wasn't functioning. It was as though the needle was on the record player but was stuck and wasn't producing music. Lee's brain wasn't releasing either the hormones required to process incoming information or those necessary for physical development. Without thyroid medication and human growth hormone, Lee's growth would have been severely impaired; he would not have grown past 5′4″. Instead, with these treatments, he grew to be 6 feet tall.

Multiple issues were avoided and repaired because Lee's parents were careful to determine exactly what was wrong. If they hadn't discovered the root of the issue, Lee would have suffered academically, athletically, and socially. Identifying the underlying cause of Lee's sudden change in behavior allowed for a more comprehensive reparative course of action. While the role of a trusted academic advisor or medical professional is crucial to helping our children identify and work with learning disabilities, it is important for parents to be involved. Our priority is the overall health of our children. As the ones who know your children better than anyone else, go with your gut—maternal and paternal instincts are real!

Societally, and particularly as parents, we are programmed to intervene quickly and want an immediate resolution, when the solution may simply be time and instruction. The short fix is often medication, which can be very effective in aiding the failing neuro-pathway. While medication might lend itself to a higher SAT score, it does not always contribute to long-term development. I often have parents come to me looking for a prescription. I recently got a text from a client who was worried about her daughter. They had been on break from school, so Maria wasn't taking her ADHD medication. On vacation, Maria's mother noticed an increase in Maria's anxiety. She wanted to know if she should look into upping the ADHD medication or adding an anxiety medication. She also noticed that her daughter was eating more than usual and had gained weight, so she wondered if she should consider some sort of medicine to address that, too.

This is very common. Maria's mother wasn't looking at the dynamics at play that might account for these differences; she just wanted to find medication that would address the issues. For one thing, they were on a family vacation, so teenage Maria was stuck in a hotel room with her parents and her annoying little brother. She was feeling anxious in part because she was off of the medication she typically took, and in part because she had college applications hanging over her head. She was eating more because her usual medication affected her appetite. She feels hungrier when she isn't taking it.

We didn't necessarily need to alter the medications she was taking. Medication might shift the observable behavior, but it can't always address the root issues. I encouraged Maria's mom to work with Maria on dealing with her anxiety and the tension of being in close quarters with her family for a week. Adolescents need help sorting out their emotions and developing the tools to deal with them. I told Maria's mom to create a plan with her to help her figure out how to manage differently, whether that meant having some independent time every day or taking some time to herself throughout the vacation. It's okay for a teenager to have a couple of "off" days or a week when they might be a little stressed or just feeling down. In some cases, there might be a need for an adjustment to their medication, but we also want to help adolescents build a tolerance for some amount of discomfort and learn healthy coping mechanisms. Medication takes several weeks to shift internal chemistry and therefore behavior, so unless we were seeing a prolonged change in Maria's mood, we didn't need to look to medication as the issue.

I want to be very clear that I am not against medication. It works wonders when there is a diagnosed need. But research consistently shows us that any medication is most effective in combination with behavioral therapy.

I encourage families to pursue medication only when necessary and not as a quick fix. It should be the last resort, not the first option. We can elicit long-term improvements by identifying the unique issue and working to develop and strengthen weaker neural connections.[15] As parents, we need to be alert and involved to determine the best course of action.

I also want to give parents a word of caution about boys versus girls. It seems that parents are quicker to diagnose boys with learning disabilities and girls with emotional disorders. We have to be careful with this. With boys, we assume we will see behavioral issues because of the mistaken assumption that "boys will be boys." More boys are diagnosed with ADHD, but it isn't totally clear whether it is more common for boys to have ADHD than for girls. With girls, we assume we will see emotional and social issues. Resist treating teens with broad strokes or assuming that boys will act one way and girls will act another. You might miss what's really going on if you operate under these assumptions. We know how to diagnose and address incredibly specific issues, so make sure that you are consistent in your own evaluation.

Another important distinction to make is that ADHD has nothing to do with intelligence. It's common for parents to actually want an ADHD diagnosis for their child so that they can have extra time for standardized tests. Extra time on tests isn't always an advantage, and it doesn't necessarily correlate with a higher score. Certain kids absolutely need extra time, but for others, extra time is too much. They are required to sustain energy for a longer period of time or they get bogged down in overthinking each answer and lose track of where they are because they can't focus for that long. A time constraint can actually be effective in keeping us on track. In the absence of a genuine learning disability, let the natural restrictions of their assignments and testing be an organizing force.

A good way to reframe learning disabilities is to consider your adolescent's brain as one that works differently from yours or from their peers. While we often see ADHD or dyslexia as disadvantages, thinking differently can actually be a great asset if it is addressed and treated in a productive way. In *David and Goliath,* Malcolm Gladwell spends a chapter on dyslexia, noting the multitude of highly successful people who struggled with the learning disability in their youth.[16] The list includes names like Richard Branson and Charles Schwab, as well as the founders of companies such as JetBlue, Cisco, Kinko's, and Gary Cohn, a longtime president of Goldman Sachs. Gladwell calls dyslexia a "desirable difficulty," arguing that the learning disability forced these individuals to develop other compensatory skills that ended up being enormous assets, such as the ability to deal with and move on from failure. In other words, kids with dyslexia have the opportunity to learn something *because of* their struggle, not *in spite of* their learning disability. This is a helpful mindset for approaching any learning disability or difference: How can your adolescent work with and around the unique makeup of their brain? Perhaps they are particularly primed for creativity, innovation, healthy risk taking, and empathy, all of which are skills that allow for immense long-term success.

Your Teenager on Social Media

Parents often counter the connection between technology and distractibility with the argument that technology can be stimulating and educational. The idea that apps and television programs are "interactive" is misleading. Interaction is engaging with another human being. Interacting is interactive! Technology is absent of eye contact, turn taking, real voices, and human attention. I don't know a single person who hasn't misinterpreted a text message because they couldn't hear the tone of the message or see the person saying the words that were written. These are the cues that allow the brain to develop social and emotional capacities, and this is an essential component of social and psychological development.[17] It never ceases to amaze me, when I am in a restaurant and I see a family with kids on devices with their headphones in or a group of teenagers who are all looking at their phones. This isn't just rude, it denies us the opportunity to experience social interaction and interpersonal relations. We see a huge reduction in situational awareness and comfort in various social settings in teenagers who are glued to their phones. In other words, these social and emotional skills aren't forming. These strong connections are key to a healthy, functional brain and mind. We are just now coming to understand the implications for a generation raised on technology; we're seeing structural, connective impairment where we haven't before. To be clear, technology isn't "bad," but we want to make sure that we are regulating our children's exposure to mitigate the harm of overuse. Remember: It's important to give your teens an explanation for why it's important that they spend time off of their phones. **Our goal is to teach them how to self-regulate as opposed to control what they do or don't do.**

Social media is wreaking havoc on teenagers' emotional health. We're seeing unprecedented levels of anxiety, depression, and suicidal thoughts among the adolescent population. Let's break this down to understand just how social media is tied to these trends. Adolescence is not only an essential period of neurological development, but is also a critical time of identity development. The formation of a healthy identity requires a multifaceted but ultimately coherent sense of self that is personally satisfying and that is recognized and affirmed by one's community.[18] A sense of self, or self-image, is based on both an internal self and the feedback we receive from others. Our internal self is shaped over time; we develop interests, hobbies, skills, and qualities of character. As we develop an internal self, we develop self-esteem, or a belief in ourself and our ability to do well. The feedback we receive from others serves to confirm or challenge how we perceive ourselves. Do our friends, family members, teachers, and coaches agree with the way we believe ourselves to be? Are we consistent across the areas of our life, such as at school, home, and work? This feedback is essential to our ability to understand and accept ourselves. Making these internal and external connections is a core piece of adolescence. Our internal sense of ourselves shapes and directs our experience of life.

A healthy adolescent will get ongoing constructive, evaluative, and comprehensive feedback from their relationships and communities that will shape who they are. As students, they are constantly submitting assignments and taking tests that demonstrate their facility with what they're learning. They get feedback on each of these, serving to reinforce what they are doing well and indicate what they can work on. They also get feedback in their activities. They might earn a leadership position on a team or a spot on the student government or a role in the school play—or they might not. And when they fail to earn these accolades or responsibilities, they have an opportunity to see where they can improve or move in a different direction. Social feedback is important, too. Adolescents are not only learning what is acceptable behavior in various situations, but they are also developing deeper friendships and relationships in which they will learn boundaries and understand give-and-take.

In all of these examples, they put a piece of themselves on the line for judgment and receive encouraging affirmation or constructive criticism. Grappling with criticism and failure is an essential component of building resilience. There is a Latin phrase, *luctor et emergo*, that means "I struggle and I emerge." Persevering through hardship allows us to develop grit, determination, and, most importantly, a belief in ourselves. Feedback, even criticism, is crucial to the construction of an inner self and the development of self-confidence. Reconciling your internal experience with your environment allows you to figure out who you are and where you want to go. Think about how you decided what career path to pursue in your own life. It was probably based, to a large extent, on positive feedback you received, role models you admired, and experiences you enjoyed and found rewarding over time. These components of growing up have been hijacked by social media.

Meaningful, genuine feedback must be be based on real experience and struggle to positively shape a teenager's identity and character. Unfortunately, social media has become a primary source of virtual feedback for teens, based on false appearances and curated images. Facebook and Instagram posts usually aren't a true reflection of who a person is and are often shared with the sole purpose of garnering attention, followers, and "likes." This feedback loop is shallow, void of substance or meaning, and chips away at the core we are trying to build.

Technology and social media distort the healthy formation of an identity because they place excessive emphasis on external approval of an inauthentic version of ourselves. Likes and followers are fleeting; the popular platform is constantly changing, and the approval isn't based on substance, value, or experience. But teenagers face constant pressure to project a popular image of themselves online. This happens all the time: An adolescent is left out of a party, a sleepover, or some other social gathering and is then inundated with Snapchats and Instagram stories of the event they are missing. This has been dubbed "FOMO," the fear of missing out, and it takes an emotional toll. It's hard enough to be excluded, but to see exactly what you're missing makes it worse. Think of yourself as a teenager. My guess is you're relieved that social media didn't exist to document some of your most awkward and fragile moments or rub salt in the wounds of being ditched or left out. You might not even have known you were missing out! But our teenagers are faced with it every single day. Today's youth increasingly feel that their lives are controlled by external social forces,[19] which leaves them feeling anxious and helpless. We're building kids up to have no sense of who they are beyond their online profile (Box 5.2).

It may seem counterintuitive, but the external focus encouraged by social media has resulted in increased narcissism among the adolescent population. When we think of narcissism, we think of selfishness, vanity, and a lack of concern for others, but narcissism is clinically defined not as a personality that loves itself too much, but as one so fragile it needs constant support and approval to feel love.[20] In individuals with narcissistic personality disorder, we often see a lack of humility, a lack of empathy, and self-absorption. These individuals scan the environment for evidence of their superiority and place great weight on the evidence they find. Think about this in terms of "likes"; a narcissist is desperate for approval and validation and cannot tolerate negative feedback. It can be hard to spot a true narcissist, because they will project

---

BOX 5.2

Smartphone Addiction

It can be hard for parents to draw a hard line around smartphones, because technology is pervasive and kids increasingly rely on devices for their school-work. So, how do we know when it has gone too far?

QUESTIONS TO ASK

- Does your teen's mood suddenly change and become intensely anxious, ir-ritable, angry, or even violent when the phone is taken away or unavailable for use?
- Does your teen skip or not participate in social events because of time spent on their phone?
- Does your teen spend so much time on their phone that it interferes with normal daily activities, such as sleep or maintaining personal hygiene?
- Do they lie, hide, or break family rules to spend more time on their phone?[27]

If the answer to one or more of these questions is yes, consider seeking the input of a therapist. It is difficult for an adolescent to learn to self-regulate without the help of an adult.

---

an outward air of superiority, yet there is an undeveloped self-identity on the interior.

We are starting to see this internal deficit in adolescents who rely on their social media for identity formation. The pursuit of constant validation and approval has created a heightened fragility at an extremely vulnerable time of life.[21] We can look to teenage celebrities for cautionary examples of what can happen when you have an outsized perception of yourself at such a fragile time in your life. We're used to seeing a child star with a DUI or tragically overdosing on drugs. Lindsay Lohan has been arrested several times and has been in and out of rehab; Mischa Barton has been arrested for DUI and drug possession; Macaulay Culkin has been found in possession of marijuana and other drugs. These are the innocent faces we remember from *The Parent Trap, The O.C.,* and *Home Alone.* Why such imbalance and volatility? When they should have been developing their internal selves, they were grappling with a high level of impersonal and often thoughtless external feedback. Regardless of their personal desires, they faced pressure to meet the standards of the media and their fanbase. We put them on a pedestal and made them feel exceptional. Then, when they made a mistake, they lost that public adoration and had no internal core to fall back on. Their sense of self-worth revolved around the love and approval of others. We see it time and again: in recent years, we've seen Justin Bieber, Miley Cyrus, and Amanda Bynes struggle with public disgrace and humiliation and turn to alcohol, drugs, and other troubling behavior.

What we have done with social media is to impose the outsized social pressure of a child celebrity onto typical American teenagers. Social media constructs a narcissistic personality that is replacing an internal sense of self and self-esteem. We even see shifts in teenage behavior based on what may elicit "likes" from one's peers. If a teenager becomes dependent on nearly constant positive feedback, the side effect will be self-obsession and self-importance. Social media undermines intrinsic confidence by placing a high value on external affirmation and thereby diminishes the value of personal fulfillment and satisfaction. It's also easy to forget that we're looking at airbrushed or otherwise curated images. We really don't know how the person feels or what their life is like, but we assume it's better than what ours are like or how we feel. I love the phrase "Don't compare your insides to their outsides." This is especially true on social media. Increased narcissistic traits correlate to moodiness, restlessness, worry, sadness, and feelings of isolation. Increasing levels of anxiety and depression among the adolescent age group actually indicate a generation-wide identity crisis.

We can't underestimate the implications of this negative trend. We have disparagingly dubbed today's teens the "selfie generation," evoking a population of vain, vapid adolescents who stare at themselves in the mirror all day. What we really have is a generation of teenagers who risk having no foundational identity with which they can cope with challenges and enjoy the successes of life. A well-adjusted adolescent is one who has a strong enough sense of themselves that they can get by and even succeed in a variety of circumstances. Our job as parents is to build our children up so that they have a strength of character to rely on when life doesn't go their way. Think about a time you were faced with a challenge or hit a bump in the road during your high school years: Your family moved, your parents got divorced, you were cut from a team or failed to get a role in the school play, your "crush" didn't like you back, you or a family member were diagnosed with a serious illness. We couldn't control the external world, but we had to move past these obstacles and not take adversity as personal failure. The sooner teens experience rejection and realize they, too, can move beyond it, the better off they'll be. It's healthy for teenagers to feel rejected and be a little bit vulnerable so that they build up the fortitude to push through it. That fortitude is based on an internal belief in themselves and their own strength. In terms of psychological development, a lack of an inner sense of self diminishes the ability to differentiate between what is internal and what is external.[22]

Teens need a sense of character and values that extends beyond likes and followers, beyond titles, accomplishments, and alma maters. While popularity on social media may provide a temporary boost, it's fleeting and not substantial enough to rely on in moments of adversity or over the long term. Think about it: You might say to yourself, "I got dumped, but I have lots of friends, I can rely on my family, and now I can spend more time on my schoolwork and my interests." Your adolescent *might* say, "I got dumped, but at least I got over 100 likes on my Instagram post last week," but it just doesn't work. It's not satisfying or reassuring over the long term. If teens lose live, experience-based identity formation, they can run into major problems. A constant connection to devices and people accessible through them weakens the ability to develop an autonomous self and contributes to aimlessness and lack of purpose.[23] On the more extreme end, we are seeing terrifyingly problematic behavioral patterns among teenagers that suggest a lack of empathy and basic humanity, including desensitization to and perpetuation of violent crimes.

AS PARENTS, WE need to pull our teenagers away from multitasking and dependence on technology so that they can develop their identities, interests, and imaginations. Constant stimulation prevents reflection and both deeper and abstract thinking. We are so fearful of boredom in our adolescent's life, but we should actually embrace rare moments of downtime and preserve unstructured time in their lives. When my kids would tell me they were bored, I would offer to find something for them to do. Most of the time, they reconsidered, as they figured I would probably come up with some sort of chore to occupy their time. But sometimes they would accept, and they actually enjoyed organizing a filing cabinet or doing the grocery shopping because their brain could rest.

Spending time off of devices and deeply engaged in an activity allows teenagers to develop interests, industry, and the internal confidence they desperately need. Even letting the mind wander is essential for recharging and developing an imagination. Several studies have shown that daydreaming leads to creativity, which in turn leads to agency, innovation, and the creation of an internal world.[24] Adolescents are naturally highly creative because of the high level of neurological activity required for brain development during this stage. The brain is wired to maximize creativity and imagination in adolescence, but it is stunted by multitasking and technology. Windows of free time allow teens to pursue various interests, and chances are they will gravitate toward something they enjoy, whether it be playing the guitar, throwing a baseball, researching animals online, or doodling in a sketchbook. These interests can become hobbies and even passions that can alter the course of a life.[25] It's time to take back unstructured time for your kids. It's worth the fight.

Consider This:
Insights & Actions

- As recently as 10 years ago, I would walk to school to pick my children up and talk to the other parents while we waited. In the same situation today, every parent would be glued to their phone. I regularly sit next to families in restaurants or pass by parents and children on the street, and it's the parents who won't look up! Be aware of the example you set for your children and adolescents. Set a goal to finish whatever you need to do on your phone before you see your kids at the end of the day so that you can devote an extended period of time to them. Give them your full focus, show them verbal and physical attention, and model solo-tasking. There is no electronic replacement for a parent's example.

- It's important to remember how many things teenagers do in any given day so that we don't compound their tasks and their stress with our own requests and "to-do"s for them. Timing is everything! At the end of a long day, your teen won't respond well to nagging. Is morning a better time? Can it wait until Friday afternoon or Sunday? Figure out when your adolescent is most receptive to your requests. Agree upon a timeline but resist the urge to nag.

- Adolescents are inherently competitive. Play a game like paddle tennis, go to a yoga or spin class, or play board games like Charades, Pictionary, or Scattergories instead of watching TV one night. Forced family fun never works, but if you add another level of interaction into their activities, like healthy competition, you gain better buy-in and, participants will bond with one another without knowing it.

- Try this experiment: Have your teenager invite a few friends over to your house. When they get there, collect their phones on the kitchen table.

Make it a challenge to see who can leave their phone for the longest amount of time. This will encourage them to make their own fun and interact with one another instead of sitting around on their devices.

- Meditation and visualization have been shown to be powerful tools to increase focus and mental clarity. With teens, visualization is often more appealing than meditation. Visualization seems to be active, while asking them to sit still and try not to think might be a challenge. Encourage them to visualize an upcoming day, a test, or a big event they might be nervous about. Get them to really see themselves performing as they hope to in that moment. The more details and tactile sensations they can bring up, the better. This can be useful for anything from tests to a party that's making them anxious. If they can take a minute to hold still, close their eyes, and visualize what they have coming up, they may feel more grounded and prepared for what's ahead.

- It's important for your teenager to conceptualize their future life. Encourage them to make lists of their goals—where do they want to be in 1, 5, or 10 years?—or even their likes and dislikes. These are important elements of identity formation and writing them down prompts them to connect the dots and find larger patterns in their interests or activities that might give them a sense of direction and purpose. They're never too young to start.

- At this stage, you probably have a sense of what types of things your adolescent is interested in. Instead of asking them "How was your day?" make an effort to share a relevant newspaper article or YouTube clip, or take them to a museum, concert, sports game, or other event related to their interest. It can be hard to get your adolescent to want to do things with you, but if you target their interests, you'll have a better chance.

- I often have parents lament that their kids don't want to come to family dinner or participate in a family outing. I always respond with: Have you asked them what they would like to do? Sometimes we impose our own desires on them instead of getting a sense of what their preferences are. It can be a little painful for you, but push yourself to meet them halfway. Maybe they don't want to go to another family dinner, but they might be happy to do something else with you. Don't constantly force togetherness; try to let it happen naturally. For example, you can all go to the movie theater and each see a different movie. That's still a family activity!

- Countless studies also show that altruism and compassion are qualities of a peaceful, happy mind; narcissism and excessive self-involvement are connected to unhappiness and dissatisfaction.[26] Have your teenager pick a socially conscious organization to participate in. It's important to expose them to the concepts of charity and "giving back" early on. This isn't about résumé building or filling openings in their schedule. This is to encourage volunteerism, self-exploration, altruism, and passion.

- In the age of the iPhone, don't let your kids hide behind the screen. Hold them accountable for the same conduct you expect when they are interacting with someone face to face. I have had numerous adolescents tell me that they sent a text to the wrong person and shared information or said something that they shouldn't have. I've done it myself! They can lie and try to talk their way out of the situation, knowing that the recipient will not believe a word they are telling them. Or they can say that they're sorry and admit that they shouldn't have done what they did and move on. Encourage them to acknowledge the mistake and offer a genuine apology.

Notes

1. Gazzaley, A., & Rosen, L. D. (2016). *The distracted mind: Ancient brains in a high-tech world.* Cambridge, MA: MIT Press.

2. Gazzaley, A., & Rosen, L. D. (2016), *The distracted mind: Ancient brains in a high-tech world.* Cambridge, MA: MIT Press.

3. Gazzaley, A., & Rosen, L. D. (2016). *The distracted mind: Ancient brains in a high-tech world.* Cambridge, MA: MIT Press.

4. Siegel, D. J. (2013). *Brainstorm. The power and purpose of the teenage brain.* New York, NY: Penguin.

5. Gazzaley, A., & Rosen, L. D. (2016). *The distracted mind: Ancient brains in a high-tech world.* Cambridge, MA: MIT Press.

6. Gazzaley, A., & Rosen, L. D. (2016). *The distracted mind: Ancient brains in a high-tech world.* Cambridge, MA: MIT Press.

7. Aiken, M. (2017). *The cyber effect: An expert in cyberpsychology explains how technology is shaping our children, our behavior, and our values—and what we can do about it.* New York, NY: Spiegel & Grau.

8. Aiken, M. (2017). *The cyber effect: An expert in cyberpsychology explains how technology is shaping our children, our behavior, and our values—and what we can do about it.* New York, NY: Spiegel & Grau.

9. Aiken, M. (2017). *The cyber effect: An expert in cyberpsychology explains how technology is shaping our children, our behavior, and our values—and what we can do about it.* New York, NY: Spiegel & Grau.

10. Collins, K. P., & Cleary, S. D. (2016). Racial and ethnic disparities in parent-reported diagnosis of ADHD: National Survey of Children's Health (2003, 2007, and 2011). *Journal of Clinical Psychiatry, 77*(1), 52–59. doi:10.4088/JCP.14m09364; George Washington University. (2015, December 8). New report finds 43 percent increase in ADHD diagnosis for U.S. schoolchildren [Press release]. Retrieved from https://publichealth.gwu.edu/content/new-report-finds-43-percent-increase-adhd-diagnosis-us-schoolchildren-0

11. Siegel, D. J. (2013). *Brainstorm. The power and purpose of the teenage brain.* New York, NY: Penguin.

12. Hallowell, E. M., & Ratey, J. J. (1994). *Answers to distraction.* New York, NY: Pantheon.

13. Healy, J. M. (2010). *Different learners: Identifying, preventing, and treating your child's learning problems.* New York, NY: Simon & Schuster.

14. Levine, M. (2003). *The myth of laziness.* New York, NY: Simon & Schuster.

15. Healy, J. M. (1998). *Failure to connect: How computers affect our children's minds—and what we can do about it.* New York, NY: Simon & Schuster.

16. Gladwell, M. (2013). *David and Goliath.* New York, NY: Little, Brown.

17. Aiken, M. (2017). *The cyber effect: An expert in cyberpsychology explains how technology is shaping our children, our behavior, and our values—and what we can do about it.* New York, NY: Spiegel & Grau.

18. Erikson, E. H. (1963). *Childhood and society.* New York, NY: W. W. Norton. (Original work published 1950)

19. Turkle, S. (2012). *Alone together: Why we expect more from technology and less from each other.* New York, NY: Basic Books.

20. Turkle, S. (2012). *Alone together: Why we expect more from technology and less from each other.* New York, NY: Basic Books.

21. Turkle, S. (2012). *Alone together: Why we expect more from technology and less from each other.* New York, NY: Basic Books.

22. Piaget, J. (1932). *The language and thought of the child* (2nd ed.). London, UK: Kegan Paul, Trench, Trubner & Co.

23. Turkle, S. (2012). *Alone together: Why we expect more from technology and less from each other.* New York, NY: Basic Books.

24. Gardner, H., & Davis, K. (2013). *The app generation: How today's youth navigate identity, intimacy, and imagination in a digital world.* New Haven, CT: Yale University Press.

25. Hallowell, E. M. (2002). *The childhood roots of adult happiness. Five steps to help kids create and sustain lifelong joy.* New York, NY: Ballantine Books.

26. Brooks, R. (2017). The request for strategies: But strategies for what? Harvard Medical School Symposium: Middle School Through College Mental Health and Education. Cambridge, MA. Course directors include Joseph Gold, Stephanie Pinder-Amaker, Mona P. Potter, Bryan C. Pridgen, and Christopher M. Palmer.

27. Homayoun, A. (2018, January 17). Is your child a phone "addict"? *New York Times.* Retrieved from https://www.nytimes.com/2018/01/17/well/family/is-your-child-a-phone-addict.html

6

The Sixth Myth

DRUGS AND ALCOHOL ONLY TEMPORARILY
IMPACT MY TEENAGER.

I MET JEN while she was home from boarding school for the holidays. Jen is prescribed Adderall and "vapes" both nicotine and cannabis oil regularly. Adderall is a stimulant, so it makes Jen feel wired and anxious. When she's taking it, she loses her appetite and struggles to fall asleep, so she buys Xanax from friends at school to take the edge off. She tells me that she can buy any drug at school from any number of "dealers."

Jen wanted to make the soccer team, but she would need to be in great shape to do so. She knew she was hurting her lungs because she struggled to keep up with her peers during workouts. She had seen her pediatrician the day before and had shared her drug use openly with her doctor. Jen's doctor told her that she could be at serious risk for a heart attack and wrote her a prescription for an EKG. Jen was getting high several times a day and taking a dangerous mix of stimulants and depressants. She admitted that her drug use had gotten out of control but she told me that, realistically, she didn't think she could fully abstain.

I asked Jen if she had considered the consequences of being found in possession of any of these drugs on campus; her prestigious boarding school has a zero-tolerance policy for illegal drugs. If caught, Jen would be expelled immediately, and her school would notify prospective colleges.

"Don't worry," she told me. "I've been doing this for a while. I know how to avoid getting caught."

When Jen talked to me, I could tell she was scared, but it was clear that she didn't fully understand the implications of what she was doing to her body or how dangerous her drug use might be. I explained to Jen that she was combining uppers and downers, in addition to taking heavy drugs that hadn't been medically prescribed to her. Teenagers often have a false sense that they are invincible and that nothing bad can happen to them. In Jen's case, she faced many risks, ranging in severity from trouble at school to damaging her health. She was not only confident she wouldn't get caught; she was also ignorant of most of these risks.

While it may seem extreme, Jen's story is actually common. Most teenagers are vaguely aware that drinking and doing drugs is risky, but they lack a concrete understanding of how those substances impact them in the short and long term. **Studies show that adolescents whose parents have talked to them about alcohol and drugs are 42% less likely to use, but only 1 in 4 teens report that they have had this conversation with their parents.**[1] This is the key to mitigating the risks teenagers face as they experiment with different substances throughout high school.

Parents can feel scared and overwhelmed at the prospect of their teenager drinking and doing drugs, so they often fall into one of two camps on the topic: "Everybody's doing it" or "Not my child." This reflects our tendency to manage our fear by assuming it's normal behavior or by denying the possibility entirely. If you fall into the "Everybody's doing it" camp, you might think that your teen can experiment with drinking and drugs and emerge from adolescence unscathed. You throw up your hands and decide to pick another battle. But the truth is, everybody is *not* doing it. In fact, many adolescents abstain or only use periodically.[2] Your involvement in this area can mitigate the risks of alcohol and drug use during the teenage years and protect your child from some of the more severe consequences. We want the message to be, "I know that some kids your age are doing this, but I'm not on board with it because it really hurts your brain and body." The best we can do is provide the facts about how these substances permanently damage their brains and bodies and set clear expectations for their behavior. If you don't have the conversation with your child, they'll interpret your silence as permission.

If you're thinking "Not my child," think again. It's likely that your teenager will experiment with at least alcohol at some point.[3] As we learned from Jen, today's adolescents have access to a wide variety of substances, and chances are high that your child will have the opportunity to drink or take drugs during high school. Ask any teenager: They'll tell you they can get their hands on pretty much anything. The worst thing you can be is naïve. As parents, we have to operate from a standpoint of not *if*, but *when*. While we may not be able to control their behavior at every turn, we can ensure that they are making informed choices when the moment arises. Whether or not they experiment, they will know they are taking a risk and will proceed with some amount of caution.

Parents hesitate to make strong decisions based on health and safety because they want to be in good standing with their child. Your kids need you to provide structure and boundaries. You aren't their friend—you're their parent. This is an important distinction to make, particularly during the adolescent years. While you might be warm and nurturing in your approach, your primary responsibility is still your child's safety and wellbeing. In this chapter, we'll give you the important information about alcohol and drugs so that you can make the ramifications clear and personal for your adolescent. It's critical that they perceive that you know what their life is like and that you're aware of what's going on. Even if they hear these facts at school or in another setting, when you are the one that directly relays this information to your teen, they will notice that you're in the know and you'll gain their respect.

Alcohol

The three primary drugs used by adolescents are alcohol, nicotine, and marijuana.[4] Let's start with alcohol, as it's the one most teenagers most commonly use and abuse. Alcohol is appealing to teenagers on many levels: It feels good, eases social anxiety, relieves stress, and is a little risky. I often meet with parents who roll their eyes and tell me that drinking can't be *that* harmful. After all, they drank throughout adolescence and they're fine. They believe that in another few years, we'll go back to saying alcohol and drugs aren't so terrible.

The truth is, we have new information based on the most comprehensive research that shows us just how harmful alcohol is for an adolescent. Alcohol impacts their cognitive and physical functioning, and their brain development. We can now definitively say that all cognitive functioning is slowed down while drinking and, most importantly, that prolonged alcohol use during adolescence results in permanent alterations to brain structure and cognitive functioning.

All mental functioning decreases under the influence of alcohol, including awareness, memory, planning, and physical regulation. Alcohol use decreases decision-making ability and slows reaction times. Adolescents who use alcohol demonstrate deficits in attention, visual and spatial skills, and executive functions.[5] Teens who consistently use alcohol do worse on memory tasks by 10%, and show less brain activity during these tasks.[6] Statistics also show that the earlier an adolescent begins drinking, the more severely they will damage their brain, and the more likely they will be to struggle with alcohol later in life. Moreover, the sooner a teenager starts to drink, the worse the overall impact on their brain and body. Research irrefutably shows that early use is a strong predictor of increased risk of substance abuse and alcohol use disorder.[7] If you start drinking before age 15, you are 85% more likely to struggle with alcohol later in life.[8] **Said another way, those who start drinking regularly by age 13 have a 47% chance of developing alcoholism, while those who don't drink until they are 18 decrease their risk to 17%.**[9] To the best of our ability, we want to delay the age at which they start drinking. If we permit them to drink at home at a young age, we increase their risk of later alcohol abuse and permanent neurological damage.

Exposure to alcohol in adolescence has long-term effects on brain development.[10] Alcohol impacts the frontal lobe most intensely, which we know is undergoing important development during the teenage years. The **hippocampus,** part of the cerebral cortex, is responsible for significant production of new neurons. Think back to chapter 1, in which we established that adolescence is a precious window for brain development and growth. The hippocampus is in overdrive during adolescence as neurons undergo pruning and myelination. Alcohol not only impairs the production of new neurons, but also kills existing brain cells. Once we lose a neuron, we can't get it back (see Box 6.1). Structural MRIs show a decrease in the volume of brain tissue and cortical thickness and lower neural connectivity in teenagers who consistently use alcohol.[11] Adolescents with ADHD are particularly susceptible,

---

BOX 6.1

Understanding Neurons

- Neurons transmit information about other parts of the body and the outside world to the brain.
- Neurotransmitters are located within a neuron and tell the neuron what to do, which in turn dictates behavior. Neuron function produces all behavior.
- Alcohol and drugs interact with neurotransmitters, which is why we behave differently when we are under the influence of any type of substance.
- The production of new neurons can be influenced by environmental factors, such as alcohol consumption. Alcohol consumption has been shown to hinder the generation of new brain cells.

as their brains develop more slowly than their peers'. Keep in mind that this is true of any learning disability that has a root in the prefrontal cortex, such as dyslexia or auditory processing disorder. From a neurological standpoint, a 14-year-old with ADHD is more like a 12-year-old without an attention disorder or learning disability. Therefore, alcohol impacts a 14-year-old with ADHD as severely as it would a 12-year-old. If your child has a learning disability, make sure they are aware of this particular risk. Alcohol is particularly harmful to a brain that is already struggling to hone these essential cognitive functions. Think about it: When women are pregnant or breastfeeding, they are advised to avoid alcohol because the fetus or baby's brain is developing, and most women heed this warning. We're likewise wrong to think it's okay for a teenager to drink while their brain and body are developing throughout adolescence. It's common sense: Anything that impairs the brain during adolescence will impair its development and thereby harm it permanently and irreversibly.

Let's review how alcohol impacts the body. It is a depressant, so it lowers our heart rate and blood pressure and slows down physical functions. Drinking impairs motor skills and results in a loss of physical balance. It also inhibits pain receptors, so we might be unaware of physical risks such as cold weather or injury while impaired. Alcohol has a serious impact on the liver, pancreas, and overall nervous system. All of these biological systems are developing in the adolescent, and regular alcohol use impairs their healthy formation. Alcohol also interferes with bone growth, as it leaches calcium from growing bones. The **brain stem**, which is the connection between the brain and the body, fails to successfully transmit messages between the two when it is flooded with booze. **Alcohol poisoning is caused by the body's inability to receive such messages, which causes essential physical functions to shut down.** It isn't as simple as passing out and not waking up. The brain is flooded with alcohol and is not sending or receiving messages critical to survival. It's especially dangerous with inexperienced drinkers (i.e., teenagers) because they don't know their limit. When the body is unresponsive to information from the brain, the result can be nothing short of deadly. Alcohol also has dangerous implications for adolescent behavior. Violence, car accidents, sexual promiscuity, and suicide attempts are all higher among adolescents under the influence.

Boys and girls absorb alcohol differently because of body weight, body fat percentage, and bone density.[12] This is important to tell adolescents because this difference can have significant implications for both sexes. Three drinks in a 120-pound female over one hour results in a 0.10 **blood alcohol content**

or BAC, which is considered to be the legal limit for intoxication in adults. The same amount of alcohol imbibed by a 160-pound male over one hour results in a 0.05 BAC. If a male and female have a few drinks over dinner, she may be twice as drunk as he is by the end of the meal. With teenagers, it's more likely that they're drinking alcohol in fast, secretive spurts and aren't tracking how much they're taking in at once. Weight-conscious adolescent girls are often drinking without having eaten much throughout the day, so alcohol is hitting their system on an empty stomach. At big events, like a school dance, it's common for kids to "pregame," or drink prior to a social gathering, particularly when there won't be alcohol available at the event. They often drink more than they can handle and end up sick or even transported to the hospital. Furthermore, girls are more susceptible to this because of their body composition.

It's helpful to use this information with your teen to encourage better decision making in the moment. If you can use the name of someone they know and reference a specific instance, you can counter their argument that it won't happen. In almost any high school in the country, kids will know about a kid who is always wasted before an athletic event or a school dance or at a house party and is most likely to get into trouble. But the ones who are more often hospitalized are the less experienced or first-time drinkers. Through the high school years, the ones who end up in the most serious trouble are the ones experimenting for the first time without any idea what their tolerance or limit might be. Gently remind your kids of a situation where this type of thing happened. It's important that you've had enough of a discussion about these issues to demonstrate a realistic awareness of what kids are doing. If your teenager feels that you have no idea what it's really like, they will write you off. If you show them that you get it, but you still expect them to behave in a certain way, this thought will register in their mind and they will be more likely to take your standards into consideration when making decisions.

Teenagers are bound to make bad decisions; if we can give them insight and help them see alternative choices, they will start making stronger decisions and exercising better judgment over time. Once they have insight, they can't unlearn it. If your teenager makes a mistake with drinking or drugs, use it as an opportunity to talk through how they were impaired and what they might do differently the next time. Use a high-structure, high-nurture approach. You still have expectations for their behavior and should impose consequences when they break a rule, but you can help them understand the reasoning behind those expectations, and push them to see how they might handle the same situation differently in the future. The good news and the bad news for parents is that teenagers will always have another opportunity because they are faced with those kinds of choices all the time.

Parents often tell me that they let their children drink at home to help them build a tolerance for alcohol. I view this as high nurture, low structure. This approach is based on a misconception of "tolerance." Adolescents are less sensitive to the sedative effects and physical impairment drinking produces. This is why you might wake up with a hangover after an extra glass of red wine, while your teenager can get away with a night of drinking and seem fine. Parents mistakenly perceive that their teenager can tolerate alcohol because alcohol affects teens and adults differently. If an impaired adult is asked to walk in a straight line, they are likely to struggle. However, if they're asked to remember a sequence of words, they might have no trouble. For a teenager, the opposite is true. They may have no difficulty walking in a straight line, but will fail to remember the words in order.[13] We need to remember that the alcohol is predominantly affecting a teenager's brain instead of their body. The teen may not show signs of physical impairment, but will struggle with recall, because alcohol is impacting their prefrontal cortex, which it isn't developed enough to overcome its impairing effects. In other words, an adolescent can't think straight.

Don't mistake an ability to "handle" a certain quantity of alcohol for a protection against damage. A tolerance is a signal that the user's brain chemicals have shifted, which causes the body to need more of a substance to feel the effects—meaning the user is actually sustaining more damage. Remember that a teenager's brain is changing rapidly throughout adolescence, so chemical changes brought on by drug and alcohol use interfere with natural brain development. With this information, you are now equipped to set strong expectations and rules around substance use.

I'm taken aback by the casual attitude many parents of young teenagers have toward drinking. I meet parents of eighth, ninth, and 10th graders who permit their children to drink and even provide alcohol for their children and their friends. This is a health and safety concern; permitting your adolescents to drink at a young age sets a very dangerous precedent that can't be reversed. It's not only illegal, and replete with major liability issues if anything goes wrong, but once you've served alcohol or sent your teen to a place where you know they're being served, you've essentially given them permission to drink, and you can't go back on this liberty.

Approval of this kind is actually low nurture, low structure because you are putting your child in harm's way. We never see good results from teens who believe they aren't fundamentally cared for, even if they are in a "loving" environment. This is a ticket to risk, danger, and potentially devastating consequences. Being strict with your teenager when you are working to have a good relationship can be hard, but adolescents want to feel safe in knowing that you are looking out for them and their best interests. You demonstrate love by being very clear with your adolescents on where you stand and why. The parental relationship is different than a peer relationship; kids need boundaries and want to feel safe and cared for. Whether or not they admit it, teenagers will hear your expectations and will struggle with some amount of discomfort if and when they choose to go against your will.

Here's an example of a low-structure, low-nurture approach to teen drinking. I had a client whose mother consistently provided alcohol for her and permitted her to have parties in her house. One Saturday night, my client was showing off to her friends and asked her mom if she would give her a bottle of vodka. Without hesitation, her mom went to the liquor cabinet and returned with a handle of alcohol for her child and her friends.

As my client told me the story, she began to cry and couldn't stop. When we talked through it, she told me that none of her friends' parents would do the same thing, so she assumed that her mom's permissiveness was the opposite of love and meant that her mom didn't care as much about her. Children don't respect a parent that lets them push the limit to this extent. Don't be the high school party house. If something goes wrong, even if you weren't home and didn't know what was going on, you are liable for what took place.

Think back to the party house when you were in high school. Where are those kids now? Chances are they have struggled with ups and downs or battled addiction. In my family, there is alcoholism on both sides, and we experienced the tragic loss of a close family friend to alcohol poisoning at a young age. I took a particularly strong stand on alcohol with my children, and they understood that while I was always there to support them, I would not condone the use of alcohol or drugs during high school. I was aware that my kids would probably drink before graduation, but I made sure they knew I was not comfortable with it. Adolescents will most likely defy you, but your job is to make it hard for them to drink and do drugs and to delay this kind of experimentation for as long as possible. Be vigilant: Check their backpacks, call their friend's parents to find out if they'll be home when your child visits their house, and insist that they check in with you when they come home from a party. They may resist and even test you, but they actually want you to push back. Stand your ground. (See Box 6.2.)

BOX 6.2

How to Have the Conversation:

I don't want you drinking alcohol or using drugs because . . .

- I don't think you're old enough. Alcohol and drugs hurt your brain and cause permanent damage. If it makes you feel impaired and out of control, it's affecting you!
- We have alcoholism in our family, which puts you at a higher risk of developing a problem.
- I'm worried you won't be able to make good decisions when you're impaired, and I don't trust others to have your best interests in mind at all times. If you can't think straight and you're interacting with others, scary things can happen.
- Everybody *isn't* doing it and I'm only concerned about you.
- You work so hard for success in school/sports/music/etc. and substance use undoes that hard work. It's two steps backward.
- Imagine how you would feel if you got caught and got in trouble at school. Would you be able to look your teachers or coaches in the eye?
- Your life can change in 30 seconds. One bad decision can change the course of your entire life.

Marijuana

Next up: marijuana. While marijuana may seem less pervasive than alcohol, it is arguably more dangerous for an adolescent to use. This is new information; we didn't know this before because we couldn't measure it. Now, we can see images of the impact of marijuana on the brain, so we can understand how it actually effects teens' neurological development. The active ingredient in marijuana is **tetrahydrocannabinol** or THC, which connects with neurological receptors and weakens connections between neurons of the hippocampus. THC disrupts a chemical in the brain called **anandamide** and rewires the developing nervous system. This, in turn, disrupts the development and maintenance of the neural connections critical for higher level cognitive functioning. When an adult smokes marijuana, their brain cells will revert to a pre-THC state after four to six weeks. **When a teenager smokes marijuana, their cells do not revert to a pre-THC state. In other words, the brain cells are *permanently* altered.** This is particularly problematic as it effects neurological development. If newly produced neurons are altered by THC, they cannot connect normally with other brain cells, resulting in lower neural connectivity and cognitive functioning. Prolonged and regular marijuana use in adolescents is shown to change the density, volume, and shape of the brain. Neuro-imaging shows significant front-brain alterations in adolescent marijuana users, which confirms that their brain cells are not forming and connecting in a normal and healthy way. This is seriously harmful.

Marijuana use has both short- and long-term impacts on the adolescent brain and body. When a teenager is high, they experience altered senses, a distorted sense of time, changes in mood, impaired movement, and difficulty thinking clearly. Studies show that individuals who smoke as teenagers lose an average of 8 to 10 IQ points over time.[14] The cumulative impact on the teenage brain and neurological development results in impaired memory, focus, and processing speed. Smokers have to use more effort to perform tasks mediated by their front brain because they have to activate additional areas of their brain in order to support their stunted frontal lobe. In the absence of THC, their brains should be forming connections to perform these tasks quickly and efficiently, but THC blocks those connections. The neurological systems most impacted in an adolescent are emotion, motivation, and memory. These systems are already vulnerable and raw in the adolescent; these are the exact systems we, as parents, want to protect and advance through adolescence.

We're discovering new information about the impact of THC on the developing brain all the time. There is mounting evidence that early marijuana use is linked to long-term impairment in the prefrontal cortex, attentional control, working memory, and executive functioning.[15] Studies show that the neural connectivity of an early onset marijuana user is disorganized and inefficient.[16] Consistent marijuana use also results in a muted response to reward and an increased sensitivity to punishment. The reward system in an adolescent brain is not fully formed, which makes it highly sensitive to substances. (For a depiction of how neurotransmitters work in the unimpaired brain, see Figure 6.1.) Think of the reward system as a network of electrical wires. When a wire is cut, you can splice it back together, but the connection remains frayed and won't be as reliable. When a teenager synthetically stimulates the reward system on a repeated basis, the system is permanently altered. This alteration weakens the brain's ability to take on tasks, manage emotion, and regulate the body. In an adult brain, the reward system is activated and is temporarily altered by marijuana, but eventually reverts to a stable structure when THC has passed through the system.[17] It just isn't the same for an adolescent.

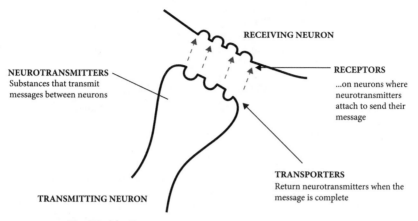

FIGURE 6.1. The Healthy Brain

Research also shows that long-term exposure to THC is linked to higher incidents of mental illness, including depression, anxiety, and suicidal ideation. It makes sense that a teenager who is looking to use various types of drugs may already be struggling in some way. They turn to a drug like marijuana because it has a calming effect and numbs their emotions. I can't tell you how many adolescents I work with who tell me that they have to get high in order to cope with the stress and pressure of their daily lives. What is so devastating about this is that regularly getting high diminishes their ability to manage what they need to do and thereby increases the stress they feel. It's not just a quick, harmless release; it increases the anxiety they will feel over time.

Continued marijuana use also prevents an adolescent from developing a tolerance for stress and an ability to respond to their emotions in a healthy way. Long-term use is linked to a higher stress response and a higher negative mood in users.[18] We also know that THC hinders an adolescent's development of learning, memory, and attention, which are crucial for overcoming anxiety. When we feel anxious, we refer to past situations to remind ourselves that we will be okay. If we can't draw on memory and shift our attention to positive emotions, anxiety becomes overwhelming.[19] While marijuana makes us feel less anxious **in the moment**, it perpetuates long-term anxiety, and we require more and more to feel okay. That short-term relief is rewiring the reward circuit in the brain so that we crave more of the drug not only to feel high but simply to feel okay (see Figure 6.2). The more of the drug we take

THC IN THE ADOLESCENT BRAIN

THC acts like a neurotransmitter and binds to receptors in the brain, permanently altering those receptors.
Once THC binds to a receptor, it sends abnormal messages to the brain.

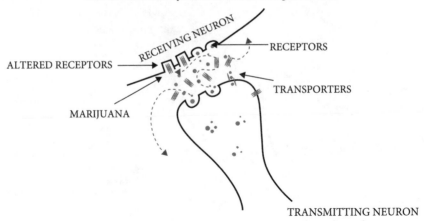

FIGURE 6.2. THC in the Adolescent Brain

in over time, the more permanently the reward circuit is damaged. What a teenager believes will make them feel better instead makes them feel increasingly worse and unable to cope with ups and downs. Regular marijuana use in adolescence is often found to be a predictive factor in the development of personality disorders in young adulthood.[20] It's helpful for adolescents to understand the difference between the sensation they feel and the actual impact: if they rely on marijuana to alter their emotions, they diminish their ability to cope with difficult feelings over time.

Physically, marijuana is harmful to lung function and capacity. We see more colds and asthma-related illnesses in teenagers who smoke regularly. Smoking marijuana impedes physical performance, too; if an adolescent is high and tries to perform a physical task, it's as though they must do it with a weight on their back. THC elevates the heart rate for up to 3 hours after using, which increases the risk of cardiac arrest. Though rare, if a teenager smokes pot and then participates in physical activity, they may be at risk for a heart attack. In males, THC impacts fertility and significantly lowers sperm count over time.

Marijuana use is on the rise: In the past 10 years, its use among the teenage population has almost doubled.[21] One in 17 high school seniors report using marijuana daily; more students consume THC than nicotine.[22] Use has increased largely because teens misperceive marijuana as less harmful than drinking. Seventy-one percent of high school seniors do not view regular marijuana use as harmful.[23] Likewise, the perception that marijuana is natural, and therefore healthy, is detrimental for adolescents. Marijuana has been legalized in several American states over the last decade, including California, Colorado, and Massachusetts. It's available in more forms than ever, from gummy bears to vaping pens to body lotion. Like most drugs, marijuana can be used therapeutically. The substance primarily sought in medicinal marijuana is cannabidiol (CBD), which is in the same class of chemicals as a neurotransmitter produced naturally in the human body and brain. CBD provides balancing and calming effects for different ailments. But medicinal marijuana use is not the same as recreational marijuana use. CBD is very different from THC, and the amount of THC in marijuana has increased. Marijuana today is 10 times stronger than the marijuana that was circulating in the '60s and '70s. The THC-to-CBD ratio has gone from 14:1 to 80:1.[24] As in the case with alcohol, those who use before the age of 18 are four to seven times more likely to develop a drug dependence later on.[25] Make no mistake: Marijuana is a gateway drug. Prolonged THC exposure causes enhanced sensitivity to heroin and opioids.[26] Any time we inhibit the reward cycle, as we do when we drink or take drugs, we crave more, so it's logical that we will look for other substances to get high (Figures 6.3 and 6.4).

ALCOHOL	MARIJUANA	NICOTINE	BENZODIAZEPINES (XANAX, ATIVAN)
EFFECT	**EFFECT**	**EFFECT**	**EFFECT**
Relaxation, reduced inhibition, delusions of grandeur	Minor euphoria, heightened sensory perception, increased appetite	Feelings of alertness, a "buzz," and increased focus	Reduced anxiety
RISK	**RISK**	**RISK**	**RISK**
Suppressed judgment and inhibition, alcohol poisoning, brain damage	Brain damage, lowered motivation, impaired mental functioning	Cancer, addiction	Addiction

FIGURE 6.3. Effects and Risks of Alcohol, Marijuana, Nicotine, and Benzodiazepines (e.g., Xanax and Ativan)

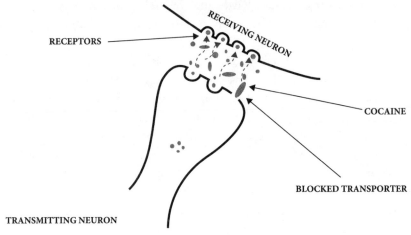

COCAINE IN THE ADOLESCENT BRAIN
Cocaine blocks dopamine from being recycled, causing the receptors to be flooded with dopamine, which creates a sense of euphoria, but blocks the reward system from functioning naturally.

FIGURE 6.4. Cocaine in the Adolescent Brain

Nicotine

Nicotine, the main ingredient in tobacco, is another culprit that can lead to additional drug use as it directly affects **dopamine** receptors, which are central to the reward circuit. Nicotine binds to receptors in multiple regions of the brain, spiking dopamine levels and mimicking a different neurotransmitter that impacts focus and arousal.[27] Nicotine is both a stimulant and a relaxant: It peps you up if you're tired and calms you down if you're anxious. For this reason, nicotine is highly addictive and easy to get hooked on. The adolescent brain is very vulnerable to addiction because substance use during development alters the structure of the brain as it forms (see Table 6.1). The younger the brain, the more easily its reward circuitry can be manipulated. Nicotine excites nerve cells and increases the rate at which nerves communicate with each other. It temporarily heightens memory, which makes us feel alert and focused. Unlike alcohol or marijuana, nicotine is a stimulant, which is chemically structured like illegal narcotics such as cocaine.

Teenage nicotine use is back on the rise in recent years, largely due to e-cigarettes and vaporizer pens. A vaporizer, often referred to by the most popular brand, Juul, looks like a long USB port, which makes it incredibly easy to hide. Smoking an e-cigarette is often referred to as "Juuling," the brand being so pervasive it has become a verb.[28] A user inhales vaporized oil through the pen, so it doesn't smell and the cloud of vapor exhaled dissipates faster than

Table 6.1. Factors Leading to Teenage Alcohol and Drug Use, and Signs Your Teen Is Using Alcohol or Drugs

Factors	Signs
Age of first use	Extreme weight loss or weight gain
Family history of alcoholism and/or addiction	Low motivation, lethargy
Childhood trauma	Excessive talking or unprecedented effusiveness
Existing anxiety, depression, or other mental illness	Elevated mood or extreme mood swings
	Signs of a hangover after being out
	Withdrawal from friends and activities
	Dropping long-time friends; change in peer group
	Skipping classes or school regularly
	Change in appearance, low hygiene
	Behavioral shifts, including sleeping or eating habits
	Missed assignments or a sudden drop in grades

cigarette smoke. Both nicotine and marijuana can be vaporized in a wide variety of flavors, from strawberry to mango to mint. While it is illegal to sell to anyone under 18, it's very easy to get. The most dangerous aspect of vaping is that teenagers are taking in the nicotine equivalent of a pack a day without any idea of how much they're inhaling. Twice as many high schoolers and middle schoolers vape than smoke.[29] They think that vaping isn't as bad for them because e-cigarettes are considered to be a safer alternative to regular cigarettes. While it's true that tar and other additives found in cigarettes are absent from the nicotine oil, the oil has also been found to have different additives, such as formaldehyde and an ingredient in windshield wiper fluid, which are carcinogenic. Remember how when we were children, we sunbathed in baby oil and tin foil and smoked cigarettes without concern? I believe that, like most addictive substances, there will be long-term damage associated with vaping that we haven't uncovered yet. Vaping can seem innocuous, but it's dangerous for teenagers as it can lead to addiction, illness, and additional drug use.

I recently met with a mother who found cannabis oil in her son's backpack. Her son struggles with depression and attempted suicide one year prior to this incident. He is on and off of antidepressants and anti-anxiety medication. When I spoke with her, she wasn't overly concerned about her son's vaping because she, too, smoked marijuana as a teenager. She wanted to know how to handle his drug use given that he had just gotten his driver's license and she had promised him a car. We're talking about a teenager who is regularly taking a mixture of powerful drugs. The promise of a car should be the least of her concerns. Antidepressants, anti-anxiety medications, and THC don't mix. Again, this is a combination of uppers and downers that can interact dangerously. A parent's primary concern should be the health and safety of their child and others. There should be no consideration of driving privileges until it's absolutely clear that drugs are out of the picture. This isn't a negotiation; teenagers need to understand that drug use is clearly out of bounds. Parents need to make it clear that they aren't okay with their adolescents smoking marijuana and that they won't get certain privileges if they do so. While it may seem extreme, I encourage some parents to consider drug testing when they feel it necessary to ensure their child's safety, particularly when it comes to driving.

Opioids

In addition to alcohol, marijuana, and nicotine, we're hearing a lot about opioid addiction in today's news. Opioid addiction is currently considered a crisis, as deaths caused by opioid overdose have quadrupled since 1999. In America, 45 people die every day from prescription painkiller overdose. An addiction to painkillers frequently leads to heroin use, which is effectively double the dose at a fraction of the cost. Like THC, heroin is more lethal than ever: in 1980, heroin was 4% "pure," while today heroin is 40% "pure," and one in four people who use heroin become addicted. Heroin reaches the brain in 7 to 8 seconds and binds to opioid receptors, giving the user a surge of euphoria, known as a **rush**.[30] One reason that heroin is lethal is because opioid receptors are involved in breathing, so users occasionally stop breathing. Studies show that 3 out of 100 high school students have tried heroin; 75% of those users began with prescription opioids, including Vicodin, Percocet, and Oxycontin. The demographic of the high school heroin user has changed: today, Caucasian students use prescription opioids and heroin more often than African American and Latino students.

Opioids, like heroin, are a form of morphine; they induce euphoria, but also cause drowsiness and confusion. Opioids are addictive because while they temporarily suppress feelings of pain, they inhibit the body's natural ability to manage pain, so regular users begin to feel generalized pain and reach for more painkillers for relief (see Box 6.3). Various studies suggest that close to 100 people die every day from overall opioid overdose—1 person every 16 minutes. (For our purposes, it's helpful to know that 40% of those deaths are among the 45- to 64-year-old population). For adolescents, an opioid addiction typically starts with a prescription painkiller, whether their own or that of a family member or friend. Opioids are increasingly available on the black market. My children have joked that they could get good money for the pain medications they have been prescribed for things like shoulder surgery and appendicitis. But it's not a joke.

It's important to be aware that this is how it happens with teens: Doctors prescribe opioids to teenagers for legitimate purposes, but it spirals beyond control. I've known several adolescent athletes who have received a prescription for a painkiller for a sports-related injury and have become unwittingly addicted to the pills. Teens don't realize the highly addictive nature of opioids and their potential to be a gateway drug to heroin. Speak to your teen about the dangers of taking painkillers for nonmedical reasons or over extended periods of time. If your child is prescribed a painkiller, be aware of their use. Adolescents prescribed opioids are more likely to use painkillers as adults, but you can control their access at home. Unlike with alcohol, marijuana, and nicotine, most adolescents are not procuring opioids independently, but we still

---

BOX 6.3

Signs of Opioid Use

- Severe mood swings that teeter between euphoria and drowsiness
- Constricted pupils
- Slowed breathing
- Constipation
- Constant runny nose
- Changes in hygiene, appearance, or sleeping habits
- Withdrawal symptoms, including diarrhea, irritability, sweating, and stomach cramps

want to be aware of the risk. Keep the medicine in your control and administer the lowest dosage that gives pain relief. Try to limit their intake and get rid of extra pills when they no longer need them. If you or another member of your family is prescribed any form of medication, make sure that it is inaccessible to your adolescent.

It's difficult to predict why some of us get addicted to certain drugs and substances while others do not, but addiction is devastating and has far-reaching consequences. What can start as use prescribed by a doctor or a recreational experiment can become a lifelong battle. Teens are unaware of the addictive nature of chemical substances and can't comprehend the fact that drug use creates a chemical reaction that is beyond their control. They think they will be able to resist subsequent use, but addiction isn't a matter of resistance and discipline. It's a chemical, physical craving in the body. Trust your instincts. If you suspect that your teenager is abusing drugs or alcohol, look into it. Addiction is characterized by behavioral excess and cannot be controlled without treatment. If you think your child is at that level, seek professional help, because addiction can't be undone with typical parental restriction or discipline.

SO, WHAT CAN we do? The most impactful thing you can do is give your adolescents precise information about how different substances affect them both in the moment and permanently. To that end, it's important for you to be familiar with various drugs and their effects (Figure 6.5). Acknowledge the reality that alcohol and drugs are appealing to our novelty-seeking teenagers. Explain to your teenager that you understand it's complicated and a highly pressured situation, but you don't think the risks are worth it. Don't hesitate to be specific and even graphic in your description of health risks. It's much more effective to show your teenager the tar-covered lung of a smoker than to tell them that smoking is bad for them. Maintain an open dialogue and take an information-seeking approach to your conversations. Ask your teenagers questions like "Do you know anyone who has done heroin?" or "Are you friends with those kids who got in trouble last weekend?" Be curious: Open-ended questions will elicit a better response than "Don't drink or do drugs." If you demonstrate an awareness of various substances and trends, such as vaping or the opioid crisis, they will perceive that you are tuned in. Point out the negative social effects of drinking and drugs, too. Acknowledge someone in a restaurant who is loud and out of control, or discuss the kid who is always high and thinks nobody is on to him. It's important that your kids see how substances can distort behavior.

FIGURE 6.5. Effects and Risks of Cocaine, Ecstasy (a.k.a. Molly, E, X, or MDMA), Heroin, and LSD

Set clear expectations for their behavior and establish consequences for if and when you catch them using alcohol or drugs. You need to be clear about what nurturing is and isn't. A nurturing environment for a teenager should be one in which they have adults in their life who will protect them from harm. Nurture isn't permission; by the same token, structure isn't cold or unloving. Setting firm boundaries for your adolescent is actually a loving gesture. Inform them of the consequences up front and hold to them. If you've told your teenager they're grounded and there's a special event they *really* don't want to miss, that's the consequence for their own behavior, and it's important that you stick to your guns to convey how dangerous you consider drinking and drug use to be. Your adolescents should know that they will be in serious trouble if you find out they've broken these rules.

When you're enforcing these rules, be creative and think of yourself as a teenager. If your teenager comes home drunk, make it uncomfortable for them. Wake them up early and ask them to complete household tasks, run errands, or exercise with you. Don't cover for them, either. If they have an obligation, ensure that they go. You want to be clear that drinking was their choice and they have to face the consequences.

At the same time, recognize good decision making. Of course, we don't want our kids to drink. But we also want our teenagers to be mature enough to navigate challenging situations. If your adolescent ends up in a situation where someone is unsafe and they take action to get that person the help they need, make sure you acknowledge the fact that they did the right thing at the time. Even if you don't approve of the situation they were in, it's important that they feel that you understand the situation they are in as a teenager. If you are black-and-white in your approach, they will assume you "don't get it" and they'll write you off.

Similarly, make sure that your children know that you're there for them, even if they're doing something they aren't supposed to do. As we discussed in chapter 3, you want your teenager to know that you will help them get out of a bad situation, even if there will be consequences for their behavior after the fact. These are tests of your relationship with your adolescent: You know they aren't perfect, you want them to try their best to make good decisions, and you're there for them if they make a mistake and need your help. Remember that your primary goals are health and safety: Try to delay the inevitable, and limit your child's exposure to risky or dangerous situations.

Consider This:
Insights & Actions

- It's accepted as the rule that a pregnant woman should not drink alcohol or do drugs of any kind because they risk impairing the developing fetus. Yet we know that the adolescent brain and body is developing and don't apply the same logic. We should view alcohol and drug use as actively harmful to healthy development.
- Be aware of access. I regularly have high schoolers tell me that they can get their hands on virtually any drug. Restrictions at school and at home won't prevent your child from the opportunity to drink and do drugs. A display of awareness on your part is an important deterrent. Also, limit your teen's finances. Juul and drugs are expensive. If they have enough of their own money to buy these things, ask them to pay for other things that you are currently financing, such as gas for the car or lunch at school, so that they have less disposable money.
- If your teenagers are going out with friends, make sure that they check in with you when they get home. Give them a hug and a kiss so that you can smell their breath and look them in the eye. They're likely to be more aware of the condition they're in if they know you'll be checking them out.
- It's a good idea to insist that your teenager sleep at home, but if they sleep at a friend's house, make sure that they check in with you when they're in for the night. Ask them to call you from a landline (you may need to explain what this is!) or turn on "Find my iPhone" so that they know that you're verifying their whereabouts.

- Teach your kids refusal skills that they can practice with you. "I'm okay for now" or "I'm not in the mood" are easy, low-key responses that don't require an explanation. If they've practiced with you, they will be able to access these responses in the moment. Holding a Solo cup full of water or soda is also a good trick to avoid being repeatedly offered a drink. The reality is, kids who are drinking or getting high aren't bothered by those that aren't; they just want to know that they won't tell on them.

- When possible, encourage your teenager to exit any situation they aren't comfortable with. If they're at school, they can always use "I'm late for class" or "I have to finish an assignment." Establish an escape plan for your teenager. They can text you a code word or call you to come get them. Tell them that they can always use "I'm not allowed" as an excuse for something they don't want to do.

- Watch *Haze* with your juniors and seniors, especially as they are college bound. *Haze* is an important, cautionary film about Greek life on college campuses.

- Talk to your teenagers about the risks and consequences in a way that resonates with them. Keep it simple: "It'll change your brain forever. Not my brain, yours. Are you okay with that?" or "Look at who you're buying drugs from—it's usually a strung-out, unhealthy, dangerous person on a street corner in a sleepy town. Is that really where you want to go?"

- If your child is college bound and you feel concerned that they haven't had any experience with alcohol, it might make sense to allow them to have a beer or a glass of wine in a safe environment, such as a family event. This is a very different scenario than prolonged exposure or permitting your child to drink recreationally in your home.

- As always, the example you set for your children will strongly influence their behavior. Children don't want to see parents getting drunk or out of control. Your kids will notice if you bring a cocktail on the road or drive after drinking throughout dinner. Even if you are clear about your expectations for their behavior, they will absorb your approach to alcohol and drugs over time.

Notes

1. Himelstein, R. (2013, September 10) Teen heroin use: An unfortunate reality. *The Inquirer*. Retrieved from http://www.philly.com/philly/blogs/healthy_kids/Teen-heroin-use-an-unfortunate-reality.html?__vfz=medium%3Dsharebar

2. Harvard Medical School Symposium: Addictions (2018, May). Cambridge, MA. Course directors include Roger D. Weiss, Shelly F. Greenfield, and Christopher M. Palmer.

3. Yule, A. (2017, November). Underage drinking and recreational drug use: Prevention, harm, reduction and treatment. Harvard Medical School Symposium: Middle School Through College Mental Health and Education. Cambridge, MA. Course directors include Joseph Gold, Stephanie Pinder-Amaker, Mona P. Potter, Bryan C. Pridgen, and Christopher M. Palmer.

4. Madras, B. K. (2017, March). Addiction, brain changes, and function: Do they intersect? Harvard Medical School Symposium: Treating the Addictions. Cambridge, MA. Course directors include Mark J. Albanese, Janice F. Kauffman, Edward J. Khantzian, and Judy Reiner Platt.

5. Yule, A. (2017, November). Underage drinking and recreational drug use: Prevention, harm, reduction and treatment. Harvard Medical School Symposium: Middle School Through College Mental Health and Education. Cambridge, MA. Course directors include Joseph Gold, Stephanie Pinder-Amaker, Mona P. Potter, Bryan C. Pridgen, and Christopher M. Palmer.

6. Spear, L. P. (2016). Consequences of adolescent use of alcohol and other drugs: Studies using rodent models. *Neuroscience and Biobehavioral Reviews, 70*, 228–243. doi:10.1016/j.neubiorev.2016.07.026

7. Jensen, F. E., & Nutt, A. E. (2015). *The teenage brain: A neuroscientist's survival guide to raising adolescents and young adults.* New York, NY: HarperCollins.

8. Yule, A. (2017, November). Underage drinking and recreational drug use: Prevention, harm, reduction and treatment. Harvard Medical School Symposium: Middle School Through College Mental Health and Education. Cambridge, MA. Course directors include Joseph Gold, Stephanie Pinder-Amaker, Mona P. Potter, Bryan C. Pridgen, and Christopher M. Palmer.

9. Yule, A. (2017, November). Underage drinking and recreational drug use: Prevention, harm, reduction and treatment. Harvard Medical School Symposium: Middle School Through College Mental Health and Education. Cambridge, MA. Course directors include Joseph Gold, Stephanie Pinder-Amaker, Mona P. Potter, Bryan C. Pridgen, and Christopher M. Palmer.

10. Spear, L. P. (2016). Consequences of adolescent use of alcohol and other drugs: Studies using rodent models. *Neuroscience and Biobehavioral Reviews, 70*, 228–243. doi:10.1016/j.neubiorev.2016.07.026

11. Madras, B. K. (2017, March). Addiction, brain changes, and function: Do they intersect? Harvard Medical School Symposium: Treating the Addictions. Course directors include Mark J. Albanese, Janice F. Kauffman, Edward J. Khantzian, and Judy Reiner Platt.

12. Barkley, R. A. (2013). *Taking charge of ADHD: The complete, authoritative guide for parents* (3rd ed.). New York, NY: Guilford Press.

13. Silveri, M. M. (2018, May). Drug use and the adolescent brain. Harvard Medical School Post-Graduate Symposium. Cambridge, MA. Course directors include Mark J. Albanese, Janice F. Kauffman, Edward J. Khantzian, Judy Reiner Platt. Cambridge, MA.

14. Madras, B. K. (2017, March). Addiction, brain changes, and function: Do they intersect? Harvard Medical School Symposium: Treating the Addictions. Course directors include Mark J. Albanese, Janice F. Kauffman, Edward J. Khantzian, and Judy Reiner Platt.

15. Silveri, M. M., Dager, A. D., Cohen-Gilbert, J. E., & Sneider, J. T. (2016). Neurobiological signatures associated with alcohol and drug use in the human adolescent brain. *Neuroscience Biobehavioral Reviews, 70,* 244–259. doi:10.1016/j.neubiorev.2016.06.042

16. Madras, B. K. (2017). Addiction, brain changes, and function: Do they intersect? Harvard Medical School Symposium: Treating the Addictions. Course directors include Mark J. Albanese, Janice F. Kauffman, Edward J. Khantzian, and Judy Reiner Platt.

17. Spear, L. P. (2016) Consequences of adolescent use of alcohol and other drugs: Studies using rodent models. *Neuroscience and Biobehavioral Reviews, 70,* 228–243. doi:10.1016/j.neubiorev.2016.07.026

18. Madras, B. K. (2017). Addiction, brain changes, and function: Do they intersect? Harvard Medical School Symposium: Treating the Addictions. Course directors include Mark J. Albanese, Janice F. Kauffman, Edward J. Khantzian, and Judy Reiner Platt.

19. Silveri, M. M. (2017). Drug use and the adolescent brain. Harvard Medical School Post-Graduate Symposium. Course directors include Mark J. Albanese, Janice F. Kauffman, Edward J. Khantzian, Judy Reiner Platt. Cambridge, MA.

20. Chadwick, B., Miller, M. L., & Hurd, Y. L. (2013). Cannabis use during adolescent development: Susceptibility to psychiatric illness. *Frontiers in Psychiatry, 4.* Retrieved from https://www.frontiersin.org/articles/10.3389/fpsyt.2013.00129/full

21. Harvard Medical School Symposium: Middle School Through College Mental Health and Education (2017).

22. Harvard Medical School Symposium: Treating the Addictions (May 2018).

23. Harvard Medical School Symposium: Treating the Addictions (May 2018).

24. Harvard Medical School Symposium: Treating the Addictions (May 2018).

25. Silveri, M. M., Dager, A. D., Cohen-Gilbert, J. E., & Sneider, J. T. (2016). Neurobiological signatures associated with alcohol and drug use in the human adolescent brain. *Neuroscience Biobehavioral Reviews, 70,* 244–259. doi:10.1016/j.neubiorev.2016.06.042

26. Silveri, M. M., Dager, A. D., Cohen-Gilbert, J. E., & Sneider, J. T. (2016). Neurobiological signatures associated with alcohol and drug use in the human

adolescent brain. *Neuroscience Biobehavioral Reviews, 70,* 244–259. doi:10.1016/
j.neubiorev.2016.06.042

27. Dwyer, J. B., McQuown, S. C., & Leslie, F. M. (2009). The dynamic effects of
    nicotine on the developing brain. *Pharmacology and Therapeutics, 122,* 125–139.
    doi: 10.1016/j.pharmthera.2009.02.003

28. Tolentino, J. (2018, May 14). The promise of vaping and the rise of Juul. *The
    New Yorker.* Retrieved from https://www.newyorker.com/magazine/2018/05/14/
    the-promise-of-vaping-and-the-rise-of-juul

29. Olmedo, P., Goessler, W., Tanda, S., Grau-Perez, M., Jarmul, S., Aherrera,
    A., . . . Rule, A. M. (2018). Metal concentrations in e-cigarette liquid and aerosol
    samples: The contribution of metallic coils. *Environmental Health Perspectives,
    126*(2). doi:10.1289/EHP2175.

30. Harvard Medical School Symposium: Addictions (2018, May). Cambridge, MA.
    Course directors include Roger D. Weiss, Shelly F. Greenfield, and Christpher
    M. Palmer.

7

The Seventh Myth

MY TEENAGER DOES RISKY AND STUPID THINGS TO IRRITATE AND DEFY ME.

I ASKED YOUNG adults of various ages and backgrounds to tell me some of the riskiest things they had done as adolescents. Here are a few of their responses:

> "At 14, I started shoplifting and stole thousands of dollars' worth of clothing from stores. I was finally caught in a Macy's and arrested at 16."
>
> "At 17, I threw a toga party while my parents were out of town and got arrested for distributing alcohol to minors."
>
> "At 18, I got hired for a great summer internship before I realized I had to take a mandatory drug test in order to work there. I had gotten high at a graduation party the week before, so I had to figure out how to fake a urine sample in order to keep the position."
>
> "At 18, I was driving alone at night and got rear-ended by two men. I pulled over right away and they pulled over behind me. I called my mom before I got out of the car and she told me to keep driving until I could get to a well-lit area with other people around. I had pulled over on an isolated road as a young woman alone and was about to get out of my car to speak to two men I didn't know. I just didn't think about how it could go wrong."
>
> "At 19, I tried mushrooms and ecstasy at the same time. It's called 'candy flipping.' The drugs were not high quality and it did not end well. We all got sick for several days—some of my friends missed work and some were hospitalized. Several years later, we realized that we had done meth."

"At 19, my friend was jaywalking in New York City on St. Patrick's Day and was hit by a taxi cab. He spent four weeks in the hospital with a broken back and the next eight months in a wheelchair. It took him almost three years to make a full recovery."

"At 20, my friend drove to Bonnaroo [a music and arts festival] with thousands of dollars worth of illicit drugs hidden in her car. On the way, she was pulled over for speeding. When the police officer asked for her ID, she couldn't provide it because it was in the backpack with all of the drugs. She opted to take the $400 fine instead."

"At 20, I was high and drunk and jumped from the top of a roof onto a bouncy house. I threw out my back and felt it for almost two years after. A friend of mine made the same jump and broke her ankle."

"At 20, my friend met an older guy on a dating app. After one date, he bought her designer shoes and flew her to Las Vegas for their second date. She found out she was pregnant three weeks later. When she asked for support, he cut ties with her and gave her nothing, so she had to pay for an abortion on her own."

"At 21, my friend joined a website called Sugar Daddies to meet someone rich. He ended up being an abusive cocaine addict and was arrested in the first six months of their relationship."

"At 21, I smoked weed in a car on the way to Atlantic City for a friend's 21st birthday. We bought alcohol on the way but she stayed in the car because she was underage (until midnight). Undercover cops stopped us in the parking lot because they smelled the weed. They tried to charge us for drug possession and distributing to a minor. They gave us the option of being searched by a drug dog (who would find other elicit drugs in the car) or getting a ticket. Luckily, a bunch of crying girls persuaded them to let us off. We drove the rest of the way in silence."

Other examples included peeing in a public alley during a St. Patrick's Day parade, drinking before a school dance after they had been warned they would be breathalyzed, streaking through a school campus, crashing a wedding, throwing or attending a party while parents were out of town, and every activity from swimming to riding a bicycle while drunk.

These incidents range from fairly innocent to reckless and harmful behaviors, but all of these stories came to me from responsible, motivated, ambitious young adults reflecting on their adolescent years. These are kids from different backgrounds, communities, families, and cultures, but I can tell you that these stories are entirely normal for the range of adolescent behavior.

Whether it was you, your child, or an adolescent you know, it should come as no surprise that teens do stupid and dangerous things in the pursuit of fun.

If I could give every parent of a teenager one gift, it would be the ability to not take their adolescent's behavior personally. The truth is that adolescents are often entirely self-focused in the choices that they make, particularly on the spot. They aren't thinking that far beyond the present moment and they don't often consider how their behavior will impact others, including you. If they have the chance to do something fun, exciting, new, or exhilarating, they'll probably want to do it. I hear exasperated pleas for an explanation from parents of teens: *I specifically told her not to do that! . . . He knew it was dangerous . . . She knew what was at stake . . . He knew he would get into trouble.* Worst of all: *How could they do this to me?*

Parents often feel that their adolescent purposefully makes poor decisions or intentionally engages in risky behavior to defy or betray them. When you devote so much time, energy, and emotion to your child, it can feel impossible to see their choices as anything other than a direct attack on you. But, the truth is, much of it isn't personal. Here's why: **The chief predictor of teenage behavior is not the perception of risk, but is instead the anticipation of reward.** Gratification is at the heart of adolescent impulsivity and is the primary motivating factor in many of their poor decisions.[1] No matter how many times you tell your teenage son or daughter *not* to do something, their brain is sending them a different message in the moment. When your teenager says "I didn't think about it" or "I know I shouldn't have done that but it didn't occur to me," they are telling you the truth. Take a minute to reflect on things you did during your own adolescence that were stupid or short sighted, whether or not you got caught. I'm sure you can think of at least a few instances in which you "just weren't thinking." At the point of decision, an adolescent is predominantly focused on the potential for reward, whether physical, social, or emotional. This is one of the keys to understanding your teenager: Adolescents are predominantly motivated by reward, which can cause them to act on an impulse and take risks without considering the consequences.

Understanding Adolescent Impulsivity

This is a crucial piece of the adolescent puzzle: The teenage brain isn't merely immature, it is actually primed for impulsivity.[2] The adolescent brain has approximately twice the number of excitatory synapses as inhibitory ones.[3] So any stimulus or impulse that enters a teenage brain is twice as likely to reach an excitatory synapse that will engage and act on it. To recall, **synapses** are tiny junctions between nerve cells across which impulses are sent via **neurotransmitters**. Some of these neurotransmitters, like **glutamate**, can be viewed as *excitatory*, meaning they encourage the brain to act on an impulse. **These excitatory connections promote brain development, so it would seem that teenagers are hard-wired to seek sensation, risk, and reward.** Other neurotransmitters are seen as *inhibitory* and are less likely to cause neurons to fire into action. **Gamma-aminobutyric acid**, or **GABA**, is the main inhibitory neurotransmitter in the brain, and is responsible for balancing the effects of various excitatory neurotransmitters, like glutamate and adrenaline. The presence of GABA allows for inhibition—the impulse to pull back—and regulates motor control. In fact, drugs that increase levels of GABA in the system have been shown to effectively treat epilepsy; GABA helps to regulate motor control and prevent seizures. An increase in this calming, inhibitory neurotransmitter allows the brain to regain control.[4] This is interesting in the context of teenagers: **Lower levels of inhibitory neurotransmitters create an overly excitable state in the adolescent brain.** It also takes adolescents longer to decide not to do something: the inhibitory response is delayed from age 8 to 20. This is because the connections between the amygdala (fight or flight) and the frontal lobe (rational thought) are still developing: the teenage amygdala can signal danger or perceive risk, but the frontal lobe doesn't respond as an adult's would.

To be clear, when an excitatory neural pathway is engaged, the corresponding action won't always lead to bad decisions or risky behavior. It's better to think of these as initiating an action or engaging with a stimulus. For example, glutamate is involved in learning and memory. This accounts for your teen's excitement to make a connection with a new person, call out an answer in class, or simply act spontaneously among family and friends. We don't want to dampen these enthusiastic and engaging impulses; we just want to direct them. The high concentration of excitatory neurons simply diminishes the work of inhibition in the brain. **Teens will receive the signal to act before they receive the signal to stop.** Therefore, we can imagine that teenagers will struggle to stop themselves before engaging in risky and dangerous behavior. Good decision making and the ability to engage inhibition is based on experience, learned responsibility, and brain development over time.

Yet because of their surplus excitatory neurons, **when a teenager is faced with a choice, *their brain is twice as likely to send a signal that tells them to go for it.*** They rarely take risk into account during the decision-making process and often completely overlook it. Risk taking and novelty seeking are actually tied to their reward circuitry, so the perception of risk often adds to the appeal. Any time an adolescent is aroused, excited, or intimidated, their decision making is short-circuited. Emotion, reward seeking, and socialization are strong influences on a relatively underdeveloped and inconsistently effective behavioral control network.[5] The thrill-seeking centers of the adolescent brain have a stronger influence over teenage behavior than their emerging control centers.[6] This sensation-seeking tendency peaks around age 19 and then declines with age; in contrast, self-regulation climbs in a gradual, linear trend until around age 23 to 24, when it plateaus at an adult level (see Figure 7.1).[7] In the teenage brain, the control center and the impulsive center are grappling with each other as decisions are made, and impulsivity often wins out.

Think about this in terms of one of the most highly anticipated milestones of adolescence: the driver's license. Driving is risky for teens because it's harder for them to conceive of potential risk. They are more likely to speed, roll through stop signs, blast the stereo, and carry too many passengers because they crave freedom and excitement and don't connect those behaviors to danger. Adults are better able to imagine the consequences and are therefore less likely to take risks while driving. Driving is less exciting for them. By contrast, the typical teenager is desperate for a driver's license and the independence that comes with it. A driver's license also offers a social reward: It's cool to drive around with a bunch of kids in your car with the music on. But distracted driving is a terrifying risk for adolescents, so the law dictates that teens start with their learner's permit, requiring that they drive only with a

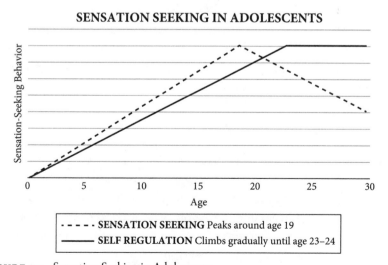

FIGURE 7.1. Sensation Seeking in Adolescents

BOX 7.1

Teen Drivers: The Facts

- Many vehicle crashes of **16- to 19-year-olds** involve only the teen's vehicle. These are typically **high-speed crashes** in which the driver loses control.
- Fatal crashes of teens aged 16 to 19 are **more likely to occur when passengers are riding in the vehicle.** This risk increases with each additional passenger.
- **Every 15 minutes**, a teenager will die due to drunk driving.
- **Sixty percent of all teen deaths from car accidents involve alcohol.**
- In 2010, **56% of teens killed in drunk driving accidents were not wearing a seatbelt.** Most teens killed in car crashes are **not wearing their seatbelts.**
- Per mile driven, the **fatal crash rate** for 16- to 19-year-old drivers is **four times as high at night** as in daytime.[15]

---

licensed driver in the car before they can drive on their own or with only unlicensed passengers. Updated driving laws have effectively reduced the number of accidents and deaths among teenagers (see Box 7.1). These restrictions don't keep teenagers off the road entirely, but they limit an adolescent driver's exposure to risk before they have experience on the road.

This is a good model for shaping teenage behavior. Providing gradual leeway allows your teen to take some risks and gain some experience, but you create the parameters in which they're able to do so (see Box 7.2). As new drivers, every teenager will experience a time when they are uncomfortable and nervous. Let them work through their discomfort in those moments; they need to have some independent experience in order to learn how to do it. This is how new neural pathways solidify.

Primed for Peer Pressure

Peer pressure also has a major influence on adolescents. Recent research shows that the presence of a teen's peers has a direct impact on the reward system in their brains.[8] Teenage actions are often quick, split-second decisions made among peers. Brain-imaging studies show that several areas of the adolescent brain are more responsive to peers than they are to adults, who are perceived as controlling and judgmental. This motivates teens to focus on their peers in decision-making situations that involve risky behavior.

BOX 7.2

What Can Parents Do?

Restrict night driving.

Restrict passengers.

Supervise practice driving.

Drive safely to **set a good example.**

Require seatbelt use.

Prohibit driving after drinking.

Choose vehicles for safety, not image.

Know the law and enforce it.

If you think back to risky things you might have done as a teen, chances are you were with your friend, acting on a "dare" or trying to impress your peers. As a teen, I can remember my friend daring me to crawl out onto a newly frozen pond. I went for it and, unsurprisingly, fell through the ice. She came after me and she fell in, too. We were lucky; she was able to get herself out and help me out after. But she was too afraid to tell her parents about what had happened, so I had to sit through dinner with their family in my freezing wet clothes. It could have been far worse, but the consequence of suffering in silence taught me an important lesson about taking stupid risks when I knew better.

At the time, I was focused on meeting her dare and caught up in the thrill of doing something risky. Again, this is largely due to the wiring of the teenage brain; adolescents have greater connectivity between the regions of the brain that respond to social stimulation.[9] Adolescents are developing a social brain, and a successful transition to adulthood requires refining and integrating these cognitive processes. It makes sense that adolescents are prone to impulsivity.

They are also hypersensitive and vulnerable. We see this in their reaction to rejection: Neuroscientists have recently discovered a part of the prefrontal cortex that is crucial for coping with negative emotions related to others, such as feelings of rejection or exclusion. Studies of peer rejection in adolescence repeatedly show a connection with worsened mood, increased distress, and elevated anxiety.[10] Remember that social rejection actually elicits a pain response in adolescents; this can result in social anxiety and avoidance, or succumbing to peer pressure. Teenagers are so desperate to avoid rejection that they might do something they don't want to do in the moment.

A client told me of an incident that took place at his house over a previous weekend. He had a few friends over and they were hanging out and watching television when his parents went to bed. Shortly after they'd gone upstairs, one of his friends suggested that they invite over a few girls. In the moment, he hesitantly agreed to the idea. The girls took taxis to his house, and soon they were out by his pool with the pool lights on and music blasting.

Of course, his parents heard the noise and saw the lights, which streamed directly into their bedroom. His parents cleverly pulled the plug on the party by shutting off the lights. Everyone panicked. All of the kids were mortified at the prospect of getting into trouble. This is often how it goes with teens: They are having a blast with not a care in the world until they get caught. Then they realize all at once the risk they've taken.

His parents were furious. *What was he thinking*? He clearly wasn't. Often, the act of getting caught is enough of a teaching moment for a teenager: His friends were embarrassed to face his parents after what they'd done and they sheepishly headed home, but returned the next day to apologize in person. It's in these moments that you need to remember that **your teen's behavior isn't personal**. Their son and his friends were thinking about how much fun they could have, not about what might go wrong. For their son's part, in the moment, the prospect of denying his friends and risking their disapproval seemed worse than a possible negative reaction from his parents, so he went for it, ignoring potential consequences.

This increased focus on peers occurs during a time when the prefrontal cortex is not yet ready to assist with mature self-regulation. These factors provide a "perfect storm" when it comes to teenagers. Peer pressure in adolescence is truly the blind leading the blind. Adolescents look to equally inexperienced peers for behavioral cues when it comes to risk taking.[11] As parents, we want to embrace the social, novelty-seeking nature of our teenager so that their ability to interact and connect with all types of people is well formed, but we want to be active in directing it. A regulatory social influence, such as a parent, mentor, older friend, coach, or teacher can encourage reflection and allow a teen to pause long enough on a decision to allow their inhibition to kick in.

The Job of Adults

It's also important for your teenager to have adults in their lives who they don't want to disappoint. It helps move their focus from *How can I avoid getting into trouble* to *How can I make the people I care about proud*? It's an essential shift we want adolescents to make over this period of their lives. This is why mentors are so impactful; they offer a connection based on understanding and interest, showing adolescents that adults can be friends and trusted confidants. An older, wiser figure can combat the pressure an adolescent faces from their peers and help guide a teen toward better decision making.[12]

Sometimes this can actually happen in the moment. I have received countless phone calls from adolescents—my kids, their friends, my clients—when they or a friend were in trouble and they needed help dealing with the situation. I once received a call from a client who had just gotten home from a football game and was planning on picking up a few friends before heading to a party. His mom wasn't around but he knew she'd been under a lot of stress, so he didn't want to bother her. He also didn't want to get into trouble or drink and drive, but he was supposed to give everybody a ride to the party.

I walked him through a few options, and we settled on a safe plan that got him out of driving after he'd been at a party and ensured that he would end up where he told his mom he was spending the night. He felt safe in telling me that he was going to drink a little bit, so I could help him solve the problem at hand. This is a tricky situation: I don't endorse underage drinking, but given that he was a senior in high school celebrating a big victory, he was going to drink regardless of what I said in that moment.

Remember that part of your job as the adult is maintaining realistic expectations of your teenager. He was calling for advice on how to responsibly handle his plans, so I kept my focus on that. If I had reprimanded him in the moment, he would have ended the conversation and wouldn't have called me again. It was more important to recognize and reward his desire to be responsible. It's important for adolescents to have someone they can seek advice from without fear of punishment or judgment. It's also important for the adults in their lives to parse out the moments of good judgment, even if we aren't thrilled with the overall behavior.

Most often, when kids make poor choices, they are only thinking about themselves. As adults, we are better able to recognize how our choices impact those around us. Therefore, throughout adolescence, it's vitally important to coach our children to consider the broader implications of their behavior, particularly with regard to other people. As our teens make choices, it's important to talk through and point out how those choices might affect their sibling, friend, parent, teacher, teammate, classmate, and others.

We can also show them how certain choices, like dangerous driving or violence, can gravely impact others. Very few adolescent boys get through high school and college without finding themselves in a physical altercation. The consequences for fighting are serious and can include criminal charges, rescinded college acceptances, and expulsion, not to mention damage done to another person. Particularly in these situations, kids often say after the fact that they are aware that what they did was wrong and that they were even cognizant in the moment that their actions would have negative consequences, but they couldn't stop themselves. They acted on an impulse. An adult in the same situation, whether at work, in a social setting, or on the sideline of a sporting event, is more often able to recognize that while they might want to punch someone in the face, they know it's inappropriate and not worth the negative outcome, so they refrain.

The same dynamic happens with teenage girls, though it's less likely to be physical. Girls are more likely to fight verbally, say harsh and mean things to each other, or exclude and ostracize peers. This social warfare can be equally damaging. They are wired for both the gratification of releasing negative feelings and of social approval, so they make decisions in the moment that might harm others but that they will regret later.

Teenagers are naturally self-absorbed. This doesn't mean that they are selfish; rather, they simply aren't used to taking others into consideration as they make choices. If you think about it, up to this point in their lives, those around them are usually providing for them or directing them. We need to expect that the ability to consider others will develop over time and with guidance. With this understanding, and a high-structure, high-nurture approach, we can engage these developing neural processes with conversations, expectations, and consequences so that they strengthen with practice.

Why is this important? We used to think that teenagers were "acting out" and viewed adolescence as the "terrible teens." If we can understand that adolescent brain circuitry lends itself to experimentation, risk taking, and stimulation, we can understand that our teenagers are simply acting according to what their brain tells them to do. Look at your teen as someone who makes decisions based on what is right in front of them in the moment. Parental expectations are rarely in the forefront of their mind, so they are rarely acting on a specific desire to defy you.

Of course, there are specific situations when a teenager will "rebel." But more often, they are pursuing gratification, immediate reward, and social approval and will therefore prioritize new, fun, and "cool" experiences over everything else. Evolutionarily, this makes sense. The teenage years are essentially a primer for adult life. Adolescence should be a time of expansive exploration in which teenagers can engage in a broad range of activities and experiences.

After adolescence, individuals begin to focus and specialize, choosing a major in college, electing a career path, making a long-term commitment to a significant other. These consequential, longer term decisions will be more informed and better researched if a teen has had the opportunity to *experience* various situations for themselves. So, as parents of teenagers, we want to find the sweet spot where we can limit the downside of risk taking while enhancing and building on the upside.

Creating Limits and Setting Boundaries

A parent's job is to influence and direct a teen's behavior—not to control what your teenager does or manipulate the consequences of their choices. However, adults are rarely present when a teenager's worst decisions are made. To influence the choices your teenager makes, you need to set limits. Part of our responsibility as parents is to do some of the legwork of perceiving risk on your child's behalf. We can't totally insulate our teenagers from risk; if we attempt to do so, we are only delaying their maturation and development. We should limit the riskiest scenarios through boundaries and restrictions, but let adolescents navigate the rest.

This comes up around big events that teens are desperate to attend, like a concert. Parents will ask me whether or not they should allow their kids to go to an event unsupervised. If you have a feeling that your teen is too young or inexperienced, it's probably a good idea to say no or arrange a chaperone to go with them. Saying no has nothing to do with how much you love your child.

By the same token, permissiveness does not communicate love. This is a key distinction to make in parenting. You can say no to a "good" kid who you typically trust to do the right thing, and you can say yes to a child who has gotten in trouble before. On the other hand, if your adolescent is 18 and headed to college in the next year, it might be a good idea to let them go with a reminder to be aware of their situation and that they can call you if they need help. I know parents who will stay upstairs during a party and "hire" one of their older children to chaperone their younger sibling and their friends. This is a great compromise! They are nearby if anything goes wrong, but they are giving their older kid some responsibility and their younger kid a little bit of rope. The older siblings most often rise to the occasion and are frequently stricter than the parents.

Teenagers are simultaneously naïve and self-confident. In response to the risk-taking behavior of the typical adolescent, many parents try to prevent their teenager from every misstep and clean up after them when they make a mistake. But now that you understand how your adolescent's brain works, you know that trying to control them is a losing battle. If you try to control your teenager, they will push back harder. Nobody wants to be controlled, especially a teenager who is developing a sense of independence and who is primed to push the limits. I work with several clients whose parents are so strict and controlling that they actually encourage defiance in their children. **Their kids also grow overly reliant on the fact that their parents will assess risk for them, so they don't feel responsible for themselves.** These kids are constantly trying to figure out what they can get away with, instead of internalizing and understanding their parents' standards. This is the nature of the battle for control: Because these parents have no tolerance for mistakes, big or small, they leave no room for their children to make minor errors or to comprehend the true implications of their behavior. Consequently, the mistakes are bigger and with higher stakes, which often requires their parents to then bail them out. Control and structure are not the same; structure leaves room for a teenager to learn how to manage for themselves.

Instead, parents should encourage their kids to begin measuring the risk for themselves as they make decisions. The only way they can do this is to give them a little bit of slack so that they can learn to figure out how to proceed. When they ask you, *What do you think I should do?*, respond with, *What do you think you should do?* It is much more productive to discuss possible options and let them decide. Try to resist micromanaging—it doesn't work. It's human nature, in the absence of psychological impairment or intoxication, to desire safety and protection. We have to trust that, in spite of excitability and curiosity, teenagers have self-preserving instincts. By giving your children some freedom with independent decision making, you have conveyed confidence in their ability to handle various situations. It will be bumpy, but it's critical that they sense that you can tolerate mistakes and simultaneously allow them to deal with the consequences of their own behavior. This is how they learn to take responsibility for themselves.

To enjoy your child's adolescence, you will need to let go of some of their errors when they are manageable, like failing a test, missing an event they wanted to attend, or being late for a flight. If you let your adolescent handle the consequences on their own, they will gain incentive to do everything in their power to avoid finding themselves in such a situation again. By giving them a sense of responsibility, you're strengthening the connection between choices and consequences in their minds. It's better to expose them to consequences instead of punishing them. You can be aligned with them and help them through it (high nurture), but you aren't preventing them from dealing with the consequences of their choices (high structure).

To limit the downside of their risk-taking behavior, have an active voice and be aware of the environments your adolescent is in. It's okay to adjust your rules based on what your child is doing and with who. When my boys were out with friends, I required that they get home earlier than when they were spending time at their girlfriends' houses, where I knew the parents were home. It's also okay to express a firm opinion in specific situations: *I don't love your going to that person's house. Those guys are trouble and it isn't going to end well.* Share your concern. Telling them they are forbidden from being friends with one kid or another typically backfires. Most adolescents will only want to do a forbidden activity more.

The same goes for child-specific parenting. Permission and lenience should be earned and deserved. It might not be the same for each one of your kids. It's okay to allow one of them to do something you wouldn't allow another kid to do. My oldest daughter had a few wild kids in her class, so I wouldn't let her go to the end-of-school party. But I encouraged my younger daughter to go because she was more of a homebody. If I had told my older son he wasn't allowed to go, he would have told me he was going to a movie and gone to the party instead. I allowed my youngest son to go for two years in a row. He tended to be more careful because he'd seen plenty of older kids get into trouble.

When you make these decisions, you're likely hear "That's not fair" or "All of my friends are allowed to go." First of all, this is seldom true, and this is where you need to hold the line and trust your judgment. Life isn't always fair, so your kids shouldn't always expect fairness. Until an adolescent demonstrates that they are consistently capable of making good decisions, it is your job to limit risk. If you feel a certain situation isn't safe for your teen, it probably isn't.

I raised my family outside of New York City, so we often took trips there to see shows or sports games. As my kids got older, they started to ask permission to go into the city unsupervised with their friends. At times, these were good opportunities to let them practice problem solving and managing independently. If there was an event during the day, I talked them through the train schedule and navigation, and made sure they checked in with me throughout the day. I was much more hesitant to allow them to venture into the city alone at night, and often went in with them so that I was nearby in case anything went wrong.

Adolescents crave independence, but the reality is that they are inexperienced and ignorant of what can go wrong. When you don't think they're ready for whatever they are asking permission to do, be honest about it. The limit-setting model that I have found to be most effective with adolescents is **ACT: A**cknowledge your child's feelings, **C**ommunicate the limit, and **T**arget the alternative. *You know I trust you and I believe you will try to do the right thing* (acknowledge their feelings), *but you've never been into the city alone before and I don't think you can handle it entirely on your own* (communicate the limit), *so I'm going to drive you and your friends to the game and bring you home when it's over. You can sit on your own and navigate the stadium without me, but I'll pick you up* (target the alternative). High structure, high nurture. If your kids don't want you to be with them, send them with a chaperone like an older sibling, babysitter, young teacher, or coach. That way, you can acknowledge their desire for independence, communicate its limits, and target the solution that will keep them safe while giving them the chance to push beyond their comfort zone.

One time, one of my sons had tickets to see the New York Rangers play at Madison Square Garden. I helped him plan what train he would take, but he and his friends were running late and realized they wouldn't make the game if they took the train, so my son decided to drive. He had no idea what driving into New York really meant; he was completely unfamiliar with the traffic, the street map, the bridges, the tolls, and the rules of city driving. He called me when they had already left the house and were on their way.

In that moment, I could have ripped him apart, reprimanded his poor time management and decision making, and insisted that he turn the car around and go home. Instead, I stayed on the phone with him and guided him through the drive. It was nothing short of harrowing for him: He saw firsthand that he had taken a risk that turned out to be scary, stressful, and pretty stupid. But he also learned how to solve a problem, gained a little driving experience, and began to respect the task at hand. And, most importantly, he knew that he could call me when he was in a bind and I would help him get through it. While it was completely nerve-racking, it was valuable to guide him through the situation, and he did not drive into the city for a long time after that. Sometimes it can help raise a child's empathy and awareness to let them stay in a problem and navigate it on their own. They learn by doing.

All of a teenager's bad decisions aren't necessarily high risk, but they often reflect impulsive, in-the-moment choices that fail to take longer term consequences into account. Remember, we want to frame behavior as choices and consequences. If you establish a curfew with your child, let them know ahead of time what will happen if they come home late. I often said to my kids, "I get that things happen. If you know you're going to be late, let me know. If you don't give me a heads-up, then you've missed curfew." This way, it's clear that they have a choice: If they miss curfew and fail to check in, they *choose* to lose the car for a few days or the following weekend, depending on the preestablished consequence. **It's important for them to make the connection that they are choosing the outcome—it's up to them.** We don't want to get into a blame game with our teen and fault them for trying to manage independently, but we do want to show them that they have control in the situation.

When you target the alternative for your teenager, they have a choice. If they choose to push or ignore the limit, they have chosen the consequence. Part of this is ensuring that consequences are proportional to the mistake made. Remember that your reaction is one of the consequences: Save your chits for the more egregious offenses. Missing curfew by 10 minutes is a different offense than throwing a party in an empty house or breaking the law. But be consistent in putting the responsibility on them—they could have made a different choice. When we target an alternative, we give adolescents the chance to rise to the occasion and improve over time. Engaging them in this way helps them see how they have control over the outcome, and clearly separates choice, behavior, and consequence.

Tactics for Handling Conflict and Enforcing Responsibility

On this note, I strongly advise you to avoid arguing with your teenager over text. As human beings, the way we know how to relate to people is by seeing their body language and hearing their tone of voice. Texting in an argument is like fighting in the dark or from separate rooms of the same house. We want to teach our teens accountability, so we need to start here; face-to-face interaction encourages accountability. It's a lot easier to shrug off a text than to ignore another person's disappointment, hurt, or anger when you're sitting across from them. Once our children become adolescents, we can't always control how they act, but we can control how we respond to them. The only way to resolve a conflict or shift your child's behavior is for them to feel your discomfort so that they can truly understand how their behavior has affected you.

When you are hurt by something your teenager has done, stay with your sadness and show them your vulnerability instead of defaulting to anger. Humans respond more strongly to an emotional connection than to harsh, blaming words. Anger shuts us down and makes us want to withdraw, while the feeling of hurting somebody that you love stays with you. Remember that teens are highly sensitive to this, so these difficult moments are crucial opportunities to show adolescents how to take responsibility for themselves and handle their relationships. This is why it's vital to have these conversations in person.

Another reason is that, as I stress with my teenage clients, anything you put in writing can be shared with anyone on any number of platforms. Texting leads to miscommunication of your feelings and misinterpretation of how the other person feels. People often avoid confrontation through text, but this is a copout. Plus, you devalue your message: Kids can ignore a text or will get used to screaming, shouting text messages that don't mean very much to them. Arguing via text negates the parent–child hierarchy and puts you on equal ground with your teen. You're no longer in charge.

When emotions are high, step back and take a minute before sending an angry text. If your child is away from you, whether down the road or away at school, being apart gives you a moment to think about the situation and gain some perspective. It's always helpful to pull back from the raw emotions that come up to think things through more clearly before we enter the conversation.

In the heat of the moment, teens will often look to deflect responsibility for their mistake. Adolescents who aren't used to being held accountable are quick to make excuses and place blame elsewhere. Immature teens don't realize that what they're doing is risky while they are doing it, and then will try to make excuses for what they have done once they are caught. If they're caught breaking a rule, they will be embarrassed and flustered.

To prevent an emotional battle in the heat of the moment, calmly state that their choices bring about consequences. Instead of reacting to their reactivity, process the issue with them later on. It's okay to help them learn to navigate these areas on their own, but don't take the blame for their inability to follow through. Simplify the situation by targeting the alternative: *You either get home before your curfew and are able to use the car, or you choose to lose your driving privileges.* When you can, let the natural consequences of a bad choice speak for themselves and resist the urge to help your child out of a difficult situation. For example, if they get a speeding ticket, there's no need to argue with or yell at them about the incident. Just make them handle the ticket on their own. The strain of coming up with the money, the hassle of figuring out how to plead guilty and submit payment, and the strikes on a license are sufficient. Take advantage of built-in consequences so that you aren't always in the position of being the disciplinarian. If you reprimand them but then take care of the situation (high nurture, low structure), your teenager will learn nothing from the incident. Instead, take yourself out of the equation as much as you can and keep it straightforward and situation specific: *I'm sorry you got that ticket. You have to take care of it, but let me know if you need me to explain anything to you or help you figure out what to do.* **The best inhibitor of risk is the reminder of the hassle and expense of dealing with the aftermath, whether it's a missed flight or a speeding ticket.**

This is also true when the consequence is more than an inconvenience. I had a client who was driving a few of his buddies to go get burgers. He sped up to beat a light, took the turn way too fast, and flipped his car. It was a disaster. Thankfully, everyone survived, but one of his friends was badly injured and another's family wanted to press legal charges against him. Of course his parents did not condone reckless driving, but I urged them to let those consequences be enough. If they had compounded his guilt and regret with further judgment or criticism, they only would have isolated him. It was an incredibly sobering moment for him; he could not have felt worse about what had happened and he couldn't change the damage he had done. That was enough.

Similarly, another client of mine was rushing to meet her boyfriend's parents for the first time and crashed her car into a tree. Chanel might have been speeding or she might have been texting—it was a little unclear—but she was lucky to be alive. She was so rattled that when she called her parents crying, they knew it would have been futile to discipline her. She was so upset and apologetic that adding their anger or additional consequences would have done very little. Don't feel like you have to punish your kids every time they make a mistake. On the other hand, acknowledge moments when they do make the right choice or are clearly working on it. Your teenager is going to make mistakes, but when we redirect their negative behavior and embrace progress, we guide them in the right direction.

Remember that, more than anything, adolescents are inexperienced. Sometimes they need to talk things through in order to gain insight and perspective. Some parents resist the idea that their child would do anything wrong, but we can't forget the impact of a group mentality, peer pressure, or simply in-the-moment decision making. It's our job to challenge teenagers to make connections between in-the-moment decisions and the associated risks or consequences. If we lean into this phase and work with our adolescent to engage their prefrontal cortex, they will start to make better decisions over time. Outside the heat of the moment, teens do have well-developed reasoning abilities. What takes them offline is arousal, excitement, and the desire for sensation. **The most effective way that we can improve their in-the-moment decision-making abilities is to preview various situations when the stakes are low so that they can think clearly and rationally.** This way, we will activate the neural pathways that will, over time, allow them to think through their choices and engage their inhibition. You can't unlearn foresight.[13]

Suppose you're going out of town for the weekend and you're concerned your adolescent will have friends over in your absence. It's far more effective to say, "If you throw a party while I'm away and the police come—which is increasingly common as they track parties on social media—you'll not only be in trouble with me and the school, you'll also face legal consequences, things will be broken, kids will get out of control, and there's a good chance you'll be cleaning up somebody's vomit tomorrow" than it is to say, "Don't you dare throw a party while I'm gone." If you ask a teenager who gets caught having a house party when his parents are away, he'll probably tell you that it unfolded like this: He invited a few friends over, they texted a few more, and suddenly his house was full of kids, many they didn't know, who were "trashing things." Only then do they realize the consequences of their choice to have a party.

Again, this is where we shift the focus of our expectations for our adolescents away from "getting caught" to the actual implications of their actions. Encourage them to focus on whether they could get hurt or get into more serious, even legal trouble. I know many teens who have been charged with an "MIP," Minor in Possession. If a teenager is caught in possession of or consuming alcohol, it's a serious offense. If convicted, the penalties can be a suspended driver's license, attending alcohol education classes, or as much as a jail sentence, depending on where they live. **Part of the task of parenting teenagers is to teach them that they don't simply answer to you; they have to be responsible for themselves in their communities and in the rest of their lives.**

In previewing scenarios with your teenager, be specific. Help them anticipate what could go wrong and what the solutions might be. Suppose you've got a kid who desperately wants to make the hockey team but also desperately wants to go skiing. No teenager wants to sit out while all of their friends are having fun together, but you have the perspective to know how disappointed they will be if they get cut from the team because they were injured skiing.

Ask them, "How will you feel if you don't get to try out for the hockey team because you got hurt skiing?" Or, "You know that the coach is excited to have you on the team this year. You'll be so bummed if you have to sit on the bench and watch your buddies play because you're hurt." These cues allow them to imagine their future selves dealing with the consequences of their choices and actions, which is an otherwise difficult task for a teen. This is challenging for many adults! The same inner urge that tells you to have an extra glass of wine or indulge in a piece of chocolate cake, even when you *know* those choices aren't good for you in the long term, is the urge that dictates most of what a teenager does, but their choices tend to have higher stakes. While you have developed the ability to (mostly) control it, they simply haven't.

Your job as a parent is to identify certain situations that your child might not be prepared for and to keep them safe from those situations to the best of your ability. But stay attuned to when and where you might promote experimentation beyond your adolescent's comfort zone so that they can grow, develop passions, and explore the world around them. Parents can get caught in saying no—and you will often need to say no as the parent of a teen—but your no will mean more if you aren't constantly preventing your teen from doing what they want to do. Plus, it's more enjoyable for everyone. **Parents make adolescence harder by feeling as though they always have to regulate and punish.** Taking healthy risks allows adolescents to learn their limits and develop self-trust and confidence. Try to get yourself out of a "no" mindset and show your kids that—sometimes—you're willing to take a risk or make an exception on their behalf.

I grew up in a ski town in the Rocky Mountains. When we were kids, they *never* canceled school. However, a few times a ski season, the school would declare a "Powder Day," and we would be allowed to head for the mountains. One year, my brother was injured and missed one of those precious Powder Days early in the season. He was a talented and passionate skier, so he took this harder than most kids might. Later that same year, the World Cup ski race came to our hometown and he was desperate to go, but it would mean missing school. My parents let him choose: If he missed school, his teachers would be mad at him and he might face a consequence with the school administrator for his absence. If he was okay with that, they would allow him to attend the World Cup. To no one's surprise, he ended up at the World Cup.

But there are a few important takeaways here. One, skiing was something my brother was passionate about; developing interests and passions is an essential component of adolescence. Two, we gain credibility with our children when we show them that we aren't black and white. Making a decision is typically multifaceted and nuanced, with pros and cons on each side. If we give teens the reins some of the time, we build trust with them and they will be willing to listen to us. Three, my parents taught my brother the important life lesson that there are moments that are more important than your day-to-day obligations. The World Cup only came to our town once in our childhoods. Seizing and celebrating these special experiences brings joy into your child's life and shows them how to have a little bit of defiance and a willingness to push back against constraints in a positive and meaningful way.

Teens are at once vulnerable and capable. Because they are vulnerable as they become capable, we want to nurture these opposing elements and keep them in balance through high structure and positive reinforcement. The adolescent tendencies toward experience, fun, and risk taking can be hugely beneficial as long as they are healthily modulated by adults. Behaviorally, adolescence is defined as a transitional period between childhood and adulthood, characterized by changes in social interaction and development of mature cognitive abilities and skills required for survival as an adult.[14] Behavioral flexibility and the ability to adapt quickly to new skills and concepts are the positive side of adolescent risk taking, and we want to embrace and encourage this element.

Adolescents have immense curiosity, high mental energy, and a desire to explore the world around them. We want to build on these aspects where we can by encouraging them to get out of their comfort zones. We've become overly focused on building our adolescents' résumés when we should be urging them to travel, try new activities, and meet different types of people. In other words, we don't want to negate their desire to seek reward and follow gratification because, during these exploratory years, there is no real downside if they aren't successful—it is simply a learning experience. We want our adolescents to learn to assess risk and develop sound judgment. When they make good decisions, they can maximize enjoyment and growth without putting themselves in danger.

Consider This:
Insights & Actions

- As much as you can, bring a sense of humor. Reflect on your own experience of adolescence so that you can empathize with and relate to your teen. Try to support their spontaneity and inquisitive nature when you can.

- With your older children, solicit their advice in how you handle their younger siblings. The best way to get them to think about choices and consequences is to involve them in these kinds of decisions. *Do you think I should let your sister go to this party?* Or *Do you think your brother should have a curfew?* You can actually get a better sense of your kids' situation from their siblings.
- I am a fan of curfews. The age-old adage "nothing good happens after midnight" is especially true for teenagers! Don't allow your teens to come and go as they please. Let them know exactly when you expect them to be home and remind them that you'll be waiting up for them or that they need to check in when they get home. Then, enact consequences if they are late without a good reason. A curfew is a good way to limit opportunities for trouble.
- With young teens (12–14 or 15), limit unsupervised time with peers. Groups of adolescents hanging out without a purpose for hours on end is nothing but trouble. Give your teenagers parameters and limits. Thirty minutes to an hour is plenty of time to grab a sandwich in town or walk around a mall.
- Emphasize progress over perfection. If your teen missed curfew last week but made it on time this week, that's progress! Don't hesitate to point it out. Let them know that you noticed their good behavior and you're proud of them for showing responsibility and holding to their word, but don't cave as soon as they meet your standards. Be consistent in your expectations so that they meet the goals you've set for them.
- To motivate your teenager, channel their reward-seeking tendency by making tasks competitive or outcome oriented. For example, add an additional reward for the completion of a task or remove a fall-back option if they fail to complete the task.
- Encourage your child to participate in various and diverse groups. Friends from summer camp, sports teams, music or theater groups, and others can create a more well-rounded social experience for your adolescent. It can also be a relief, when social tensions are high, to have different friends to rely on in different moments.
- For younger adolescents, encourage safe activities that meet their need for sensation seeking and promote positive peer relationships. Outdoor activities such as rock climbing, zip-lining, and paintballing are great opportunities for healthy fun with limited risk.

- A driver's license is a good tool to encourage responsibility. Ask your adolescent to run some errands for you or manage the car's maintenance, such as getting it inspected or making sure it is full of gas.
- Use real examples of things that have happened within your community to point out what can go wrong with risky behavior. Teenagers offer endless teaching opportunities, and you don't want to let these pass unnoticed. When we associate an emotion with a memory, it becomes more ingrained in our mind.
- It's excruciating for parents to watch their child be bullied, excluded, or left out, but it's important that you resist the urge to become overly permissive to try to compensate for their social angst. Don't let your desire for your child to "fit in" get in the way of providing the structure that they need.

Notes

1. Jensen, F. E., & Nutt, A. E. (2015). *The teenage brain: A neuroscientist's survival guide to raising adolescents and young adults.* New York, NY: HarperCollins.
2. Hunt, P. S., Burk, J. A., Barnet, R. C. (2016). Adolescent transitions in reflexive and non-reflexive behavior: Review of fear conditioning and impulse control in rodent models. *Neuroscience and Biobehavioral Reviews, 70,* 33–45. doi:10.1016/j.neubiorev.2016.06.026
3. Jensen, F. E., & Nutt, A. E. (2015). *The teenage brain: A neuroscientist's survival guide to raising adolescents and young adults.* New York, NY: HarperCollins.
4. Treiman, D. M. (2001). GABAergic mechanisms in epilepsy. *Epilepsia, 42*(Suppl. 3), 8–12. doi:10.1046/j.1528-1157.2001.042suppl.3008.x
5. Stevens, M. C. (2016). The contributions of resting state and task-based functional connectivity studies to our understanding of adolescent brain network maturation. *Neuroscience and Biobehavioral Reviews, 70,* 13–32. doi:10.1016/j.neubiorev.2016.07.027
6. Damour, L. (2017, March 8). Teenagers do dumb things, but there are ways to limit recklessness. *New York Times.* Retrieved from http://nyti.ms/2m1xHkB
7. Jensen, F. E., & Nutt, A. E. (2015). *The teenage brain: A neuroscientist's survival guide to raising adolescents and young adults.* New York, NY: HarperCollins.
8. Kilford, E. J., Garrett, E., & Blakemore, S.-J. (2016). The development of social cognition in adolescence: An integrated perspective. *Neuroscience and Behavioral Reviews, 70,* 106–120. doi:10.1016/j.neubiorev.2016.08.016
9. Stevens, M. C. (2016). The contributions of resting state and task-based functional connectivity studies to our understanding of adolescent brain network maturation. *Neuroscience and Biobehavioral Reviews, 70,* 13–32. doi:10.1016/j.neubiorev.2016.07.027

10. Kilford, E. J., Garrett, E., & Blakemore, S.-J. (2016). The development of social cognition in adolescence: An integrated perspective. *Neuroscience and Behavioral Reviews, 70,* 106–120. doi:10.1016/j.neubiorev.2016.08.016

11. Stevens, M. C. (2016). The contributions of resting state and task-based functional connectivity studies to our understanding of adolescent brain network maturation. *Neuroscience and Biobehavioral Reviews, 70,* 13–32. doi:10.1016/j.neubiorev.2016.07.027

12. Bowlby, J. (1969). *Attachment and loss, Vol. I* (2nd ed.). New York, NY: Basic Books.

13. Daumor, L. (2017, March 8). Teenagers do dumb things, but there are ways to limit recklessness. *New York Times.* Retrieved from http://nyti.ms/2m1xHkB

14. Spear, L. P. (2000). The adolescent brain and age-related behavioral manifestations. *Neuroscience and Biobehavioral Reviews, 24,* 417–463.

15. Insurance Institute for Highway Safety. (2019, May). Teenagers. Retrieved from https://www.iihs.org/topics/teenagers

8

The Eighth Myth

TODAY'S ADOLESCENTS STRUGGLE WITH MENTAL
HEALTH DISORDERS BECAUSE THEY'VE HAD IT EASY.
THEY DON'T WANT TO DEAL WITH THE REALITY OF
LIFE BECAUSE THEY'RE SPOILED.

WHAT DO YOU want to be when you grow up? We pose this question to our children almost as soon as they can speak, as though their identity is fixed from birth. We are so focused on where they'll end up, from nursery school through college and into the working world, that we leave out crucial elements of identity formation. Actually, childhood and adolescence should be a time of exploration and self-discovery through trial and error and a willingness to learn. The final "psychological crisis" of adolescence is termed **identity versus role confusion**, the process by which a person masters various tasks and challenges of society.[1] Before adolescence, these are primarily school related. By adolescence, your child should be interacting with society on a much broader basis. Teens start to experience success in certain areas, which feeds further interest and effort. It is also during adolescence that we start to see independent agency: work ethic, integrity, and higher functioning thinking arise. These are integral pieces of adolescence, because they will determine how hard teens will work and how committed they are to what they care about. Adolescents should be struggling with making choices, navigating social interactions, and developing a sense of right and wrong. For the first time, it's up to the teen to make these choices for themselves and then enjoy (or regret) the consequences. For the first time, our teens begin to experience achievement and failure.[2]

In today's world, adolescence is largely viewed as preparation for getting into college. The focus is on attributes and accomplishments that can be measured externally—the teen years have become oriented toward an out-come. With so much pressure placed on the end result, the process is rendered insignificant.[3] There is little emphasis on personal psychological awareness or development of intrinsic qualities that are essential for "solid growth" toward adulthood. We are robbing our teens of learning how to fail, how to negotiate their place in the world, how to stand up for themselves, and even how to succeed with grace.

While we as parents can recognize that college is undoubtedly an impor-tant step in the lives of many, we also should strive to focus on the goal of raising capable and well-adjusted adults. When we force our children onto paths that are strictly focused on results and outcomes, we deny them the op-portunity to develop an independent identity and explore the many facets of themselves. They fail to develop a core that they can fall back on when something goes wrong. The goal of adolescence is not admission to college, but rather the formation of a unique identity, the ability to build and enjoy various relationships, and the development of industry in various areas of one's life. If we allow ourselves to be overly focused on teens' achievement, particularly as it pertains to the college process, we don't equip ourselves for the possibility of raising an adolescent who, for one reason or another, cannot achieve in the way we would like them to, or has a different set of interests that they want to pursue. **When we prescribe our own definition of success or achievement for our children, we often prevent them from developing their own goals and interests.**

Instead, we should create an environment for adolescents to develop a sense of themselves based on more than academic, athletic, or artistic suc-cess. Thirty percent of today's high school seniors describe feeling completely overwhelmed with their lives, compared with 18% in 1985.[4] High school should be manageable; these years are a rare time to experiment, explore, and discover oneself. In today's adolescents, we see increased anxiety along-side aversion to risk. Teens are plagued by "what if": what if this goes wrong, what if nobody likes me, what if something bad happens? They are deprived of the experience of getting through something uncomfortable and realizing that they will be okay. This is essential to the development of self-trust. **If we are raising teenagers in a world where they feel their value is connected to where they are able to attend college, they become unwilling to take a chance or risk failure.** They suffer from "planning delusion," the idea that if they make careful, practical plans, they will face no obstacles or challenges to success. Their lives are so structured that they are not learning about failure. Constant self-projection and self-tracking leaves little time for private contemplation and identity construction. The prominence of an internal sense of self is dwindling, perhaps to the point of nonexistence. **If young people prematurely foreclose their identities, or worse, never develop them, they are less likely to achieve a fully realized and satisfying life.**

To counter this, parents need to stop shielding their children from unhappiness or hardship. Teens need to struggle and figure out how to right themselves on their own in order to develop a tolerance for unhappiness and discomfort. When we intercede and shield them from these experiences, we prevent them from developing autonomy and the ability to cope. It's an important marker of maturity to understand that, ultimately, they are accountable for themselves. They don't do their homework, study for their exams, clean their rooms, or do the right thing for your sake. They need to have a sense that these daily habits will set them up for success in whatever area they decide to pursue. This way, you allow them to develop industry and purpose instead of creating a dynamic in which they answer to you. Besides, you've already been a teenager! You don't need to live through it again. Most importantly, squeaking by or evading their responsibilities will catch up to them, and it will be theirs to answer for sooner or later. When we set up a dynamic with our teenagers in which they are simply trying to get away with bad behavior and avoid punishment (high structure, low nurture), they fail to comprehend the larger implications of their choices. If they cut corners and take unnecessary risks, they're setting themselves up for long-term disappointment.

As parents, we can embrace our role in shaping the mentality our teens use to view the world around them. We want to strive to promote a growth mindset in our children, rather than a fixed mindset. A **growth mindset** is inherently process oriented, whereas a **fixed mindset** depends on results for validation.[5] A fixed mindset supports the idea that a teen either has certain qualities and abilities or doesn't; this can limit them and provide them fewer options for a productive life. Setting up the idea of desirable skills that one either has or lacks creates a standard against which an adolescent might feel they can never measure up. By contrast, a growth mindset promotes a willingness to try various things and a comfort with failure, a desire for curiosity, and a commitment to apply oneself, learn what is not known, and figure it out. Room for exploration allows those with a growth mindset to experience more throughout their life because they are adaptable to various situations and demands.[6]

Adolescence is a critical time to develop a healthy identity, a multifaceted but ultimately coherent sense of self that is both personally satisfying and affirmed by the surrounding community. **Identity formation** is defined as the development of a persona or image that fits comfortably with one's sense of self and fits into their community. A sense of oneself, or an identity, is the foundation of a healthy mindset that allows adolescents to work through difficult experiences. If the identity is not properly formed and thereby expressed throughout adolescence, we see teenagers and young adults who struggle to find their way in the world. In some cases, we start to see symptoms of depression and anxiety, which prevent these individuals from functioning at full capacity. These same individuals may have trouble forming intimate relationships, forging a path, finding satisfaction in the work world, and raising the next generation of contributing adults, all of which may be considered the foundation of a happy life.[7]

Mental Illness in Teens

As parents, we know that adolescent behavior can be unpredictable and erratic, but when should we be concerned about the ups and downs? With the rise of depression and anxiety in the adolescent population, it's important to know what to look for in your teenager so that you can anticipate a chemical imbalance before it becomes severe.

The stigma around mental health disorders is detrimental to our understanding of these imbalances and hinders the steps we can take to help those affected. Some parents worry that if they seek help for their child's mental health, it's a poor reflection on them. There should be no shame in needing support. Intervention in these areas is especially important for teens because some of the symptoms, such as low energy and poor concentration, have a far-reaching impact on social and academic functioning. Depression and anxiety can be so pervasive that it becomes difficult to break the cycle, and once these symptoms take hold, they can erode a teenager's confidence and self-image.

If we look at mental health as one component of our overall health, we can begin to approach issues in a more holistic way. If your child had a fever that lasted for more than two weeks, you would absolutely take them to see a doctor. If you had a kidney infection, you wouldn't ignore it. Why should the health of the brain be approached any differently? **The brain is the only organ in the body that is responsible for behavior.** The brain dictates every aspect of our experience of the world, so it should be treated with the highest care.

We often see the first symptoms or presentations of mental health issues in adolescence because of the neurological and hormonal changes taking place. Anxiety, depression, and suicide have escalated alarmingly in the adolescent population.[8] Approximately 11% of youth will experience depression at some point,[9] and research shows that if it isn't resolved in a healthy manner, depression can have significant consequences in adulthood: 75% of individuals who experience depression in adolescence will make a suicide attempt in adulthood.[10] Most alarmingly, we are seeing 40,000 teenaged suicides per year. In 2016, some sources estimated that 62,000 adolescents died by suicide.[11] This is a true public health crisis.

Whether these numbers point to greater awareness of mental health issues or higher incidences of these abnormalities, we need to pay attention. As parents, we want to play an active role and engage with our teenager to understand how they are feeling as they navigate the physical and emotional shifts of adolescence. Paying close attention to behavior is crucial to ensuring that changes don't indicate something more serious. Have in mind where your teenager should be: Consider their temperament, their strengths and weaknesses, and their social setting. Watch for abrupt or worrisome changes in these areas. While teenage behavior can be irregular and even erratic, if we assume all irregular behavior simply indicates "a phase," we might miss a more significant issue and face a devastating consequence.

Mental health disorders and teen substance use often go hand in hand. Kids with emotional, learning, or behavioral challenges are particularly tempted and often turn to alcohol or drugs to cope with difficult feelings. Mental health professionals widely employ the general statistic that almost half of adolescents with an untreated mental health disorder will have a problem with substance abuse; further, "a 2016 study of 10,000 adolescents found that two-thirds of those who developed alcohol or substance use disorders had experienced at least one mental health disorder."[12] This is a hugely problematic statistic because we know how vulnerable the adolescent brain is to alcohol and drugs. This is yet another reason to seek support if you are concerned about your teen's mental health. The risk is too great to let them suffer unnecessarily.

Depression and anxiety are two of the most common and frequently diagnosed mental health issues for adolescents. They are also particularly problematic for teens because mental illness prevents learning, so it is particularly important to understand how serious the mental illness is before figuring out what we can do about it. Depression and anxiety can present in similar ways, so we often conflate the two, assuming that the presence of one indicates the other. But it's important to note the nuanced differences between the two so that we can ensure we are addressing the right issue.

Depression

Depression is not simply sadness; it impacts every aspect of life. There is a difference between a "low," or a bout of sadness, and depression. When someone is depressed, they are in a dark place almost all of the time and it's very difficult to pull them out—they can't "snap out of it." Depression is a state in which the lack or excess of a certain brain chemical is often a factor. In many cases, depression can be considered a blunted reward response. Depression manifests in the front of the brain and, as we know, the front of the adolescent brain is under construction. Psychiatric testing has advanced so that we can now see depressive emotions in the frontal cortex through an MRI, so we can determine with greater certainty whether an individual is experiencing disproportionately negative feelings.

Adolescents are particularly susceptible to depression because they react more strongly to rejection and negativity. Those suffering from depression often report increased feelings of rejection, which is especially difficult for a teenager to face.[13] Depression is particularly dangerous for adolescents because it diminishes concentration and focus, and creates feelings of worthlessness in an already vulnerable individual.

As adults in the lives of adolescents, we must do a better job of teaching skills to handle and correct this negative trajectory. Teens are already primed for emotionality and volatility, so an added imbalance must be addressed. If you are dealing with an adolescent who is clinically depressed, keep in mind that the chemical impairment is so strong that they will struggle to manage their physical and emotional response. In conjunction with aligning teachers and counselors with mental health professionals, we can teach adolescents preventive skills such as emotional regulation, mindfulness, and problem solving, which can be very helpful in dealing with mental health disorders.[14] It's crucial that those who suffer from these chemical imbalances receive the appropriate treatment *for them*.

Various courses of action, including behavioral therapy and medication, can be incredibly effective. **Cognitive behavioral therapy** (CBT) is a particularly helpful therapy that can help teens learn how to get themselves out of negative thought patterns. CBT can not only help teenagers overcome depression, but it also gives them a skill set to use at any other time in their life when they are struggling with patterns of negativity. There are also many helpful antipsychotic and antidepressant medications, but it can take time to determine what an individual's chemistry needs to regulate itself. If a doctor recommends medication for your child, consult an psychiatrist specializing in adolescent care to determine the best course of action. Don't simply ask your pediatrician for a medication you read about online or that your friend's child takes. Remember that you are medicating a developing brain, so you need the guidance of a professional who will tailor the prescription to your teen's unique chemistry, height, and weight. Teens are growing and changing, and we often fail to adjust dosage or prescriptions to match. Consult someone who does this for a living to find the right solution, and monitor medication on a regular basis.

Adolescent depression can look different for boys and girls. Depressed boys often show signs of withdrawal and/or bouts of anger and aggressive behavior. Girls tend to display depression through withdrawal and shutting down. For instance, I worked with a teenage girl who was severely depressed. Carmen was having dark thoughts, had lost her appetite, and began writing poetry about hurting herself and feeling like an outsider. She began cutting her thighs and having occasional suicidal thoughts. Carmen's family had recently immigrated to the United States, so they were dealing with the challenges of assimilating to their new community while trying to preserve elements of their own culture. They had a strong, almost rigid set of cultural and religious values that left little room for Carmen's feelings. It seemed that anything that brought joy into her life was at odds with her parents' rules, so she felt very misunderstood. She would often go into her room, shut the door, and not get out of bed or engage in any activities.

Carmen's parents were also very resistant to the idea of a therapist. It wasn't until Carmen attempted suicide that a religious mentor stepped in and insisted that she seek psychological help. With a combination of professional help (for both Carmen and her parents) and medication for Carmen, she managed to come out of her depression. Eventually, she was able to find peace in yoga and mindfulness. This wasn't an easy solution; her parents did not support her pursuing these outlets, but they were necessary to her ability to grapple with her depression. Today, she is healthy, teaching yoga, and doing well in college, but it was a long road to where she is now.

I also work with an adolescent boy who continually struggles with serious depression. Damian is a serious athlete and dreamed of playing a sport in college. Unfortunately, he suffered several serious injuries that sidelined him during the season he would have been recruited. Damian has gotten increasingly angry and has become emotionally belligerent in fights with family and friends. He breaks things at home, throws furniture, and instigates conflict in social interactions. His athletic performance has dropped and he's largely given up on athletics altogether. Damian blames everyone else for his issues.

According to him, his friends have excluded him, his coaches have screwed him over, and his parents have ruined his life. He has certainly been through a lot: He had two major injuries, struggled through a long road of rehab, took heavy painkillers, and has had to come to terms with letting go of a long-held dream.

Because Damian's anger was so prevalent and extreme, nobody considered that there might have been an underlying condition like clinical depression. It's very common for someone who has gone through physical turmoil to become depleted and depressed. A short-term prescription of an antidepressant along with counseling could have enabled him to rebound completely, but because it went untreated for so long, he has struggled much longer than necessary. He wasn't raised to accept responsibility for any of his behavior and there was no attempt to resolve his issues. He is big, strong, violent, and most importantly, miserable.

As much as we might not want to admit that our child might be depressed, we need to encourage our teens to get the help they need before the consequences become serious. As parents, we need to be more proactive in seeking professional help when a teen's behavior becomes disruptive in their life or your family's. We have the tendency to obscure our issues and act like everything is okay, but this typically results in worsened symptoms and destruction. You might need to be the driving force that gets your adolescent the treatment and support that they need. You might be met with resistance, and you might need to be somewhat forceful in pushing your teen toward help, but don't back off. It doesn't always have to be a formal consultation with a therapist; you can seek out a school counselor, teacher, coach, mentor, or religious figure to share your concerns and gain their insight. Sometimes a simple shift or suggestion can help everyone get back on track.

It can be normal for adolescents to experience bouts of anxiety or depression or to display some of the symptoms without having a clinical diagnosis of one or the other. As parents, we can try to help our adolescents manage these imbalances through encouraging healthy habits such as exercise, rest, meditation, and nutritious eating. If you notice your kid is upset about something, check in with them about what they've eaten and how much sleep they've gotten. Encourage your teenager to notice how they feel when they make different choices.[15] Did they get enough sleep? Are they hydrated? Have they eaten a good meal? In this way, you can affirm them in making healthy choices so that they are better equipped to take care of themselves.

I have had several clients who find themselves depressed in their first and second years of college. During these years, adolescents are often taking care of themselves on their own for the first time, right when academic and social demands are high. It can be hard to adjust to a different academic workload and standard; successful students often struggle to accept that what they thought of as a good grade is much harder to come by in college. Their schedules wear them out: They are studying and partying at all hours, drinking too much beer and eating too much pizza, and trying to rest in noisy dorm rooms with unfamiliar roommates. Meanwhile, everyone around them seems to be having the time of their lives, and they interpret their depression as their own inadequacy and begin to experience a pervasive sense of loneliness.

I had a client who went to an academically rigorous college that was far from where she'd grown up. She suffered with a bit of social anxiety, and the school was one where many of her classmates seemed to know each other before they arrived on campus. As academic work began to mount and she struggled to adjust to her new environment, she started to gain weight (more than the typical "freshman fifteen"), was frequently sick with colds or stomachaches, and would stay in her room instead of going out on the weekends. This trend worsened over her first two years of school, but she explained her challenges by saying she was sick because she was in a different climate than she was used to, she gained weight because the food at school was bad, and she struggled academically because her professors were unfair.

After her second year of school, she came to see me. After a thorough consultation, it became clear that this wasn't a dietary issue but was actually a combination of depression and anxiety. I referred her to a psychiatrist who prescribed her with a low-dose antidepressant and urged her to seek out counseling at school. She did, and she was able to learn coping skills and establish a connection with someone who she could check in with when she was feeling overwhelmed. It was remarkable to see what a difference these simple shifts made in her life.

College is often the first time that willpower can't get an adolescent through something, and they don't have immediate access to their family at home to help them cope. Or perhaps they previously hadn't hit all that many bumps in the road, and now find themselves among hundreds of kids who can match their accomplishments and skills. If we are aware of this heightened time of risk, we can guide our college-age children, encouraging them through medical, behavioral, and therapeutic solutions that can help them get through it. To be clear: Healthy habits can't prevent mental health issues, but they can have a positive impact on our overall emotional wellbeing. If your adolescent is practicing healthy habits but seems withdrawn and uninterested in their activities, it might be a signal that there is a larger issue at play.

Signs of Depression[16]

If at least five of the following symptoms are present for two or more weeks and represent a change from your child's previous functioning, they may be suffering from depression. Even if your child is feeling or displaying three of these signs, it's always worthwhile to consult a mental health professional if you have concerns.

- A depressed mood for most of the day, nearly every day. Friends, teachers, parents, and siblings observe a change from previous behavior.
- Description of negative emotions, such as feelings of sadness or emptiness inside.
- Diminished interest or pleasure in daily activities, particularly hobbies they previously enjoyed such as playing sports, reading, shopping, socializing, or eating.
- Significant weight loss without dieting, or sudden weight gain. A marked increase or decrease in appetite.
- Insomnia or hypersomnia. If not sleeping, do they have problems falling asleep or staying asleep? If oversleeping, how many hours are they sleeping?
- Agitation or inhibition. Feelings of restlessness and an inability to sit still or an immobility and complete lack of engagement.
- Fatigue or loss of energy nearly every day.
- Withdrawal from peers and a lack of desire to socialize.
- Feelings of worthlessness or excessive, inappropriate guilt paired with low self-esteem (i.e., they blame themselves for things beyond their control).
- Diminished ability to think or concentrate, or general indecisiveness. A lack of focus or concentration, particularly in class, or an inability to read, watch television, or follow a conversation. Difficulty making a decision, particularly small, insignificant choices such as what to eat or what to wear.
- Recurrent thoughts of death or suicidal ideation with or without a plan.

Anxiety

I used to primarily see anxiety in older adolescents, but today, I meet with clients anywhere from 8 to 22 who suffer from extreme anxiety and are consumed with fear of underachievement, failure, and inadequacy. Anxiety has nothing to do with a lack of courage, character, or bravery. Everybody experiences anxiety at some level, particularly adolescents. Anxiety is the body's natural warning system; there's a primitive part of the brain that's geared to sense threat. When the brain perceives a possible danger in our environment, it activates the anxiety response to push us into awareness and action. When the brain sends this signal of danger, the body surges with cortisol (the stress hormone) and adrenaline to prepare the body to run or fight for its life. This is the "fight or flight" response, and it's in everyone, but the "go" button is more sensitive for people with anxiety. When an anxiety disorder is present, this system is overactive.[17] The brain is sending frequent and intense danger signals in low-risk situations. If a paralyzing fear is consistently triggered at inappropriate times, we see a shutdown, which must be addressed so that it does not hinder productivity and healthy functioning. Anxiety disorder is obsessive worry or constant fear of uncertainty and danger, and it becomes detrimental when it gets in the way of normal behavior.[18]

We know teens are already struggling with high levels of stress and, given their hectic schedules and daily demands, it is natural that at moments, they will become fractured and anxious. When anxiety isn't clinical or paralyzing for a child, parents can be impactful in helping them organize a plan to work through anxiety and manage anxious feelings in a healthy way. We often see adolescents avoid whatever makes them anxious, so we want to encourage them to approach the source of their anxiety with a different perspective. As a parent, your child's anxiety may not make sense to you, because it is irrational and nonsensical, but it's not helpful to point that out. **We want to teach them to acknowledge what they fear about a certain situation and approach it with curiosity instead, by calmly and slowly breaking the anxiety into manageable pieces.**[19] Ask them to talk it out with you so that you can balance their fears with reality. Ask them: *What is the worst thing that could happen?* Once they give you an answer, ask them: *How likely is that to happen?* and *Could you live with it if it did happen?* Talking through fear in this way can diminish the uncertainty and allow us to see that, even if the worst outcome is realized, we will probably survive. If your child can't seem to break out of irrational worry and fear, they might be dealing with clinical anxiety disorder.

Feelings of anticipation before a big event and even nervous energy can be healthy as a motivating and invigorating force, prompting preparation or a heightened attention to detail. But anxiety isn't helpful when it becomes a paralyzing cycle of worry and fear. We often see anxiety and panic disorder originate from excessive worry. Everybody worries; we worry about specific things that might or will take place in the future. For example, your child might worry about an upcoming test or athletic event. But excessive worry creates a progression that can't be contained, building from worry → fear → anxiety → panic.[20]

Anxiety becomes unhealthy when we begin to avoid or withdraw from a task or when our fear prevents us from performing. If your adolescent studies for their upcoming test and seems comfortable with the material but then does poorly, they might struggle with anxiety. When they are anxious, they are stuck in their back brain and can't access the higher cognitive functions of the front brain. Anxious individuals find it difficult to stay grounded in the present moment. They need to learn how to calm themselves under pressure so that they can access a different neural pathway. If you're trying to differentiate between nervousness and anxiety, look at its result. If it creates focus and attention and enhances performance, it's healthy. If it creates irrational worry, panic, or avoidance, or brings down performance, it isn't healthy.

I work with a boy named Colin who has all the trappings of a high school all-star: he is a high-achieving student, plays two varsity sports, and has a girlfriend. He will most likely be recruited to an Ivy League school to play at the Division I level. He's in an intense and high-pressured environment in his school life, and on top of that, his father is extremely anxious and overbearing. He is overly involved in every aspect of his son's life and demands that he excel in every area. Colin feels that he is on a hamster wheel where no amount of effort or success is enough to satisfy his father. Here is a boy who has nearly perfect board scores and is a top performer in a nationally ranked athletic program, but he does not see himself as successful. He is paralyzed by a fear of what might go wrong in his life. *What if I don't get into the college where my father wants me to go? What if my girlfriend breaks up with me? What if I don't play well in my game?* He is swimming in feelings of inadequacy and experiences little joy in his life. Not to mention, he is exhausted and stressed out. As soon as one issue resolves, he begins to worry about something else. While it seems logical to tell Colin to stop worrying about one of these things, he actually needs professional help to break the cycle in his brain.

When an adolescent (or anyone for that matter) gets stuck in a cycle of anxiety, breaking out of it independently can be a struggle. It's also common to see episodic panic attacks in adolescents. Regardless of what their parent, teacher, or coach might tell them, if they are experiencing an inordinate amount of anxiety, they have engaged the amygdala and the "fight or flight" response in their brain. They are in survival mode and are unable to access their higher reasoning to see the reality of a situation. When the amygdala is engaged, the brain is operating on cortisol. Higher levels of cortisol tend to elicit irritability and crankiness and prevent feelings of pleasure. Anxiety exhausts the body and wears the adolescent down, and this level of activity can have long-term effects.[21]

In adolescents, anxiety often presents as avoidance, whether they fail to get their assignments done or skip social events that they feel nervous about. One function of the prefrontal cortex that develops later in adolescence is initiation: the ability to start something. Parents often tell me that their adolescent is failing to complete their homework or turn it in on time. They are concerned that their teen has a learning disability, but it's frequently anxiety. It's hard for anybody to get started on tasks or projects, but it's particularly hard for adolescents because initiation is a skill that is refined over the teenage years. They don't know where or how to begin, and then they avoid it and the panic becomes worse. A therapist can help them figure out what triggers their anxiety so that they can learn to manage it. This doesn't take several months on a therapist's couch to address. In even as few as a couple of sessions, they can learn to work around the angst they feel . . . and start to develop a skill set that they can rely on when they inevitably have the next anxiety attack.

During exam periods, I see a lot of adolescent clients who are so afraid of underperforming on their upcoming tests that they cannot sit down and study effectively. Their fear of the result prevents them from taking the steps to achieve the desired outcome. Even if they are staring at their books, nothing registers. Help them "break it down" into pieces and make a plan of attack that feels manageable. I am adamant that the plan, list, or calendar be written down into a tangible, three-dimensional list. The physical act of taking something from your brain and putting it on paper is proven to relieve some of the stress and anxiety, because it's literally "off your mind" and you've put it somewhere you can do something with it. It's neurobiological: Once we can look at what we have to do on a calendar and assure ourselves that we have the time needed to get through our workload, or plan how to approach it, we feel less anxious. As humans, we are visual learners. Color coding is especially effective because it allows the brain to make a picture. Try having your teen do this, even with just two colors. Time management is a lifelong skill, as well as a helpful antidote to performance anxiety. Letting them look at what they have to do on paper instead of imagining it disproportionately in their mind is soothing. When you don't have a clear picture in your mind of what needs to get done, it's difficult to initiate action. The same is true for the act of studying; it should be an interactive process with notes, color-coded Post-its and index cards, and printed documents (see Box 8.1). I know this is not environmentally friendly, but brain development is more important!

Many teens also experience social nervousness and angst, particularly around big events like a school dance or an athletic event. Some adolescents are more outgoing and extroverted, while others tend toward insularity and

---

BOX 8.1

Test Preparation

- Studying should be a three-dimensional process: see, hear, say, and repeat. Sound and vision provide access to language and memory recall.
- Active note taking triggers memory responses and color coding engages vision. Use markers, index cards, and Post-its to visually record information.
- Quiz yourself on information. If you're reading through notes or memorizing terms or equations, say them aloud to speak and hear the words.

TEST-DAY TIPS

- A lot of kids read over a test and panic about what they don't know. Encourage them to go into the test with the mindset: **"What *do* I know?"**
- Before you start, jot down a few quick memory notes to rely on through the test.
- Read the directions carefully, underlining important words that tell you what to do.
- With multiple choice, use the process of elimination: Eliminate answers that are ridiculous, inaccurate, or too general, and usually you'll end up with a choice between two instead of four.

---

introversion. A tendency toward alone or quiet time is not necessarily cause for concern, unless you see a marked difference from previous behavior.[22] If your child is consistently withdrawing from their peers and avoiding social interactions, they may be struggling with social anxiety. While adults tend to experience anxiety brought on by financial, marital, professional, and health-related issues, among others, adolescents experience anxiety brought on by their academics and their social lives.[23] Social anxiety is more frequently diagnosed in adolescent girls; however, based on my work, I believe that social anxiety is equally prevalent in adolescent boys. Girls may be able or willing to articulate their feelings in a way that boys are not, but it's just as important for adolescent boys to feel they have an outlet to express fear and insecurity and receive reassurance from a parent or adult.

Girls and boys respond differently to social anxiety; girls might plan to go to an event, but then panic and break down immediately before or during the event, while socially anxious boys tend to withdraw and isolate from their peers. Girls will often plan ahead for an event: They'll shop with friends for an outfit or arrange to "get ready" at someone's house, but then become overwhelmed with fear as the event approaches and suddenly not want to go. *What if I wear the wrong outfit? What if nobody asks me to dance? What if I'm offered a drink and I don't want one?* Boys, on the other hand, might worry about the same questions, but will act uninterested in situations that might make them uncomfortable. We often see a shift in boys after the ninth and 10th grades, when they have more independence and feel more comfortable among their peers.

If you see your adolescent avoiding social interactions once or twice, this is fairly normal. If avoidance and isolation become a pattern, you need to look into what your teenager might be feeling and experiencing so that their anxiety doesn't become debilitating and manifest more seriously. Ask them if there's a reason they don't want to go to a certain event; sometimes, kids will avoid certain situations for good reason and we don't want to push them to go against their judgment.

Parents of one of my female clients expressed concern that she wasn't as social as they wanted her to be. They told me she preferred staying home on the weekend instead of going on dates or hanging with her friends. This client is a good athlete and a top student in a small private school. Her parents insisted that there must be something wrong with her. When I checked in with her about this, she told me that she doesn't really love the high school party scene and she feels more comfortable at home. There's nothing wrong with that. It's not the worst thing if your teenager doesn't have the urge to push every limit! Some adolescents are more introverted or are late social bloomers and that's okay, too. Just check it out with them. If they seem afraid or like they want to go but are nervous that it won't go well, that's different.

There are other times when they may have a bad feeling about an upcoming party or a particular group of kids. I remember a moment with one of my daughters when we were new in town and she'd been invited to a big party. She had gotten a present and a dress, but just before the event she told me she wasn't going. She'd always been pretty comfortable in social situations so I wasn't entirely sure what was up. I pushed her to go because I felt that it was in poor form to bail after committing, but she was firm so eventually I let her stay home. It turned out to be a wild party and kids got in all kinds of trouble. Even the parents who gave the party got into trouble! If your teenager has a bad feeling about something, let them listen to it. They probably know more about what they're getting into than you do. But if it seems like there isn't a specific reason, encourage your teens to try smaller interactions at different times. In this way, they take on trials of socializing. Avoid excessive praise for their progress, as teens don't want to *feel* that they are different from their peers or struggling socially.

Signs of Anxiety

When your child demonstrates excessive anxiety and worry on more days than not, they might be struggling with more anxiety than is typical for their age group. The *Diagnostic and Statistical Manual of Mental Disorders* suggests consulting a professional if the symptoms in the following list are present for over six months, but I recommend a consultation any time these symptoms continue to resurface. If you notice a pattern, go with your instinct. Six months is a long time in a teen's life; we don't want to let these symptoms go unchecked for longer than necessary.[24]

- Consistent, unrealistic anxiety and worry about several things in their life, and an inability to control feelings of anxiety and worry.
- Feelings of restlessness, difficulty sitting still, perception of being on edge.
- Fatigue or a tendency to tire easily.
- Difficulty concentrating.
- Feelings of irritability.
- Feelings of tension; aching and soreness in muscles.
- Difficulty falling asleep and/or staying asleep.
- Anxiety or worry causes significant distress or impairs social, academic, or extracurricular performance.
- Panic attacks, feelings that they might faint or have a heart attack, sweatiness, trembling, numbness, difficulty breathing.

Figure 8.1 demonstrates the overlap of symptoms common to both depression and anxiety. In certain cases, these disorders can present similarly. The most important thing is to seek treatment when these symptoms are present.

Eating Disorders

High school is a common time for adolescents to develop eating disorders, as the stress from academics, the college process, and social pressure are at an all-time high. The need to fit in and be accepted can trigger insecurities that lead to abnormal behavior around food. An **eating disorder** is best defined as an overwhelming desire to be thin or an irrational fear of weight gain. Research has found that over half of teenage girls and nearly one-third of teenage boys

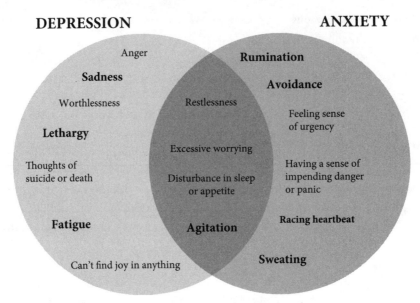

DEPRESSION   ANXIETY

Anger

Sadness

Worthlessness   Restlessness

Lethargy

Excessive worrying

Thoughts of
suicide or death   Disturbance in sleep
or appetite

Fatigue   **Agitation**

Can't find joy in anything

Rumination

Avoidance

Feeling sense
of urgency

Having a sense of
impending danger
or panic

Racing heartbeat

Sweating

FIGURE 8.1. Shared vs. Distinct Symptoms of Depression and Anxiety

use unhealthy methods to control their weight. These can include crash diets, vomiting, fasting, excessive exercise, and even laxatives or diet pills.[25] Obsessive or excessive exercise has become more common in recent years, particularly among college-age females. The newest fad gaining popularity for rapid weight loss is cryotherapy, a treatment for physical ailments that claims to burn up to 800 calories per session.

An eating disorder is especially detrimental in adolescence because there is such crucial neurological and biological development taking place. If a teenager is crash-dieting or exercising excessively, their body perceives this as starvation and focuses only on survival, letting other processes of development go by the wayside. Eating disorders exacerbate anxiety, depression, social isolation, and low self-esteem. It's very difficult to help a person get better if they are nutritionally compromised; we have to address that issue first because that's where the brain will remain focused in order to survive.

Different eating disorders present different behaviors and symptoms. Two of the most common eating disorders are anorexia nervosa and bulimia nervosa. An individual who suffers from **anorexia** may have a distorted body image, low body weight, or endocrine disturbance.[26] Excessive restriction results in malnutrition, which causes the brain to shrink over time and the receptors within the brain to change. Anorexia is difficult to treat with medication and it's particularly bad for adolescents because it slows their thinking, impairs their concentration, and lowers their comprehension. Signs and behaviors to watch for include hiding or discarding food, altered self-image, obsessive calorie counting or restriction, denial of hunger, obsessive rituals around food preparation or eating, avoidance of eating around others, compulsive or excessive exercise, hair loss, skin discoloration, pronounced emotional changes, irritability, abnormal menstrual cycle, exhaustion, dizziness, or fainting.

An individual who suffers from **bulimia** may also have a distorted body image but will binge-eat and then purge through vomiting or misuse of laxatives.[27] The misleading thing about bulimia is that purging is not an effective method for eliminating calories.[28] Yet, the individual is wreaking havoc on their system. The physical impact can include burst blood vessels, tooth decay, throat swelling, and hemorrhoids, among others. Signs to watch for include eating unusually large amounts of food with no apparent weight gain; hiding food, wrappers, or packages; frequent trips to the bathroom after meals; impulsive behaviors; frequently clogged showers or toilets; bad breath; vomit-like odor; discolored teeth; stomach pain; fatigue or weakness; and irregular or absent menstrual cycles.

Orthorexia is worth mentioning as it has become more common, and health and wellness are more mainstream topics now. It's hard to scroll through Instagram without seeing several feeds full of green juices, salads, and fit selfies. Orthorexia is considered to be an unhealthy obsession with healthy eating. It includes behaviors such as the restriction of cheeseburgers and nachos or other "junk" foods, a preoccupation with nutrients and quantities, and/or obsessive meal-planning. These behaviors can reach isolating extremes. Orthorexia is a particularly common eating disorder among men. Boys who restrict their food intake obsessively will often show low levels of testosterone and vitamin D, which can then result in depression. Often, additional conditions such as depression and anxiety underlie these behaviors, so it's important that any treatment plan address these core issues.[29]

There is undoubtedly a connection between the notion of a "perfect body" and eating disorders, but we don't have a consensus on a single root cause. For many teenagers, disordered eating is a coping mechanism to deal with stress and anxiety. Eating disorders can result from behavioral, biological, or social factors including peer pressure, bullying, low self-esteem, genetics, and association with others who suffer from an eating disorder. Dietary restriction can be an expression of perfectionism, asceticism, or competitiveness. The behaviors can spiral out of control and the physical and emotional impact, whether the disorder presents as anorexia or binge eating, can be severe.[30]

It's important for parents to be aware of their own behavior around food or around their kids' food. Some parents who have unhealthy relationships to food struggle to establish healthy eating habits in their house. Remember: There's a difference between what you eat and how you eat. Eating is often a social behavior. My sons give me a hard time if we go out to dinner and I order a salad. At times, it offends them if I don't participate in sharing plates or enjoying a special meal together. It's okay for you to make healthy choices, but your kids will notice if you abstain or constantly restrict yourself. They are so susceptible to these cues. Adolescent girls, in particular, receive all kinds of messaging that they need to watch what they eat and lose weight. Boys, too, might feel pressure to "make weight" or slim down for a particular position on an athletic team. Wrestling is notorious for this, because athletes will go to drastic measures to make their weight class. It's not worth it; severe calorie restriction impacts physical performance, as well as mental capacity. We want to emphasize that food is fuel for the brain and body; it's not just calories.

I've also worked with several female athletes who struggle to balance the physical demands of their sport and their desire for the "perfect body." It's very common to see a girl playing a sport at the high school or college level who struggles to keep up because she isn't properly fueling her body or doesn't want to get "too strong." For female athletes in particular, their desire to succeed in their sport can actually be somewhat therapeutic, because it becomes a sacrifice they aren't willing to make. One of my clients began to develop anorexic behaviors over her junior year of high school. By her senior year, the stress of the college process, her desire to look good, her athletic endeavors, and parental pressure were completely overwhelming her, and her eating disorder spiraled out of control. She told me that initially, her friends and family told her that she looked good, so she began to restrict her intake even more severely. Her hair began to fall out, she struggled to concentrate in class, her grades slipped, and she couldn't keep up athletically. She was very resistant to the idea that she had an eating disorder, so much so that she isolated the friends who approached her with genuine concern. In adolescence, appearance is tied into identity and self-esteem, so these behaviors are difficult to unwind, but it's crucial to address as early as possible. A medical and/or psychological professional can help devise a plan for recovery.

Eating disorders are difficult to diagnose because the person afflicted may appear to be a normal weight. People often judge physical appearance when it's really about the habit or the behavior. Teens can be secretive and demonstrate typical eating habits in front of others, but on their own, they are purging, vomiting, binging, or exercising excessively. If you feel that your teen has an abnormal relationship with food, it's important to have them assessed by a professional. Seek medical and/or therapeutic help when you see, along with disordered eating habits, any associated depression, anxiety, or compulsive behavior. They will deny that they have an eating disorder, so simply asking your teenager is not enough. If you notice restrictive behavior at certain times or around certain people, it's a signal that there's an issue you need to address. This behavior is usually a reaction to a problem, so look for patterns or triggers. Is it a cover for social anxiety, is it helping them fit in, or do they feel out of control? Food is a good dissociator—it can divert attention from stress or anxiety. It might help to ask other parents to ask their kids, because a teenager's peers often notice these behaviors first and have a better idea of what's really going on.

In a society that places high value on appearance, parents are often in denial about their own child's problem. It's extremely important to seek professional guidance because eating disorders are difficult to control. They tend to recur throughout life until the underlying causes are addressed. A multidisciplinary and gender-sensitive approach is best; this can include individual and family therapy, psychiatric evaluation, medical treatment, and nutritional assistance. The National Eating Disorder Association helpline can be reached by texting NEDA to 741741.

Suicide

We are seeing a lot in today's media about adolescent suicide, so it's important to look at the numbers to understand the facts. Suicide rates have increased in recent years, but it is still a rare occurrence. Adolescent suicide is the third leading cause of adolescent death in the United States behind automobile accidents and homicide; 15% to 25% of adolescents think about suicide, and there are 15 to 20 nonfatal attempts for every completed suicide.[31] However, most adolescents who commit suicide have been suffering for a while. The main risk factors for adolescent suicide include a previous attempt, an underlying mood disorder, and substance abuse. **Most importantly, one of the most consistent predictors of an adolescent suicide is a firearm in the house.[32] Over the past decade, the rate of firearm suicide among children and teens has risen by 61 percent.[33]** This is not a political statement, it is simply a fact. Most completed suicides for adolescents include a firearm and consumption of alcohol. Adolescents who attempt suicide and survive almost always regret the attempt, but there is no margin of error with a bullet.[34] If you have a firearm in your house, you need to have it locked securely and be inaccessible to your teenager. It is a safety issue that could mean the difference between life and death for your child.

Suicidal thinking is a symptom that something is wrong. When we know that somebody is having suicidal thoughts, we look for what is wrong. It's difficult to eradicate suicidal thinking because we can never be entirely sure that we have eliminated the risk. We don't treat suicidal thinking; we manage suicidal thinking. We want to be extremely careful around suicide with teenagers. It's shockingly common to see families who won't address a child's depression or threat to themselves because of their moral or religious beliefs about suicide. Adolescents are impulsive; remember that their internal chemistry is extremely volatile and they are not always able to access their rational brain functions. If you suspect or fear that your child is contemplating suicide, ask them in a straightforward way if they have considered taking their own life. If they tell you that they have or if they planned to at one point in time, seek professional help. Likewise, if your child demonstrates signs of depression or shows an increase in risk-taking behavior, a disengagement from their life, or an abnormal obsession with dark topics, seek professional help. (Also, see Box 8.2 for a discussion of adolescent self-harm.)

We need to work against the idea that suicide is a common or natural response to depression, social isolation, bullying, and other triggers we might see on television or read about in the news.[35] Your child will watch how you respond to suicide, so be wary of what you say on the topic. It can be difficult for teens to grasp the permanence and irrevocability of suicide. Talk to your child about the concept of death and being "gone," not to be morbid, but to make sure they understand the severity of such an action. For adolescents, who are experiencing a changing chemistry and its highs and lows for the first time, we want to reiterate that suicide is not a viable option. It doesn't ever solve a problem; there is always another solution. We want the message our children receive to be that suicide is a tragedy that devastates families, friends, and communities.

It's also important to reiterate that suicide is never the fault of another person. If someone completes suicide, whether or not they suffered from a chemical imbalance or mental illness, it was the only option they could consider at the time. It can often be hard for families to make sense of suicide after the fact and it is always unbearably sad, but in the moment, the person who takes their own life didn't see any other way out of their pain.

It's incredibly difficult to discuss suicide with your teenagers but, unfortunately, it's likely they know somebody who has been affected by suicide,

---

BOX 8.2

Self-Injury

Self-harming behaviors are becoming more common among the adolescent population. Cutting, or scratching the skin with anything that can draw blood, qualifies as self-injury. This behavior is more frequent in girls, but many adolescent boys also self-harm.

Self-harming is an attempt at communication or is used as a maladaptive coping tool. Kids rely on it to deal with their painful feelings. Many describe that the actual cut provides relief. I have had clients describe cutting as punishment for something they feel bad about, while others say that the pain allows them to feel something. It can be a reaction when a teen feels rejection, extremely low self-esteem, and/or isolation.

It's important for parents to be aware of the signs of cutting, which include:

- Talking about self-injury
- Suspicious-looking scars that they explain with odd, incongruent excuses
- Wearing long-sleeved shirts or pants in warm weather
- Increased isolation/withdrawal

If your teenager is harming themselves, it's important to seek professional medical and/or psychological help as soon as possible.

---

even if peripherally. Share your feelings with your teenager and allow them to share theirs with you. These honest and emotional conversations can build a bridge with your adolescents and allow you to develop a meaningful connection with them. There doesn't always need to be a lesson or a solution in these conversations. It's powerful to share in the pain and discomfort.

MANY PEOPLE LIVE with depression and anxiety in manageable ways. These imbalances can fluctuate over a lifetime—symptoms will be worse at some time than they are at others. I encourage you as parents of teenagers to have a low threshold for seeking professional or medical advice. Be vigilant. It is not your job to pretend your child is perfect. When in doubt, go ahead and ask for help. Your job is to oversee your child's development, and both depression and anxiety disorder can impede them significantly.

Consider This:
Insights & Actions

- Knowing that adolescence is a time of high absorption and neurological activity, we can tap into their creativity and help shape their ability to problem solve. As parents, we can encourage our teens to think for themselves and imagine the various directions they can go in, asking questions such as "What would you try next time?" or "What might you have done differently to produce a different outcome?"

- When your child opens up to you about feelings of anxiety, be careful not to dismiss their worry as insignificant or temporary. If you start a sentence with "In my day," you may as well not finish it. You want your adolescent to feel understood, seen, and heard. Listen to their worries and help them construct an approach for tackling what they are afraid of. Don't dismiss or diminish what troubles them. Validation is important in and of itself. Just hear them.

- If your child can identify what they are worried about, ask them: What's the *worst* thing that could happen? Then ask them, how likely is it? Naming the worst case scenario empowers us to feel that, even if our fears were realized, we would most likely survive. Then make a plan so that they feel the worst case scenario is unlikely to unfold, and move down the line from there. What's the worst? What's the second worst? Then test these against reality. Is this likely to happen? If it does, can you live with that?

- Avoid avoiding. As soon as we take one small action toward a big task, it diminishes the scope of what is ahead of us and helps us to feel that we can accomplish what we need to do. Once you've helped your teen break down what needs to be done, encourage them to take on the first small task. Post-its or lists are great because there is empowerment in crossing something off. Momentum is key.

- If anxiety and worry are keeping your teen from falling asleep, help them establish a nightly routine to calm their nervous system before bed. Make them a cup of warm milk, urge them to read a fun or fantastical novel, or allow them to play soothing music in their bedroom. Ritual is calming and makes us feel safe and in control.

Notes

1. Erikson, E. H. (1963). *Childhood and society.* New York, NY: W. W. Norton. (Original work published 1950)

2. Erikson, E. H. (1963) *Childhood and society*. New York, NY: W. W. Norton. (Original work published 1950)

3. Levine, M. (2008). *The price of privilege: How parental pressure and material advantage are creating a generation of disconnected and unhappy kids*. New York, NY: HarperCollins.

4. Twenge, J. M. (2017). *iGen: Why today's super-connected kids are growing up less rebellious, more tolerant, less happy—and completely unprepared for adulthood—and what that means for the rest of us*. New York, NY: Atria.

5. Dweck, C. S. (2006). *Mindset: The new psychology of success*. New York, NY: Random House.

6. Dweck, C. S. (2006). *Mindset: The new psychology of success*. New York, NY: Random House.

7. Erikson, E. H. (1963). *Childhood and society*. New York, NY: W. W. Norton. (Original work published 1950)

8. Sugarman, J. (2017, Fall/Winter). The rise of teen depression. *Johns Hopkins Health Review, 4*(2). Retrieved from https://www.johnshopkinshealthreview.com/issues/fall-winter-2017/articles/the-rise-of-teen-depression; Data Resource Center for Child & Adolescent Health. (n.d.). The National Survey of Children's Health. Retrieved from https://www.childhealthdata.org/learn-about-the-nsch/NSCH; Heid, M. (2019, March 14). Depression and suicide rates are rising sharply in young Americans, new report says. This may be one reason why. *Time*. Retrieved from http://time.com/5550803/depression-suicide-rates-youth/

9. Mental Health America. (n.d.). 2017 state of mental health in America—youth data. Retrieved from http://www.mentalhealthamerica.net/issues/2017-state-mental-health-america-youth-data

10. Nock, et. al. , M. K., Gren, J. G., Hwang, I., McLaughlin, K. A., Sampson, N. A., Zaslavsky, A. M., & Kessler, R. C. (2013). Prevalence, correlates, and treatment of lifetime suicidal behavior among adolescents: Results from the National Comorbidity Survey Replication Adolescent Supplement. *JAMA Psychiatry, 70* (3), 300–310. doi: 10.1001/2013.jamapsychiatry.55.

11. World Health Organization. (2018, September 18). Adolescent mental health. Retrieved from https://www.who.int/news-room/fact-sheets/detail/adolescent-mental-health

12. Miller, C. (n.d.). Mental health disorders and teen substance use. Child Mind Institute. Retrieved from https://childmind.org/article/mental-health-disorders-and-substance-use

13. Verduyn, C., Rogers, J., & Wood, A. (2009). *Depression: Cognitive behaviour therapy with children and young people*. New York, NY: Routledge.

14. Auerbach, R. P. (2015). *Depression, impulsivity, and suicide prevention*. Harvard Medical School Symposium: Middle School Through College Mental Health and Education.

15. Jensen, F. E., & Nutt, A. E. (2015). *The teenage brain: A neuroscientist's survival guide to raising adolescents and young adults*. New York, NY: HarperCollins.

16. American Psychiatric Association. (2013). *Desk reference to the diagnostic criteria from DSM-5*. Arlington, VA: Author.

17. Szymanski, J. (2017). *Anxiety disorders and OCD*. Harvard Medical School Symposium: Middle School Through College Mental Health and Education.

18. Harvard Medical School Symposium: Middle School Through College Mental Health and Education (2015).

19. Szymanski, J. (2017). *Anxiety disorders and OCD*. Harvard Medical School Symposium: Middle School Through College Mental Health and Education.

20. Stallard, P. (2009). *Anxiety: Cognitive behavior therapy with children and young people*. New York, NY: Routledge.

21. Stahl, S. M., & Moore, B. A. (Eds.). (2013). *Anxiety disorders: A guide for integrating psychopharmacology and psychotherapy*. New York, NY: Routledge.

22. Crone, E. (2017). *The adolescent brain: Changes in learning, decision making, and social relations*. New York, NY: Routledge.

23. Jensen, F. E., & Nutt, A. E. (2015). *The teenage brain: A neuroscientist's survival guide to raising adolescents and young adults*. New York, NY: HarperCollins.

24. American Psychiatric Association. (2013). *Desk reference to the diagnostic criteria from DSM-5*. Arlington, VA: Author.

25. Gowers, S. G., & Green, L. (2009). *Eating disorders: Cognitive behavior therapy with children, adolescents, and families*. New York, NY: Routledge.

26. Wachter, A. (2016). *Getting over overeating: A workbook to transform your relationship with food using CBT, mindfulness, and intuitive eating*. Oakland, CA: New Harbinger Publications.

27. Wachter, A. (2016). *Getting over overeating: A workbook to transform your relationship with food using CBT, mindfulness, and intuitive eating*. Oakland, CA: New Harbinger Publications.

28. Marks, J. (2018, October 16). Bulimia 101: What you need to know about this common eating disorder. *Everyday Health*. Retrieved from https://www.everydayhealth.com/bulimia-nervosa/guide

29. Varga, M., Konkolÿ Thege, B., Dukay-Szabó, S., Túry, F., & van Furth, E. F. (2014). When eating healthy is not healthy: Orthorexia nervosa and its measurement with the ORTO-15 in Hungary. *BMC Psychiatry, 14,* 59. doi:10.1186/1471-244X-14-59

30. Gowers, S. G., & Green, L. (2009). *Eating disorders: Cognitive behavior therapy with children, adolescents, and families*. New York, NY: Routledge.

31. Schlozman, S. C. (2017, November). Depression and suicide. Harvard Medical School Symposium: Middle School Through College Mental Health & Education, Cambridge, MA. Course directors include Joseph Gold, Stephanie Pinder-Amaker, Mona P. Potter, Bryan C. Pridgen, and Christopher M. Palmer.

32. Schlozman, S. C. (2017, November). Depression and suicide. Harvard Medical School Symposium: Middle School Through College Mental Health & Education,

Cambridge, MA. Course directors include Joseph Gold, Stephanie Pinder-Amaker, Mona P. Potter, Bryan C. Pridgen, and Christopher M. Palmer.

33. Centers for Disease Control and Prevention, National Center for Injury Prevention and Control. (2019). Welcome to WISQARS.™ Retrieved from https://www.cdc.gov/injury/wisqars/index.html. WISQARS = Web-Based Injury Statistics Query and Reporting System. A yearly average was developed using 5 years of most recent available data: 2012–2016. Children and teens were defined as 0 to 19.

34. Schlozman, S. (2017). *Resilience in youth.* Harvard Medical School Symposium: Middle School Through College Mental Health and Education.

35. Coloroso, B. (2003). *The bully, the bullied, and the bystander: From preschool to highschool—How parents and teachers can help break the cycle.* New York, NY: William Morrow.

Conclusion

SO, WHERE DO we go from here?

As we've discussed, adolescence is difficult for parents because they feel they are losing the struggle for control. This is inevitable. Your adolescent wants to be in the driver's seat now—they want to take control over their own life, and they will be so much better off if you support them and guide them in doing so instead of battling them for the reins. I hope this book has convinced you.

Part of a parent's task is grappling with the idea—which is intimidating and even painful—that we can't control what happens to our children. As hard as we may try, we can't protect them from everything that could go wrong in their lives. Instead, we want to equip them to tackle those obstacles on their own by creating the structure within which they will learn to take responsibility for themselves. It's not easy, but the shift from control to connection will free you to be on your adolescent's side as they develop into an independent person. When you're in a partnership with your child, they will respect you and listen to you instead of take you on as an opponent. As Harvard psychiatrist Dr. Hallowell says for difficult times: "In connection we stand a better chance. We do not have to flee. We can hold our ground against the tide that always wants to wash us away. In connecting to other people, to great causes or small moments, we can sink our ankles into the sand against the constant undertow of loss and pain."[1]

Try to pull back and take the long-term view as much as possible. Your job is to shape and mold the human being that this energetic, curious, and creative individual will become. Curfews and driving privileges and SAT scores and athletic statistics are all pieces of the puzzle, but don't get too caught up in any one of them. Focus on teaching your teenager how to have positive social interactions, how to behave, and how to delay gratification. Focus on your child's strengths and show them that you're confident in their ability to find satisfaction in their endeavors and in themselves. The way you will do this is by using the strategies in this book to put a solid foundation under your child that will support and sustain them through their lifetime.

Martin E. P. Seligman has a theory that states that wellbeing is comprised of five elements: positive emotion, engagement, relationships, meaning, and achievement. As you now know, adolescence is the phase of life during which these elements are put into place. If we focus our effort on encouraging and building these components in our children, we will build more sustainable, resilient, and healthy individuals. An adolescent with a solid foundation under them will be able to recognize where they have choice and will be in a position to take advantage of those moments and make positive decisions. Where they will live, what they will do for work, who they will spend their time with, and the issues they will care about are really a sum of the choices they make. How they adapt and adjust to life's ups and downs, and their capacity for flexibility, will determine the depth of joy they find in their lives. When all is said and done, our choices become our lives, and how we make our choices determines how we live our lives.

We are constantly reading negative reports of today's youth—millennials and members of iGen—describing a generation that is ill equipped for the workplace, that lacks the resilience of previous generations, and that expects everything to be handed to them. I don't agree with these generalizations. In working with today's adolescents every day, I find them to be engaged, eager to connect, and hoping to build a satisfying life. But moreover, whose children are they? Ultimately, the responsibility falls back to the parents. We have raised this generation and we will raise the next one. We, as parents, are in a position to make a profound impact and initiate lasting change in the world. If we raise a generation of adolescents who enjoy deep and long-term wellbeing, think of how the world will look then.

A final note: Psychologist John Bowlby says that parenting will not work if the parent does not derive joy from the endeavor.[2] I love working with adolescents. They are engaged, vulnerable, creative, and eager to please. When we take a step back, we can see the privilege of raising these incredibly raw, developing people. If you can find the joy and the humor in parenting adolescents, your role as a parent will be the source of immense and lasting gratification. Control has a right and a wrong, a winner and a loser—or more often, losers all around. Connection is about lasting meaning, engagement, and relationship. As soon as you have an end point, you lose the dialogue, you lose the connection, and you end up with an antagonistic framework.

It's the good news and the bad news: Your job as a parent never ends. You want to be in a position to enjoy watching your children take life on independently. You also want to have a relationship in place so that they will seek your guidance, and it will be incredibly gratifying when they do. When you form a connection with your child, it will grow, expand, and strengthen through every phase of life.

Notes

1. Hallowell, E. M. (1999). *Connect: 12 vital ties that open your heart, lengthen your life, and deepen your soul.* New York, NY: Pantheon Books.
2. Bowlby, J. (1969). *Attachment and loss, Vol. I* (2nd ed.). New York, NY: Basic Books.

Acknowledgments

They say there is no substitute for experience, so I would like to thank my four children for providing me with endless and invaluable opportunities to practice what I preach.

Thank you to Dana Bliss and his incredible team at Oxford University Press for their support of this book.

Thank you to Shay Pantano for her ongoing guidance and encouragement.

Thank you to Dr. Habib Sadeghi for his belief in this mission and in me, and for writing a powerful foreword to this book.

And most importantly, this project would never have come to fruition without Julia Ireland. Her writing and editing skills were as strong as her devotion to the work.

References

Ahrons, C. (2004). *We're still family: What grown children have to say about their parents' divorce*. New York, NY: HarperCollins.

Aiken, M. (2016). *Cybereffect: An expert in cyberpsychology explains how technology is shaping our children, our behavior, and our values—and what we can do about it*. New York, NY: Spiegel & Grau.

Altman, D. (2014). *The mindfulness toolbox, 50 practical tips, tools, and handouts for anxiety, depression, stress, and pain*. Eau Claire, WI: PESI Publishing & Media.

Ambron, S. R. (1978). *Child development* (3rd ed.). New York, NY: Holt, Rinehart and Winston.

American Psychiatric Association. (2013). *Desk reference to the Diagnostic Criteria from DSM-5*. Arlington, VA: Author.

Barkley, R. A. (2013). *Taking charge of ADHD: The complete, authoritative guide for parents* (3rd ed.). New York, NY: Guilford Press.

Barkley, R. A., & Robin, A. L. (2014). *Defiant teens: A clinician's manual for assessment and family intervention* (2nd ed.). New York, NY: Guilford Press.

Berlin, I. N., & Stone, L. A. (Eds.). (1979). *The basic handbook of child psychiatry* (Vol. 4). New York, NY: Basic Books.

Blos, P. (1962). *On adolescence: A psychoanalytic interpretation*. New York, NY: The Free Press.

Bowlby, J. (1969). *Attachment and loss, Vol. I* (2nd ed.). New York, NY: Basic Books.

Brand, S., & Kirov, R. (2011). Sleep and its importance in adolescence and in common adolescent somatic and psychiatric conditions. *International Journal of General Medicine, 4*, 425–442. doi:10.2147/IJGM.S11557

Brick, J., & Erickson, C. K. (1998). *Drugs, the brain, and behavior: The pharmacology of drug use disorders* (2nd ed.). New York, NY: Routledge.

Brooks, D. (2015). *The road to character*. New York, NY: Penguin Random House.

Brown, B. (2012). *Daring greatly: How the courage to be vulnerable transforms the way we live, love, parent, and lead*. New York, NY: Gotham Books.

Brown, Stuart M. (2009). *Play: How it shapes the brain, opens the imagination, and invigorates the soul.* New York, NY: Avery.

Call, J. D., Noshpitz, J. D., Cohen, R. L., & Berlin, I. N. (Eds.). (1979). *The basic handbook of child psychiatry* (Vol. 1). New York, NY: Basic Books.

Campbell, I. G., Kraus, A. M., Burright, C. S., & Feinberg, I. (2016). Restricting time in bed in early adolescence reduces both NREM and REM sleep but does not increase slow wave EEG. *Sleep, 39*(9), 1663–1670. doi:10.5665/sleep.6088

Caplan, G., & Lebovici, S. (Eds.). *Adolescence: Perspectives.* (1969). New York, NY: Basic Books.

Casey, B. J., Jones, R. M., & Hare, T. A. (2008). The adolescent brain. *Annals of the New York Academy of Sciences, 1124,* 111–126. doi:10.1196/annals.1440.010

Coles, R. (1997). *The moral intelligence of children: How to raise a moral child.* New York, NY: Penguin.

Collins, K. P., & Cleary, S. D. (2016). Racial and ethnic disparities in parent-reported diagnosis of ADHD: National Survey of Children's Health (2003, 2007, and 2011). *Journal of Clinical Psychiatry, 77*(1), 52–59. doi:10.4088/JCP.14m09364

Coloroso, B. (2003). *The bully, the bullied, and the bystander: From preschool to high school—How parents and teachers can help break the cycle.* New York, NY: William Morrow.

Cozolino, L. (2006). *The neuroscience of human relationships. Attachment and the developing social brain.* New York, NY: W. W. Norton.

Crone, E. (2017). *The adolescent brain: Changes in learning, decision making, and social relations.* New York, NY: Routledge.

Csikszentmihalyi, M. (1997). *Finding flow. The psychology of engagement with everyday life.* New York, NY: Basic Books.

Damour, L. (2017, March 8). Teenagers do dumb things, but there are ways to limit recklessness. *New York Times.* Retrieved from http://nyti.ms/2m1xHkB

Duckworth, A. (2016). *Grit: The power of passion and perseverance.* New York, NY: Scribner.

Dweck, C. S. (2006). *Mindset: The new psychology of success.* New York, NY: Random House.

Dwyer, J. B., McQuown, S. C., & Leslie, F. M. (2009). The dynamic effects of nicotine on the developing brain. *Pharmacology and Therapeutics, 122,* 125–139.

Erikson, E. H. (1963). *Childhood and society.* New York, NY: W. W. Norton. (Original work published 1950)

Essau, C. A., & Petermann, F. (Eds.). (2001). *Anxiety disorders in children and adolescents: Epidemiology, risk factors, and treatment.* New York, NY: Taylor & Francis.

Faber, A., & Mazlish, E. (2012). *How to talk so kids will listen and listen so kids will talk.* New York, NY: Scribner.

Fonagy, P., Target, M., Cottrell, D., Phillips, J., & Kurtz, Z. (2002). *What works for whom? A critical review of treatments for children and adolescents.* New York, NY: Guilford Press.

Garbarino, J., & deLara, E. (2002). *And words can hurt forever: How to protect adolescents from bullying, harassment, and emotional violence.* New York, NY: The Free Press.

Gardner, H. (2006). *Five minds for the future.* Boston, MA: Harvard Business School Publishing.

Gardner, H., & Davis, K. (2013). *The app generation: How today's youth navigate identity, intimacy, and imagination in a digital world.* New Haven, CT: Yale University Press.

Gauld, L., & Gauld, M. (2002). *The biggest job you'll ever have: Find the right balance between character and achievement for your child.* New York, NY: Scribner.

Gazzaley, A., & Rosen, L. D. (2016). *The distracted mind: Ancient brains in a high-tech world.* Cambridge, MA: MIT Press.

Gladwell, M. (2009). *What the dog saw: And other adventures.* New York, NY: Little, Brown.

Gladwell, M. (2015). *David and Goliath: Underdogs, misfits, and the art of battling giants.* New York, NY: Little, Brown.

Gowers, S. G., & Green, L. (2009). *Eating disorders: Cognitive behavior therapy with children, adolescents, and families.* New York, NY: Routledge.

Hall, E. (1982), and Lamb, M. E, & Perlmutter, M. (Advisory Eds.). *Child psychology today.* New York, NY: Random House.

Hallowell, E. M. (1999). *Connect: 12 vital ties that open your heart, lengthen your life, and deepen your soul.* New York, NY: Pantheon Books.

Hallowell, E. M. (2002). *The childhood roots of adult happiness. Five steps to help kids create and sustain lifelong joy.* New York, NY: Ballantine Books.

Hallowell, E. M., & Ratey, J. J. (1994). *Answers to distraction.* New York, NY: Pantheon Books.

Healy, J. M. (1990). *Endangered minds: Why children don't think and what we can do about it.* New York, NY: Touchstone.

Healy, J. M. (1998). *Failure to connect: How computers affect our children's minds—and what we can do about it.* New York, NY: Simon & Schuster.

Healy, J. M. (2010). *Different learners: Identifying, preventing, and treating your child's learning problems.* New York, NY: Simon & Schuster.

Himelstein, R. (2013, September 10). Teen heroin use: An unfortunate reality. *The Inquirer.* Retrieved from http://www.philly.com/philly/blogs/healthy_kids/Teen-heroin-use-an-unfortunate-reality.html

Hindle, D., & Sherwin-White, S. (Eds.). (2014). *Sibling matters: A psychoanalytic, developmental, and systemic approach.* London, UK: Karnac Books.

Hoffman, J. (2014, June 23). Cool at 13, adrift at 23. *The New York Times.* Retrieved from https://well.blogs.nytimes.com/2014/06/23/cool-at-13-adrift-at-23/

Homayoun, A. (2018, January 17). Is your child a phone "addict"? *New York Times*. Retrieved from https://www.nytimes.com/2018/01/17/well/family/is-your-child-a-phone-addict.html

Huit, Z. T., Holt, N. R., & Hope, D. A. (2018). Enhancing queer and transgender resilience: Review of a self-help workbook. *The Behavior Therapist, 41*(8), 353–354.

Hummer, D., & Lee, T. (2016). Daily timing of the adolescent sleep phase: Insights from a cross-species comparison. *Neuroscience & Biobehavioral Reviews, 70,* 171–181.

Hunt, P. S., Burk, J. A., & Barnet, R. C. (2016). Adolescent transitions in reflexive and non-reflexive behavior: Review of fear conditioning and impulse control in rodent models. *Neuroscience and Biobehavioral Reviews, 70,* 33–45. doi:10.1016/j.neubiorev.2016.06.026

Jensen, F. E., & Nutt, A. E. (2015). *The teenage brain: A neuroscientist's survival guide to raising adolescents and young adults.* New York, NY: HarperCollins.

Kennaway, D. J. (2015). Potential safety issues in the use of the hormone melatonin in paediatrics. *Journal of Paediatrics and Child Health, 51*(6), 584–589. doi:10.1111/jpc.12840

Kestenbaum, C. J., & Williams, D. T. (Eds.). (1988). *Handbook of clinical assessment of children and adolescents* (Vols. I & II). New York, NY: New York University Press.

Kilford, E. J., Garrett, E., & Blakemore, S.-J. (2016). The development of social cognition in adolescence: An integrated perspective. *Neuroscience and Behavioral Reviews, 70,* 106–120. doi:10.1016/j.neubiorev.2016.08.016

Kindlon, D., & Thompson, M. (2000). *Raising Cain: Protecting the emotional life of boys.* New York, NY: Ballantine Books.

Lee, K. A., Mcenany, G., & Weekes, D. (1998). Gender differences in sleep patterns for early adolescents. *Journal of Adolescent Health, 24*(1), 16–20. doi:10.1016/S1054-139X(98)00074-3

Levine, M. (2003). *The myth of laziness.* New York, NY: Simon & Schuster.

Levine, M. (2005). *Ready or not, here life comes.* New York, NY: Simon & Schuster.

Levine, M. (2008). *The price of privilege: How parental pressure and material advantage are creating a generation of disconnected and unhappy kids.* New York, NY: HarperCollins.

Levitt, S. D., & Dubner, S. J. (2009). *Freakonomics: A rogue economist explores the hidden side of everything.* New York, NY: HarperCollins.

Lichtenberg, J., Bornstein, M., & Silver, D. (1984). (Eds.). *Empathy I.* New York, NY: Routledge.

Mah, C. D., Mah, K. E., Kezirian, E. J., & Dement, W. C. (2011). The effects of sleep extension on the athletic performance of collegiate basketball players. *Sleep, 34*(7), 943–950. doi:10.5665/SLEEP. 1132

Marston, S. (1990). *The magic of encouragement: Nurturing your child's self-esteem.* New York, NY: William Morrow.

Midgley, N., & Vrouva, I. (Eds.). (2012). *Minding the child: Mentalization-based interventions with children, young people, and their families.* New York, NY: Routledge.

Nock, M. K., Gren, J. G., Hwang, I., McLaughlin, K. A., Sampson, N. A., Zaslavsky, A. M., & Kessler, R. C. (2013). Prevalence, correlates, and treatment of lifetime suicidal behavior among adolescents: Results from the National Comorbidity Survey Replication Adolescent Supplement. *JAMA Psychiatry, 70*(3), 300–310. doi:10.1001/2013.jamapsychiatry.55

Norsigian, J. (2005). *Our bodies, ourselves: The Boston women's health book collective* (4th ed.). New York, NY: Touchstone.

Olmedo, P., Goessler, W., Tanda, S., Grau-Perez, M., Jarmul, S., Aherrera, A., . . . Rule, A. M. (2018). Metal concentrations in e-cigarette liquid and aerosol samples: The contribution of metallic coils. *Environmental Health Perspectives, 126*(2). doi:10.1289/EHP2175

Paruthi, S., Brooks, L. J., D'Ambrosio, C., Hall, W. A., Kotagal, S., Lloyd, R. M., . . . Wise, M. S. (2016). Recommended amount of sleep for pediatric populations: A consensus statement of the American academy of sleep medicine. *Journal of Clinical Sleep Medicine, 12*(6), 785–786. doi:10.5664/jcsm.5866

Piaget, J. (1932). *The language and thought of the child* (2nd ed.). London, UK: Kegan Paul, Trench, Trubner & Co.

Pink, D. H. (2005). *A whole new mind. Moving from the information age to the conceptual age.* New York, NY: Riverhead Publishers.

Pipher, M. (1994). *Reviving Ophelia: Saving the selves of adolescent girls.* New York, NY: Berkley.

Rimm, S. (1996). *How to parent so children will learn.* New York, NY: Three Rivers Press.

Rosenberg, M. (1965). *Society and the adolescent self-image.* Princeton, NJ: Princeton University Press.

Satir, V. (1972). *People making.* Palo Alto, CA: Science and Behavior Books.

Sax, L. (2013). *Why gender matters: What parents and teachers need to know about the emerging science of sex differences.* New York: Harmony Books.

Seligman, M. E. P. (2011). *Flourish: A visionary new understanding of happiness and well-being.* New York, NY: The Free Press.

Sheff, D., & Sheff, N. (2019) *High: Everything you want to know about drugs, alcohol, and addiction.* New York, NY: Houghton Mifflin Harcourt.

Siegel, D. J. (2012). *The developing mind: How relationships and the brain interact to shape who we are.* New York, NY: Guilford Press.

Siegel, D. J. (2013). *Brainstorm. The power and purpose of the teenage brain.* New York, NY: Penguin.

Siegel, D. J. (2017). *Mind: A journey to the heart of being human.* New York, NY: W. W. Norton.

Siegel, D. J., & Bryson, T. P. (2011). *The whole brain child: 12 revolutionary strategies to nurture your child's developing mind.* New York, NY: Bantam Books.

Siegel, D. J., & Bryson, T. P. (2014). *No drama discipline: The whole-brain way to calm the chaos and nurture your child's developing mind.* New York, NY: Bantam Books.

Siegel, D. J., & Hartzell, M. (2004). *Parenting from the inside out: How a deeper self-understanding can help you raise children who thrive.* New York, NY: Tarcher.

Siegel, J. P. (2000). *What children learn from their parents' marriage: It may be your marriage, but it's your child's blueprint for intimacy.* New York, NY: HarperCollins.

Silveri, M. M., Dager, A. D., Cohen-Gilbert, J. E., & Sneider, J. T. (2016). Neurobiological signatures associated with alcohol and drug use in the human adolescent brain. *Neuroscience Biobehavioral Reviews, 70,* 244–259. doi:10.1016/j.neubiorev.2016.06.042

Singer, D. G., & Revenson, T. A. (1978). *A Piaget primer: How a child thinks.* New York, NY: Penguin.

Spear, L. P. (2000). The adolescent brain and age-related behavioral manifestations. *Neuroscience and Biobehavioral Reviews, 24,* 417–463.

Spear, L. P. (2016). Consequences of adolescent use of alcohol and other drugs: Studies using rodent models. *Neuroscience and Biobehavioral Reviews, 70,* 228–243. doi:10.1016/j.neubiorev.2016.07.026

Stahl, S. M., & Moore, B. A. (Eds.). (2013). *Anxiety disorders: A guide for integrating psychopharmacology and psychotherapy.* New York, NY: Routledge.

Stallard, P. (2009). *Anxiety: Cognitive behavior therapy with children and young people.* New York, NY: Routledge.

Stevens, M. C. (2016). The contributions of resting state and task-based functional connectivity studies to our understanding of adolescent brain network maturation. *Neuroscience and Biobehavioral Reviews, 70,* 13–32. doi:10.1016/j.neubiorev.2016.07.027

Steyer, J. P. (2012). *Talking back to Facebook: The common sense guide to raising kids in the digital age.* New York, NY: Scribner.

Tarokh, L., Saletin, J. M., & Carskadon, M. A. (2016). Sleep in adolescence: Physiology, cognition and mental health. *Neuroscience & Behavioral Reviews, 70,* 182–188. doi:10.1016/j.neubiorev.2016.08.008

Telzer, E. H., Fuligni, A. J., Lieberman, M. D., & Galvan, A. (2013). The effects of poor quality sleep on brain function and risk taking in adolescence. *Neuroimage, 71,* 275–283. doi:10.1016/ j.neuroimage.2013.01.025

Tolentino, J. (2018, May 14). The promise of vaping and the rise of Juul. *The New Yorker.* Retrieved from https://www.newyorker.com/magazine/2018/05/14/the-promise-of-vaping-and-the-rise-of-juul

Tough, P. (2012). *How children succeed: Grit, curiosity, and the hidden power of character.* New York, NY: Houghton Mifflin Harcourt.

Treiman, D. M. (2001). GABAergic mechanisms in epilepsy. *Epilepsia, 42*(Suppl. 3), 8–12. doi:10.1046/j.1528-1157.2001.042suppl.3008.x

Turkle, S. (2012). *Alone together: Why we expect more from technology and less from each other.* New York, NY: Basic Books.

Twenge, J. M. (2017). *iGen: Why today's super-connected kids are growing up less rebellious, more tolerant, less happy—and completely unprepared for adulthood—and what that means for the rest of us.* New York, NY: Atria.

Varga, M., Konkolÿ Thege, B., Dukay-Szabó, S., Túry, F., & van Furth, E. F. (2018). When eating healthy is not healthy: Orthorexia nervosa and its measurement with the ORTO-15 in Hungary. *BMC Psychiatry, 14,* 59. doi:10.1186/1471-244X-14-59

van Duijvenvoorde, A. C. K., Peters, S., Braams, B. R., & Crone, E. A. (2016). What motivates adolescents? Neural responses to rewards and their influence on adolescents' risk taking, learning, and cognitive control. *Neuroscience and Biobehavioral Reviews, 70,* 135–147. doi:10.1016/j.neubiorev.2016.06.037

Van Veen, M. M., Kooij, J. J., Boonstra, A. M., Gordijn, M. C., & Van Someren, E. J. (2010). Delayed circadian rhythm in adults with attention-deficit/hyperactivity disorder and chronic sleep-onset insomnia. *Biological Psychiatry, 67*(11), 1091–1096. doi:10.1016/j.biopsych.2009.12.032

Verduyn, C., Rogers, J., & Wood, A. (2009). *Depression: Cognitive behaviour therapy with children and young people.* New York, NY: Routledge.

Wachter, A. (2016). *Getting over overeating: A workbook to transform your relationship with food using CBT, mindfulness, and intuitive eating.* Oakland, CA: New Harbinger Publications.

Willard, C. (2010). *Child's mind: Mindfulness practices to help your children be more focused, calm, and relaxed.* Berkeley, CA: Parallax Press.

Wolf, A. E. (2002). *Get out of my life, but first could you drive me and Cheryl to the mall? A parent's guide to the new teenager.* New York, NY: Farrar, Straus and Giroux.

Index

References to boxes, figures, and tables are denoted by an italicized *b*, *f* and *t*.

For the benefit of digital users, indexed terms that span two pages (e.g., 52–53) may, on occasion, appear on only one of those pages.